AN IRISH BISHOP IN PENAL TIMES

BY THE SAME AUTHOR
View from Mount Pelier
The Last Citadel (a three-act play)
Bíonn an fhírinne searbh (a collection of short stories in Irish)
Fíon an Ghrá (three one-act plays in Irish)
Éigse na hIarmhí (Gaelic poets from Westmeath)
The Second City: Portrait of Dublin 1700-1760
A Georgian Celebration: Irish poets of the Eighteenth Century
Dublin's Turbulent Priest: Cornelius Nary (1658-1738)

An Irish Bishop
in Penal Times

THE CHEQUERED CAREER OF
SYLVESTER LLOYD OFM,
1680-1747

PATRICK FAGAN

This book was typeset by
Koinonia Ltd, Manchester for
FOUR COURTS PRESS LTD
Kill Lane, Blackrock, Co. Dublin, Ireland.

© Patrick Fagan 1993

ISBN 1-85182-130-9

A catalogue record for this book
is available from the British Library.

Printed in Ireland by
Colour Books Ltd., Dublin

PREFACE

My sincere thanks are due, firstly, to Fr Hugh Fenning OP for reading the original manuscript and for his advice and assistance thereon, and for bringing to my attention some additional sources of information. For the use of material from the Stuart Papers in the Royal Archives at Windsor Castle the permission of Her Majesty, Queen Elizabeth II, is gratefully acknowledged. I should like specially to thank Fr Benignus Millett OFM, editor, *Collectanea Hibernica*, for the use of material from the Vatican Archives edited or calendared in that journal by the late Fr Cathaldus Giblin OFM, and to acknowledge the assistance of Fr Feargal Grannell OFM in putting at my disposal copies of Sylvester Lloyd's translation of the Montpellier Catechism held in the Franciscan House of Studies, Killiney. My thanks also to my son, Desmond, for helping with the checking of the proofs.

I am indebted to the staff of the following institutions for their help and cooperation in my research work: National Library of Ireland; Royal Irish Academy, Dublin; Gilbert Library (a branch of the Dublin Public Libraries); National Archives, Dublin; Representative Church Body Library, Dublin; Dublin Diocesan Library, Clonliffe, Dublin; King's Inns Library, Dublin; British Library, London; Registry of Deeds, Dublin; Franciscan House of Studies, Killiney, Dublin and the Library of Trinity College, Dublin.

CONTENTS

Preface 5
List of illustrations 8
A note on sources and dates 9
1 Road to Damascus 11
2 The Montpellier catechism 20
3 The Franciscan 33
4 The quest for a mitre begins 47
5 The question of an oath 74
6 The Congress of Soissons 103
7 Bishop of Killaloe 123
8 Bishop of Waterford and Lismore 166
Index 199

LIST OF ILLUSTRATIONS

1 Jeronimos (Hieronymites) monastery at Belem, Lisbon   15
2 Title page of Part II of Lloyd's translation of the Montpellier catechism   27
3 St Isidore's College, Rome, view of aula   37
4 Manuscript of poem in Irish on Lloyd's return to Ireland, *c.*1723   51
5 Section of Rocque's map of Dublin, 1756   79
6 James Francis Edward Stuart, 1745   107
7 Map of the Austrian Netherlands   143
8 View of Waterford city, 1736   177

CREDITS

Illustration 1: Portuguese National Tourist Office, London: nos. 2 and 3: Franciscan House of Studies, Killiney, Co. Dublin: nos. 4, 6 and 8: National Library of Ireland.

A NOTE ON SOURCES AND DATES

The principal source of material for this biography has been the Stuart Papers at Windsor Castle, or, in other words, the official correspondence of the court in exile of James III, *de jure* King of Great Britain and Ireland, commonly called the Pretender. Since the Stuart Papers are most readily accessible through microfilm copies in the British Library, London, it should be noted that, for the convenience of those interested, I have in qouting references given the number of the British Library microfilm reel (MFR) in addition to the Windsor Castle volume and item number.

Under the Julian Calendar in operation in Britain and Ireland up to September 1752, the New Year began on 25 March. Furthermore, the Julian Calendar was by the eighteenth century eleven days behind the Gregorian Calendar by then in operation in most west European countries. Something of the order of 50% of the correspondence used in this biography originated on the continent and is, therefore, dated in accordance with the Gregorian Calendar, while the remainder originated in Britain or Ireland and is dated in accordance with the Julian Calendar. I have not attempted to bring the latter into line with the Gregorian Calendar (called the New Style), except to the extent that, where dates fall between 1 January and 24 March (inclusive), the year is such cases is rendered according to the New Style (for example, 1 March 1728 becomes 1 March 1729). The discrepancy of eleven days, however, between the two calendars is a factor that has to be kept in mind.

I

ROAD TO DAMASCUS

Of the Irish catholic bishops of the first half of the eighteenth century, Sylvester Lloyd stands out as by far the best documented. This derives from the fact that quite a substantial amount of his correspondence has been preserved in the Stuart Papers at Windsor Castle, and, in addition, there are extensive references to him in the Vatican Archives, in particular in the records of the Brussels nunciature. And yet his early life, despite some tantalising clues, must be a matter for considerable speculation. It appears that the fact he was born a protestant and converted to the catholic faith as a youth, made him extremely reticent about his background; for not only did he change his religion, he also changed his politics, and from being a soldier in the army of King William on the continent, he transferred his allegiance to James II and, in later life at any rate, supported the Jacobite cause with all the proverbial zeal of the convert.

The first problem, then, to be faced by the biographer of Sylvester Lloyd is his parentage and place of birth. In this connection Gillow's contention that he was a Welshman[1] can be dismissed out of hand, for Lloyd himself on a number of occasions provides evidence that he was an Irishman, while he did on one occasion point out that his great-grandfather was born in Wales.[2] As to what part of Ireland he was born in, we are faced with two conflicting pointers—one to the province of Munster, the other to County Kilkenny. The most substantial evidence for a Munster birthplace occurs in a poem in Irish, written by Tadhg Ó Neachtain, celebrating Lloyd's return to Ireland in 1723 or 1724, following his visit to France to elicit French support for the quashing of the 1723 Popery Bill.[3] At one point in this poem Lloyd is addressed as 'a bhile

[1] Joseph Gillow, *A literary and biographical history or bibliographical dictionary of the English Catholics* (London and New York, no date), vol. 4, p. 291.
[2] Stuart Papers RA SP(M), vol. 96/101, MFR 763.
[3] National Library of Ireland (N.L.I.) MS G 132, p. 103. A translation of the poem in question into English is included as an appendix to Chapter 4.

curtha Críche Cuirc', that is, 'O scion of the warriors of the territory of Corc'. Now, Corc was king of Munster in the fifth century and was the reputed founder of Cashel as the seat of the Munster kings. According to *Onomasticon Goedelica*[4] 'Críche Cuirc' was generally understood to mean North Munster, or the counties of Clare, Limerick and Tipperary. At a more specific level Corc is associated with Corcomroe in County Clare, with Bruree in County Limerick and, as we have seen, with Cashel in County Tipperary. According, then, to Tadhg Ó Neachtain who must have known him well, Lloyd came from somewhere in the counties mentioned.

A further pointer to a Munster birth-place was Lloyd's appointment to the bishopric of Killaloe in the ecclesiastical province of Cashel. It was normal practice for priests to be appointed bishops in a diocese in their native ecclesiastical province, although there were exceptions to this practice, and indeed Lloyd's first bid for promotion was to the archbishopric of Dublin. The ecclesiastical province of Cashel is conterminous with the province of Munster, but with the exception that the former includes some half-a-dozen Leinster parishes in south Offaly.

When we come to consider Lloyd's parentage, the evidence again points to a Munster birthplace. It will be seen in Chapter 4 that, in connection with the appointment of an archbishop of Dublin in 1724, two gentlemen 'noted for their learning, standing and holiness'—and who were determined that Lloyd would not be appointed archbishop—asserted in a letter to the nuncio in Brussels that Lloyd was born of a protestant father 'who was not ashamed to have two wives at the same time'.[5] Earlier, in a dispatch to the Vatican, the nuncio mentioned that Lloyd's father had been a protestant minister.[6] On the basis of this latter information, according to Canon Leslie's *Succession list of Church of Ireland clergy*,[7] there were two clergymen, William Lloyd and Edward Lloyd, who could, at first sight, have been Sylvester Lloyd's father. William Lloyd was a son of Thomas Lloyd of Tuogh (also known as Towerhill) near Cappamore, County Limerick. This Thomas was an army officer who was one of the County Limerick commissioners of the poll tax in 1660. His descendants down to the present day are well documented in Burke's *Irish families*, from which it is apparent that his son, William, had only one son, also

4 Robert Hogan, *Onomasticon Goedelicum* (Dublin and London, 1910; reprinted Dublin, 1993), p. 304.
5 Cathaldus Gilbin, 'Catalogue of Material of Irish interest in the collection Nunziatura di Fiandra, Vatican Archives' in *Collectanea Hibernica*, no. 11 (1968), p. 76.
6 Ibid., p. 76.
7 N.L.I. MS 1776.

named Thomas, who was ordained in the established church.[8] William Lloyd can, therefore, be ruled out of contention as Sylvester Lloyd's father, who must, then, be assumed to have been Edward Lloyd.

According to Canon Leslie's *Succession list*, Edward Lloyd was collated prebendary of Killeedy, County Limerick, in 1663, and was at the same time appointed vicar of Castlerobertgore, Kilfergus and Shanagolden with the church of Kilcolman, near which he presumably lived. He was vicar of Kilmoylan in 1667-8 and of Kilbroderan, Cloncoragh and Kilscannel in 1668-77.[9] All these parishes are centred around the villages of Glin and Shanagolden in west Limerick near the border with County Kerry. This Edward Lloyd may possibly be the same man who, according to *Alumni Dublinenses*, hailed from County Limerick, entered Trinity College, Dublin in 1670, graduated BA in 1673 and obtained an MA degree in 1678, although this would mean that he was a very mature student indeed (at least thirty years old) when he entered TCD and that his age at entry ('about sixteen'), as shown in the Entrance Book of the college, is incorrect. In this connection it should be said that it was not unknown for Church of Ireland clergy to be allowed time off to pursue their studies in TCD. During the Cromwellian period, when Edward Lloyd would in the normal course have attended TCD, the Anglican church was subjected to a degree of oppression, entailing the prohibition of their liturgy and the suppression of their episcopacy. The education of their clergy was necessarily haphazard during that period, and efforts would have been made to rectify the situation when matters returned to normal with the Restoration.

Edward Lloyd vacated his prebend, resigned his parishes and disappears from the clerical scene in 1677, and was succeeded by a John Vesey.[10] It may have been some scandal in his private life that forced this step upon him; presumably there was some basis for the report, already mentioned, of his having 'two wives at the same time'. On the other hand, it may be simply that he abandoned the church for some other career, perhaps teaching, a career which was always popular with protestant clergy. At all events, he apparently succeeded in regularising his matrimonial difficulties, for there is evidence that he married a second time. This evidence is provided by Sylvester Lloyd's will, executed in Waterford in

---

8   H.M. Massingberd (ed.), *Burke's Irish family records* (London, 1976). Burke does not state that William Lloyd was a Church of Ireland clergyman. For confirmation that he was see N.L.I. MS 1776 and the entry for Thomas Lloyd, son of William, in *Alumni Dublinenses*.
9   N.L.I. MS 2686, passim.
10 Ibid., p. 116.

1743, in which he cut off with the customary shilling each of his nephews and nieces by his half-sisters, Jane and Rebecca Lockington.[11] At first sight it might appear from this that it was Sylvester Lloyd's mother who married a second time to a man named Lockington. But this would mean that the names Jane and Rebecca Lockington are the maiden names of these two ladies. However, in legal documents such as wills, married women require to be referred to by their married names, and accordingly it would appear that the maiden name of these ladies was Lloyd and that they married husbands, perhaps brothers, with the same name of Lockington.

In regard to Edward Lloyd's first marriage, *Alumni Dublinenses* provides us with what may be a clue in an entry in respect of a John Lloyd, born in Shannell, County Limerick, whose father was named Edward Lloyd, and who (i.e. John) was aged eighteen when he entered TCD in June 1680. Shannell, as a Limerick place-name, appears neither in *Index of the townlands of Ireland* (1901) nor in the index to Sir William Petty's maps c.1655-59. However, in Petty's Down Survey map a Kilshannell is shown in the vicinity of Kilcolman, where Edward Lloyd had his church. Bearing in mind the practice of abbreviating place-names common throughout Ireland, it is quite possible that Shannell was used as an abbreviation of Kilshannell. It seems then that John Lloyd was indeed a son of our Edward Lloyd, and the conclusion must be that Edward Lloyd first married as a young curate in his early twenties and had a son, John, and two daughters, Jane and Rebecca, by this marriage.

As to when Edward Lloyd married a second time, it is on record that an Edward Loyd (*sic*) married an Elizabeth Simpson (where not stated) in 1676,[12] and that an Edward Lloyd married an Elizabeth Tailor in Cashel cathedral on 17 January 1679 (i.e. 1680 New Style).[13] Either of these couples could possibly be the parents of Sylvester Lloyd, but the couple married in Cashel cathedral appear by far the more likely in view of other pointers to south Tipperary as Lloyd's birthplace. Firstly, there is evidence of a friendship between Lloyd and two catholic nobles from the area, Lord Cahir and Lord Dunboyne. Both were to sign a postulation in 1724 in favour of Lloyd's bid for the Dublin archbishopric.[14] In the case

11 William Carrigan, 'Dr. Sylvester Lloyd' in *Journal of the Waterford Archaeological Society* vol. 3, (1897), pp. 38-9.
12 National Archives, *Index of prerogative administrations*. Although the venue of this marriage is not stated, the spelling 'Loyd' would suggest Dublin where this form of the name was generally found.
13 Cashel Cathedral Parish Records, N.L.I. microfilm Pos. 1390.
14 Stuart Papers, RA SP(M) vol. 74/108, MFR 753.

1 Jeronimos (Hieronymites) monastery at Belem, Lisbon

of Lord Cahir there is the further point that Lloyd escorted Cahir's eldest son on at least two occasions to the English College at Douai.[15] It is of some significance, too, that a letter dated October 1732 from Lloyd to the historian, Thomas Carte, was written in a place named Rehill, which can apparently be identified as a townland located between the towns of Cahir and Clogheen in south Tipperary. Rehill formed part of the estate of Lord Cahir. Lloyd in this letter excused himself from going to Dublin to meet Carte because of the loss of his sight, and it appears that he was sojourning in Rehill in the hope of some improvement. Secondly, the reference in Tadhg Ó Neachtain's poem, already mentioned, to Críche Cuirc could be construed more specifically as the Cashel area, while the phrase 'a chláir Eumainn' (i.e. from the plains of Edward/Edmund) in the same poem could be construed as referring to Edmund Butler, the then Lord Dunboyne. As to the year of Lloyd's birth, the date of his later defection from the army (1697 at the latest) postulates a date of birth not later than 1680. This would mean that Lloyd was probably born in the closing months of 1680, his parents having wed in January of that year.

It seems unlikely that he was christened Sylvester. An Anglican clergyman would scarcely name a child of his after a pope of the fourth century. A second name, Lewis, is to be found in Franciscan documents and in the Stuart Papers, and this was probably the name given him at

15 Ibid., vol. 116/152, MFR 772 and vol. 96/101, MFR 763.

birth. It is likely that he acquired the name Sylvester when he joined the Hieronymite order in Lisbon, since it was by that name he was known when he was ordained a priest in that order in 1711. Later, when he joined the Franciscans, he appears to have reverted to the name Lewis, for it is in the Latin form of this name, Ludovicus, that he appears in the Franciscan records, with the sole exception of the mention of his death, when he is called Sylvester.[16]

Let us now turn to the claim, mentioned above, that Lloyd was born in Kilkenny. In a lecture on Lloyd, given by Fr Feargal Grannell OFM to the Clare Archaeological and Historical Society in Ennis, County Clare in January 1972, Fr Grannell stated that an early source suggested that Lloyd was a native of Kilkenny.[17] However, he has been unable to recall, after a lapse of twenty years, what this early source might be. While it has to be said that the evidence available does not point in the direction of Kilkenny as Lloyd's birthplace, it is possible that the family moved to Kilkenny during Lloyd's boyhood. Furthermore, it may be of some significance that there were living, one at least in Kilkenny city, at the relevant time two brothers named John and Edward Lockington.[18] Could these be the husbands of Lloyd's half-sisters, Jane and Rebecca? Extensive searches of various sources have not revealed any marriage between a Lockington and a Lloyd and the relevant marriage licence records, which might have settled this matter one way or the other, were burned in the fire in the Public Record Office in 1922.

Lloyd's evident proficiency in the Irish language points to a rural upbringing. A protestant boy brought up in a city or a town at that time would scarcely have had the opportunity or the inclination or the need to acquire Irish. But a protestant with a knowledge of Irish would not have been at all unusual in the country areas. A knowledge of the language would indeed have been very desirable if only for the purpose of conversing with the servants and the labourers. We have no information as to Lloyd's early education. It is quite evident from his many letters and from his translation of the Montpellier catechism that he had a very sound education, but it may be that he got most of this at St Bonaventure's College, Douai or during his years as a monk. His suggested connection with Kilkenny prompts the question as to whether he attended Kilkenny

16 Anselm Faulkner (ed), *Liber Dubliniensis – chapter documents of the Irish Franciscans 1719-1875* (Killiney, 1978), p. 1.
17 Feargal Grannell, 'The strange story of Sylvester Lloyd O.F.M.', lecture given in the Old Ground Hotel, Ennis as reported in *The Clare Champion* of 15 January 1972.
18 National Archives, Betham's Abstracts of Wills, BET 1/41, p. 100 and Primm papers. John and Edward were sons of Richard Lockington who died c.1686.

College. However, a search of the college register, which dates from 1684, does not reveal his name.[19]

It appears that, while still only a youth, Lloyd found himself a soldier in the army of King William. Whether he undertook this career as a duty expected of his class, or whether there was an element of compulsion or conscription about it, we do not know. His military involvement is disclosed in a dispatch from Nuncio Spinelli in Brussels to his superiors in Rome on the subject of Lloyd's candidature for the archbishopric of Dublin.[20] We gather from this that Lloyd was so smitten by a crisis of conscience after he had killed one of the enemy, that he left the army, cast aside his protestant religion and became a catholic. The date of his defection from the army and conversion to Catholicism can be fixed with some accuracy as 1697, for in a letter dated 25 August 1726 to the Pretender's secretary of state he reveals that he had at that date been 'near thirty years a Roman Catholic and above three and twenty in religion'.[21] If the suggested year of birth, 1680, is correct, then Lloyd was a youth of only about sixteen years when he joined the army. Lloyd's assertion in later life that 'it has next my duty to God *ever since I came to any kind of knowledge in the world* been my greatest study how to be of service to your Majesty' (i.e. the Pretender) is evidence that he was still a callow youth when he defected from the army.[22]

The war in which Lloyd found himself reluctantly taking part was the War of the League of Augsburg, also known as the War of the Grand Alliance. The league had been put together largely by William of Orange to counter the aggrandising designs of Louis XIV of France. It was a league of catholic and protestant states, the main partners being Austria, Holland, Spain, and Sweden, with the pope giving secret support. Later, when James II had been ousted from the throne, Britain came in as a further important ally. William's British (and Irish) army, once the Jacobites had been defeated in Ireland, saw service mainly in the Netherlands, and it is there one would expect Lloyd to have been soldiering when he had his crisis of conscience. This would certainly tie in with Gillow's contention that Lloyd was educated at St Bonaventure's College at Douai,[23] a college of the English Franciscans near the Belgian border in north-east France.

19 Trinity College, Dublin MS 2019, *Registrum Collegii Kilkenniensis*.
20 C. Giblin, op. cit., no. 11 (1968), p. 76.
21 Stuart Papers, RA SP(M) vol. 96/101, MFR 763.
22 Ibid., vol. 114/136 MFR 771. The italics are mine.
23 J. Gillow, op. cit., vol. 4, p. 291.

There is a period of about six years between the date of Lloyd's conversion and the date he joined the Hieronymites in Portugal. Some of this period could be accounted for by his attendance at St. Bonaventure's, but his friendship with the Irish lawyer, Thomas Power O'Daly, to whom he dedicated his translation of the Montpellier Catechism (see next chapter), implies a lengthy sojourn in Ireland[24] before joining *c*.1703 the Hieronymites at their monastery at Belem, today a suburb of Lisbon. The Spanish Congregation of Hermits of St Jerome, commonly known as Hieronymites or Los Jerónimos, was organised by Pedro Fernandez Pecha, the royal chamberlain, who died in 1374. Pope Gregory XI gave the order his approbation in 1373, and soon after numerous houses were established in Spain, including one at Yuste, to which Emperor Charles V retired following his abdication in 1556. King Manuel of Portugal set up a monastery of the order at Belem in 1499; it remains to this day one of the architectural delights of Lisbon. The Hieronymites followed the rule of St Augustine under the direction of a general elected every three years by a general chapter. Each monastery retained a high degree of autonomy but observance of the rule was strict. While Philip II succeeded in uniting all the monasteries in Iberia under a single superior, problems of discipline and organisation later set in. The order was suppressed in 1835 but re-appeared at Segovia in Spain in 1957.[25]

The archives of the Patriarcado, Lisbon reveal that Friar Sylvester Lloyd of St Patrick of the order of St Jerome was ordained a priest on 30 May 1711 by the bishop of Tagaste in his oratory at Lisbon.[26] Fr Feargal Grannell in the course of the lecture already mentioned was of the view that Lloyd qualified as a lecturer with the degree of licentiate in sacred theology. Certainly, he is described on two occasions in Franciscan records as Sacrae Theologiae Lector (i.e. professor of sacred theology).[27] It does not seem likely that he spent all his time in Belem. It will be seen from the next chapter that Luke Fagan, later successively bishop of Meath and archbishop of Dublin, encouraged Lloyd early in the century to undertake the translation of the Montpellier catechism. It seems likely

24 The following extract from the Dedication is indicative of a close friendship between Lloyd and Power O'Daly, which could only have developed following his defection from the army and conversion to Catholicism (the italics are Lloyd's): 'My own inclination and love for your person might perhaps have byassed me in my choice of a Patron; but I cannot be suspected of having acted according to any such prepossession, when I assure the world that all my *Friends* joined with me in this choice; and unanimously pointed out Mr *Power* [*recte* Power O'Daly] as the man to whom I ought to make this *Dedication*. '
25 *New Catholic Encyclopaedia* (Washington D.C., 1967).
26 I am indebted to Fr Hugh Fenning OP for this information.
27 A. Faulkner, op. cit. pp. 1 & 11.

that Lloyd and Fagan met in Seville, a diocese with which Fagan was connected and where the Hieronymites had a monastery.

Lloyd remained with the Hieronymites for only about a year after his ordination. He then transferred to the Franciscan order and, having completed scarcely six months probation in the Irish Franciscan college of St Isidore in Rome, he was sent to Ireland.[28] The short period of probation can be explained by the fact that he had already been a monk for about nine years and his translation of the Montpellier catechism must have added greatly to his standing as a cleric.

---

28 C. Gilbin, op. cit., no. 11 (1968), p. 76.

2

THE MONTPELLIER CATECHISM

The original Montpellier catechism, published in Paris in 1702, was the work of François Pouget (1666-1723), a doctor of the Sorbonne and a member of the Oratorian order. He spent some years in Paris before returning to his native Montpellier in the south of France, where he became rector of the diocesan seminary there. His catechism is subtitled *Instructions générales en forme de catéchisme où l'on explique en abrégé, par ecriture sainte et par la tradition, l'histoire et les dogmes . . . les morales . . . les sacraments, les prières*. It is no ordinary catechism, but more a comprehensive cyclopaedia of Christian doctrine. It quickly achieved a *succes fou*, and within a short time was translated into German, Dutch, Latin, Spanish and English. This was, of course, before it came under the scrutiny of the Holy Office because of its alleged Jansenist tendencies.

Pouget's catechism is said to have come under the disfavour of Rome, not so much because of what it contained but because of Pouget's patrons. One of these, Bishop Colbert of Montpellier, was openly sympathetic to Jansenism. Another patron, Cardinal Noailles, archbishop of Paris, had earlier in his career taken part in the assembly of the French clergy in 1682 which adopted the Four Gallican Articles, thus giving the French Church a measure of independence from Rome. Furthermore, Noailles was quite ambivalent to Jansenism. For instance, he forbade the Jesuits, noted for their stand against Jansenism, to preach or hear confessions in the archdiocese of Paris, and he did not formally accept until 1728 the bull *Unigenitus* (issued in 1713), which declared the Jansenist propositions of Quesnel to be heretical.[1]

Thus suspect from the outset, as far as Rome was concerned, Pouget's catechism could not have stood much of a chance when its orthodoxy came under the scrutiny of a Holy Office, haunted by the twin spectres of

[1] *New Catholic Encyclopaedia* (Washington D.C. 1967)

Gallicanism and Jansenism. Placed on the Index of Prohibited Books in 1721, it has remained somewhat controversial down even to our own day. While, for example, one contributor, G. S. Sloyan, in the *New Catholic Encyclopaedia* (1967) pronounces the catechism to be 'unexceptionable',[2] another contributor, P. Mulhern, states that 'even those who attempted to vindicate the catechism and its author had to note that the condemned editions contained expressions that were distinctively Jansenist in connotation'.[3]

It has been accepted by several writers that Sylvester Lloyd's translation into English of the Montpellier catechism was first published in 1712, but none of them quote any authority for this date and no copies of this edition can now be traced. I can find no evidence to support this date of 1712 other than a reference, in Lloyd's prefatory note to the reader, repeated in the 1723 edition, to the fact that the Rhemish English translation of the Bible (1582) had been published 130 years previously.[4] This certainly points to the year 1712 as the year of publication, and for our purposes it will be convenient to adhere to that date, although actual publication may not have been effected until a year or two later. In any event, it appears that the preparation of this work took place before Lloyd joined the Irish Franciscans and while he was still a member of the Hieronymite order, which he had joined, as we have seen, *c.*1703.

It was later argued, when Lloyd's translation came under the scrutiny of the Holy Office, that it was an English translation, not of the original French catechism, but of a Spanish translation of that catechism. However, Lloyd's note to the reader, already mentioned, clearly indicates that the 1712 edition *was* a translation from the French original. Lloyd states:

> I cannot say much for the Translation, but that I have endeavoured to keep as near as possible to the sense of the original, and make it speak English, so as to be understood by every Capacity.[5]

He goes on at some length to deal with the difficulties in translating works such as this from the French, but there is no mention at all of having got any help from the Spanish translation.

The dedication to Thomas Power O'Daly, appearing in the second edition, can be assumed also to have appeared in the first edition. Like the

2 Ibid., vol. 3, p. 329.
3 Ibid., p. 229.
4 S. Ll., *General Instructions, by way of catechism* (London, 1723), Part 1, preface entitled 'Translator to the Reader', p. 2.
5 Ibid., preface, p. 2.

generality of dedications of that period it is fulsome in the extreme. Having dealt more than handsomely on why he is dedicating the translation to O'Daly, Lloyd goes on:

> Accept it therefore, Sir, as the public Acknowledgement of your Country; but especially of that Body of Men, whose Ministry makes the propagation of Religion their more immediate concern. You have by a thousand instances of Zeal distinguished yourself in their Defence; you have been all along the Universal Refuge of those who have been distressed upon that Head; you have very often risked both Liberty and Fortune for their Relief. . . You have studied the Laws of your Country, not to enrich yourself at its expense, but to be useful to your Countrymen; you have studied Religion, not to be more wise than you ought, but to be wise unto Sobriety. . . All agree that politeness and Piety meet in your character; and that the same man may be a Statesman, fine Gentleman and good Christian too.[6]

Lloyd's familiarity with Portugal is underlined by references in the dedication to members of the O'Daly clan who had achieved fame in that country:

> I could show you an O'Daly in the Court of Portugal, in all the secrets of that Prince's cabinet, more than once his Ambassador to Foreign Courts, and at the same time founding and endowing Seminaries and Religious Houses for the Service of his distressed Country in the City of Lisbon, where he died in an Opinion of Sanctity, and Bishop elect of Conimbria [sic]; I might show you another (and a very near kinsman too) promoted to the greatest Employments of one of the most Illustrious Societies of the Church, very often Superior, and at length Provincial of his Order in that same Kingdom.[7]

---

6   Ibid., dedication, p. 2. Thomas Power O'Daly was a younger son of Denis Daly, chief justice of the common pleas during the reign of James II. He was named after his maternal grandfather, Thomas Power of County Limerick, and was a lawyer by profession.

7   Ibid., dedication, p. 3. The first O'Daly referred to was Daniel O'Daly (1595-1662), who was a native of Kerry. As a youth Daniel entered the Dominican order in Spain but was educated in Bordeaux. He set up an Irish Dominican college in Lisbon of which he was appointed rector in 1634. He was also instrumental in setting up a convent for Dominican nuns at Belem, in the Lisbon area, in 1639. Sylvester Lloyd would have been familiar with this convent, since it was at their Belem monastery that he first entered the Hieronymite order. Daniel O'Daly was later Portuguese ambassador to the courts of Charles I and Charles II. In 1662 he was appointed bishop of Coimbra, but died before consecration. A side note describes the second O'Daly mentioned by Lloyd as 'late Provincial of the Augustines in Portugal, a man of eminent learning and piety'.

In his prefatory note to the reader Lloyd states that he undertook this work 'for the good of my Countrymen, who are, or may be destitute of Instruction in matters of Religion; I began it by the Advice of some very learned and Pious Men, and it is with their Approbation that I now publish it.'[8] One of these learned and pious men must have been Bishop Luke Fagan, whose connection with Lloyd was touched upon in Chapter 1, for Fagan was later to write to Lloyd:

> When I received your translation together with the Spanish I had not much leisure to peruse 'em, but at last have done it with great pleasure. In my opinion you have performed it to a great advantage, and the public is much obliged to you, it being a most useful work; as I was the first who encouraged you to undertake it, so I shall exert myself in my walk [visitation] to recommend it to the clergy and laity.[9]

Fagan was educated at the Irish College in Seville, which he entered, already ordained, in 1682. He was later a confessor in the diocese of Seville and is said to have returned to Ireland in June 1689.[10] However, he apparently returned later to Spain for his name does not appear in the lists of priests who registered under the act of 1704 for registering catholic clergy, indicating that he was absent from Ireland at that time. It would have been about this period that he encouraged Lloyd to undertake the translation.

On Lloyd's return to Ireland in 1713 he must have quickly become known for his translation of the Montpellier catechism, and the speed with which he obtained various appointments within the Franciscan order from preacher and confessor of the laity in 1716 to deputy provincial in 1723 is an indication of the high esteem in which he was held. In Dublin in particular the catechism was highly thought of and appears to have been in general use throughout the diocese. How far it could be used in

8   Ibid., preface, p. 2.
9   Cathaldus Giblin, 'Catalogue of material of Irish interest in the collection Nunziatura di Fiandra, Vatican Archives' in *Collectanea Hibernica*, no. 5 (1962), p. 107. It might be argued that Fagan's letter (first line) implies that Lloyd's translation was made from the Spanish translation. However, I believe Lloyd's reason for sending Fagan the Spanish translation instead of the French original was that Fagan had little or no knowledge of French while he was proficient in Spanish.
10 John J. Silke, 'The Irish College, Seville' in *Archivium Hibernicum*, vol. 24 (1961), p. 131. A letter from Archbishop Byrne of Dublin to the Vatican in December 1707 indicates that Fagan had returned to Dublin earlier that year and was awaiting assignment to a parish. (See note by John Brady 'Luke Fagan, archbishop of Dublin' in *Reportorium Novum*, vol. 2 (1960), p. 378)

other dioceses would depend on the extent to which English was spoken, and at this time, apart from Dublin and the larger towns and cities, Irish was still in general use and the ordinary people's knowledge of English would scarcely be such as would enable them to comprehend catholic dogma as expounded in Lloyd's catechism.

In any event, the catechism was such a bulky tome—Parts 1, 2 and 3 of the 1723 edition running to almost 900 pages—that it can scarcely have been popular with the ordinary people, even those with a good knowledge of English. It was probably more in the nature of a reference book for the clergy, from which they could expound catholic doctrine to their parishioners. No doubt copies would also be found in more well-to-do catholic homes, for the better-off generally took their religion very seriously, and catechisms and works of religious controversy enjoyed a wide sale.

When the original Montpellier catechism was condemned by Rome in 1721, it must have been plain to Lloyd and the Irish church authorities generally that Lloyd's translation would also be suspect. There must, then, have been a rush to get out a new edition where questionable passages would be expunged and the translation brought into line with the Spanish translation, which was apparently in good standing with the church. Part 1 of the new edition was accordingly described on the title page as 'translated from the original French and carefully compared with the Spanish approved translation'. It was further significantly described as 'The Second Edition, corrected and amended by S.Ll.' With the publication of the First Part of this second edition early in 1723, there must have been a scramble to withdraw from circulation copies of the first edition. This would account for the fact that no copies of this first (1712) edition can now be traced.

Such was the haste to get out this amended second edition that little or no thought appears to have been given to the retention of Lloyd's note to the reader apparently as it had appeared in the first edition. It proved a major faux pas to have retained it without amendment, in that it referred in the following highly laudatory, not to say incriminating, terms to the original Montpellier catechism, placed on the Index of Prohibited Books two years before:

> This Catechism was first published in France, in the Diocese of Montpellier, by order of Mr Colbert, Bishop of that See, in the year 1702. It was everywhere received with the greatest applause, and there were a great many editions of it in a very little time. . . . It is an epitome of the Sacred Annals of the Church from the Creation to the

present time, in which a brief but satisfactory account is given of the various Vicissitudes of the Faithful in the Old, and of the Christians in the New Law. . .

It is a history of all the Errors, Schisms and Heresies that troubled the Church from the beginning of Christianity to this very Day. . . . and it is an explanation of the Christian Morality, Sacraments, Prayers, Ceremonies and Rites of the Church, in which her doctrines are faithfully delivered without entering into those nice disputes, which rather puzzle the Understanding, than mend the Heart. . ..

Those who are in Error or wavering in their Faith, may in this Book find sure and incontestable Principles whereby to clear their Doubts and satisfy their Scruples; those who are true Believers will find certain and infallible Rules for living holily in every State and Condition of Life, and for avoiding a thousand Evils that Men daily fall into either through Ignorance or Superstition; . . . so that the Reader will on serious perusal find that he never read a Book more proper to strengthen his Faith and compose his Manners, or to instruct him in every good Word and Work.[11]

After such solecisms it was just as well that Lloyd included at the end of the note the saving clause that he submitted 'every Word and Work of mine to the Judgment of our Holy Mother, the Church' and was ready 'to retract anything in this Translation, which may be contrary to her Sentiments'.[12]

The note for the reader could also have done with updating in other respects. While it refers to the Spanish translation of 1709, it fails to mention the German translation of 1718 and the Dutch of 1719. In maintaining that the most recent translation into English of the Bible was the Rhemish translation of 1582,[13] and in apologising for having to make use of that translation in Scripture references, he ignored the translation of the New Testament published in 1718 by Cornelius Nary, a man to whom, it will be seen, he was to owe some debt of gratitude.

In his attempt to forestall action by Rome by getting out this new edition, Lloyd must have secured the cooperation of Archbishop Byrne of Dublin, for the latter arranged, as soon as it was published, for the first part of the 1723 edition to be examined by three separate groups of theologians. A group drawn from the secular clergy of the Dublin

11 S. Ll., op. cit., preface p. 1.
12 Ibid., preface p. 2.
13 Ibid., preface p. 2

archdiocese and consisting of John Clinch, vicar general and parish priest of St Michael & John's, Cornelius Nary, doctor of laws of Paris university and parish priest of St Michan's, John Linegar, parish priest of St Mary's, and James Redmond and John Harold, both doctors of sacred theology, in their Opinion dated 21 August 1723, declared that, on the order of the archbishop of Dublin, they had read with all possible care the first part of the English translation made by Sylvester Lloyd of 'that golden book' entitled *General instructions by way of catechism*. Remarking that Lloyd was commissary provincial and actual definitor of the Irish Franciscans, they pointed out that the English translation was made from the French original, but was carefully collated with the Spanish translation which had been approved by the Holy Office. They declared that they found nothing in Lloyd's translation which was contrary to faith and morals and indeed remarked that Lloyd's skill was especially noticeable in the way he ingeniously omitted whatever was superfluous or dubious in the French original or emended such passages to bring them into line with catholic teaching. Consequently, they considered this translation, which took so much study and hard work, suitable to provide knowledge of salvation to those who sit in darkness and in the shadow of death.[14]

A second Opinion dated 3 September 1723 from two Augustinian theologians—Edmund Byrne, provincial of the Irish Augustinians, and bachelor of sacred theology and Laurence Gernon, prior of their Dublin convent—declared that they had carefully read the first volume of the work entitled *General instructions by way of catechism* and found nothing in it that was contrary to the true faith; indeed they considered it a useful book for all catholics.[15]

A third Opinion, dated 22 August 1723, was given by a group of Dominican theologians consisting of Stephen MacEgan, doctor of sacred theology, protonotary apostolic and prior provincial of the Irish Dominicans, Terence Kennedy, doctor of theology of the Sorbonne, and James Cormick and John Byrne, both professors of theology. They declared that they had carefully read and examined the first volume of the *General instructions* which had been translated into English from the French and at the same time collated with the Spanish version which was examined and approved by the Inquisition. They stated that they had found nothing in the translation which was opposed to faith and morals and that the doctrine outlined in it was in keeping with sacred Scripture and the

14 C. Giblin, op. cit., no. 5 (1962), pp. 107-8.
15 Ibid., p. 108.

General Instructions,
BY WAY OF
CATECHISM,
IN WHICH THE
History and Tenets
OF
𝕽𝖊𝖑𝖎𝖌𝖎𝖔𝖓,
THE
Christian Morality, Sacraments, Prayers, Ceremonies, and Rites of the CHURCH, are briefly EXPLAIN'D, by Holy-Scripture and Tradition.

Translated from the Original French, and carefully Compar'd with the Spanish Approv'd Translation.

SECOND PART.

By *S. Ll.*

LONDON:
Printed in the Year, MDCCXXIII.

2 Title page of Part II of Sylvester Lloyd's translation of the Montpellier catechism, 1723 edition

teaching of the Fathers. It was their honest opinion that the translation was most useful to catholics and indeed extremely necessary; that those who were well-versed in the mysteries of which it treats would admire with delight the profundity of its thought; and that ordinary people would easily accept the principles of the catholic faith and the rules governing christian morality because of the clear method used in setting forth these things. Furthermore, they pointed out that the translation would furnish priests with safe nourishment for their flocks, that it would encourage parents to bring up their children on principles based on christian discipline and teach young people to have love and respect for their parents from an early age. The translation would make everybody so conversant with the teachings of moral theology and give people such a clear insight into the truths of religion that a person could not deviate from the right path with this book as a guide.[16]

Copies of these three Opinions, together with Bishop Fagan's letter to Lloyd already mentioned, were forwarded to the nuncio in Brussels for transmission to Rome. Fagan's letter is dated simply 'Thursday' and it is not clear whether it was solicited specially for the occasion or had been written some time before. The Dominicans and Augustinians were asked for Opinions presumably because these were the two largest orders in Ireland after the Franciscans, who would have been ruled out of consideration because Lloyd was a member of that order.

What is called the Second Part of this new edition, but in fact includes Part II (275 pages) and Part III (155 pages), was evidently published later in 1723 for it bears the legend 'Second Part/ by S.Ll./London/Printed in the year MDCCXXIII'. The dedication and the translator's note to the reader have been omitted, but rather significantly the volume is prefaced by the following 'Advertisement':

> It having been industriously given out, since the publication of the first Volume of this Translation, that it contained some of the pernicious errors of Jansenius and Quesnelle; and it having been further insinuated that this work was never translated by any Catholic Hand into the Spanish Language, I have therefore thought fit to assure the Reader, First, that it has been approved by most of the eminent Divines of this City, as they have attested by Instruments under their Hands, and are ready to acknowledge when required: and Secondly, that it has been carefully compared with the Spanish

16 Ibid., pp. 108-9.

Translation now in the Printer's Hands, a Translation which is in the greatest Esteem in Spain, where it was published by Authority, as will appear from the following Approbation of an eminent Father of the Society of Jesus. I have made choice of this Approbation among many others of no less note, because its learned author is of an illustrious and religious Body of Men, who cannot be suspected of any private understanding with Jansenism: It is as near as our language would bear, Word for Word, with the Spanish original.[17]

This 'Advertisement' is followed by an English translation of the approbation, mentioned above, by Fr Joseph Casani SJ, qualificator of the Supreme Council of Inquisition in Madrid.

There is no evidence that this Second Part of the 1723 edition was ever examined by teams of theologians, as the First Part had been examined. A copy does, however, appear to have been sent to Internuncio Spinelli in Brussels, for the latter in a dispatch to Rome, dated 24 March 1724, in the course of some very unfavourable comments on Lloyd's bid to be archbishop of Dublin, remarked that Lloyd was the author of an English version of the Montpellier catechism, although he knew the work was condemned by the Holy See, and he had the second part of the catechism published despite the papal prohibition.[18] This remark shows that Spinelli had completely misread the situation.

Despite the apparent show of solidarity by the teams of theologians in favour of Lloyd's translation, the reality was that, following the condemnation in 1721 of the original Montpellier catechism, there were deep divisions amongst the Dublin clergy as to the acceptability of the translation. Indeed, the venom engendered by the altercations over the catechism was to manifest itself anew in the bitter wrangles in the Dublin chapter over appointments of vicar capitular and archbishop which occurred on three occasions between 1724 and 1734. Those who defended the catechism claimed that the English translation was not a literal translation from the original French, but was made from a Spanish translation which had been corrected and approved by the Holy Office. They further cited the approval given to the translation by many sound Irish theologians. On the other hand, those who opposed the translation pointed out that the preface to it composed by Lloyd was sufficient in itself to have the work condemned, since Lloyd spoke of the original

17 S. Ll., op. cit., Part 2, 'Advertisement'. The position of qualificator held by Fr Casani in the Supreme Council of the Inquisition meant he was a censor of the press.
18 C. Giblin, op. cit., no. 11 (1968), p. 76.

Montpellier catechism as if it were a second gospel, and in fact claimed that he did his utmost in the translation not to deviate in the slightest from the meaning of the original version.[19]

Eventually, the dispute in Dublin over the catechism became so notorious and so public that the London *Postman* felt obliged to take note of it in its edition of 27 February 1724:

> They write from Dublin that great disputes are arisen among the Popish clergy concerning the catechism of Montpellier, lately translated from the Spanish into the English tongue. It is believed by some men of judgment that those disputes have been industriously set on foot to prevent the Government's taking notice of it as a book that is indeed a complete magazine of refined Popery. Or as others think, perhaps to stir up the curiosity of Protestants to read their doctrine.[20]

The sequence of events leading up to the condemnation of Lloyd's translation would appear to be:

(a) During the autumn of 1723 Archbishop Byrne of Dublin forwarded to Spinelli, the internuncio (later nuncio) in Brussels with responsibility for Irish affairs, the opinions of the Dublin theologians on the new 1723 edition (Part I).

(b) On 13 December 1723 the Congregation de Propaganda Fide issued orders to Spinelli to have the condemnation of the original Montpellier catechism published in Ireland.[21]

(c) The response from Dublin to Spinelli was that the condemnation applied only to the original catechism but not to Lloyd's translation.[22]

(d) Spinelli replied that Lloyd's translation was also prohibited at least until it had been examined by the Holy Office and adjudged otherwise.[23]

(e) Russell, vicar capitular in charge of the Dublin diocese following the death of Archbishop Byrne in February 1724, deferred to the internuncio's wishes, but referred to the deep divisions amongst the clergy of Dublin on the subject of Lloyd's translation.[24]

19 Ibid., no. 5 (1962), p. 107.
20 *London Postman*, 27 February 1724, quoted in John Brady *Catholics and catholicism in the eighteenth century press* (Maynooth, 1965) p. 42
21 C. Giblin, op. cit., no. 11 (1968), p. 77.
22 Ibid., p. 78.
23 Ibid., p. 78.
24 Ibid., p. 78.

The Montpellier Catechism

(f) Spinelli repeated that the prohibition on Lloyd's translation was to stand until such time as new directions were received from Rome.[25]

(g) By dispatch dated 9 June 1724 Spinelli submitted the case with supporting documents to Rome. He requested the cardinals to speed up their examination of the case as the translation had given rise to very serious divisions and scandals especially in Dublin.[26]

(h) Lloyd's translation was condemned by a decree of the Index dated 15 January 1725. A dispatch dated 27 January 1725 from Cardinal Spinola to Spinelli stated that, as the Congregation of the Index had prohibited Lloyd's translation, Spinola enclosed a printed decree of the Congregation so that it would be at Spinelli's disposal to use as he sees fit.[27]

(i) On 16 February 1725 Spinelli informed the Holy See that news of the condemnation had been spread in England and Ireland, so that any harm which could result from reading such 'an evil book' will be checked.[28]

(j) On 21 May 1725 Spinelli noted in his diary that the translation of the Montpellier catechism by Lloyd had been banned at last. He has sent a copy of the ban to England and another to Ireland and has informed the archbishops and the vicars apostolic of the decision.[29]

The decision of the Holy Office might appear to have been unfair to Lloyd in that, in condemning his translation, no distinction appeared to have been made between his original translation of 1712 and the amended translation of 1723. However, it appears from a letter in August 1728 (see Chapter 6) from Cardinal Imperiali to the Pretender that the 1723 edition was also found wanting by Rome. We gather from this letter that it was the Vatican view that, while Lloyd in the 1723 edition had corrected various errors in the 1712 edition, other errors had crept into the 1723 edition, for which reason both editions were prohibited.

Lloyd nevertheless accepted the ban on his translation with a good grace; indeed he made a point of announcing the ban himself from the pulpit and of publicly retracting his translation.[30] But despite this full and loyal submission to the church authorities, he was to find the catechism a black mark against him when he came to be considered for appointment as

25 Ibid., p. 78.
26 Ibid., p. 78.
27 Ibid., no. 14 (1971), p. 39.
28 Ibid., no. 5 (1962), p. 113.
29 Ibid., no. 15 (1972), p. 34.
30 Stuart Papers, RA SP(M) vol. 120/130, MFR 774.

bishop or archbishop. In 1724 it was one of the reasons advanced by Spinelli for not considering him for the vacant archbishopric of Dublin.[31] In 1728, when the Pretender had nominated him for the bishopric of Killaloe, Cardinal Imperiali, Protector of Ireland, initially demurred, citing his translation of the Montpellier catechism against him. However, Imperiali later relented and agreed to Lloyd's appointment as bishop of Killaloe.[32]

The discomfiture of the catholic Church establishment in Dublin in having to condemn outright a catechism which they had previously wholeheartedly approved was seized on with glee by elements of the regular clergy—to put it mildly, there was no love lost between the secular and regular clergy, especially in Dublin. S.J., an anonymous member of the regular clergy, in a sermon said to have been preached in Dublin in 1728 had this to say:

> As to Mr Lloyd's translation of Montpellier's catechism, this city and kingdom is sensible how they recommended it to be read by all Christians as both excellent, pious and edifying; and soon after to forbid it again as pestiferous and heretical. A fine proof of their infallibility.[33]

The fact of its being placed on the Index Librorum Prohibitorum and indeed being branded as an evil book ensured the removal of the catechism from libraries etc. to such an extent that it has become a very rare book. I have failed to trace the whereabouts of any copy of the 1712 edition. The Franciscan House of Studies, Dún Mhuire, Killiney, County Dublin possesses two copies of the 1723 edition, but the title page, dedication and the preface entitled 'The Translator to the Reader' is missing from Part I of one set. Only Part I of the 1723 edition is in the British Library, London.

---

31 C. Giblin, op. cit., no. 11 (1968), p. 76.
32 Stuart Papers, RA SP(M) vol. 119/55, MFR 773 and vol. 120/130, MFR 774. It will be seen from Chapter 6 that, after the Pretender had confirmed in 1728 that Lloyd had publicly retracted his translation in 1725, Imperiali had the retraction registered in the Secretariat of the Index, so as to close the mouths of all on this question.
33 S.J., Popish priest, *Sermon in vindication of Mr Francis Lehey, against the Romish clergy of the city of Dublin; which sets forth their cruelty to their poor brethern, particularly to the said Mr Lehey* (Dublin, 1728). Ref. P. gg. 9. no. 33, Trinity College, Dublin library.

3

THE FRANCISCAN

Founded by Francis of Assisi in 1209, the order of Friars Minor rapidly spread throughout Europe and even during Francis's own lifetime missionaries of the order were advancing further afield to North Africa and the Middle East. The original rule drawn up by Francis prescribed a life of Christ-like poverty with the members of the order wandering about preaching, and working among the poor, and begging for their bread. They owned no land and lived in very simple dwellings. Later, however, the order began to acquire land and build large convents. Disputes over the rule led eventually to the splitting up of the order into three main branches—the Observants, the Capuchins and the Conventuals.

There is some doubt as to when the first Franciscans arrived in Ireland, and they may even have arrived here before the death of Francis in 1226. However, it is generally accepted that, following the arrival here of the English Franciscan, Richard Ingworth, in 1231-2, the order quickly spread throughout the country. If we exclude the Capuchins, who can be regarded as a separate order, the vast majority of Irish Franciscans by the time the monasteries were suppressed c.1540 belonged to the Observant branch of the order, the Observants and the Conventuals between them accounting for sixty-two convents. There were an additional forty-seven convents approximately belonging to a lay brother branch called the Third Order Regular. Following the suppression of their convents and the confiscation of their land and property, most Franciscan communities continued to lead a hunted, hand-to-mouth existence in the vicinity of their old convents, endeavouring to practise their rule as far as practicable and secretly holding regular chapters of the Irish province[1]

---

1   Aubrey Gwynn & R. Neville Hadcock, *Medieval religioius houses in Ireland* (London, 1970; reprinted Dublin 1988), passim.

Their extreme loyalty to the pope as well as the fact that they were looked upon as an unnecessary burden on the poor (and indeed were so regarded by some secular clergy) ensured that the regular orders in general were an easy target for the Irish administration. Following the collapse of the Jacobite cause in 1691, the Irish parliament accordingly began to think in terms of banishing the regular clergy from the country altogether, and in 1697 King William approved a draft bill with this effect, presented to him by the Irish administration. Later the Irish Parliament expanded the bill to bring bishops and persons exercising ecclesiastical jurisdiction within its ambit. Under the resulting Banishment Act 1697 all regular clergy, bishops and those exercising ecclesiastical jurisdiction were required to leave the country by 1 May 1698 on pain of treason; if they returned to the country they could be charged with high treason.[2]

A census of the catholic clergy carried out by the authorities in 1697 showed that there was a total of 872 secular and 495 regular clergy in the country at that time. The actual expulsion of the regulars was carried out in a highly efficient manner, 424 of them being recorded as having been actually transported from Irish ports. Of the eight bishops in the country in 1697, two (Ossory and Kildare) left of their own accord and the majority of the remainder were arrested over the ensuing years. Of the regulars who remained in the country, some found refuge in wealthy catholic houses, while others were able to pass themselves off as secular clergy and to register as such under the act of 1704 for registering catholic clergy.[3]

Measures by the Irish authorities against catholics such as the Banishment Act were often in subsequent years to prove an embarrassment to the British government in their relations with catholic countries in Europe, who were their allies or with whom they wished to maintain good relations. In the case of the Banishment Act it is not surprising then to find catholic Austria, William's ally in the recent war with France, taking up with the British government through its ambassador in London, Count Auersperg, the expulsions under the act. On 9 May 1698 the count informed the internuncio in Brussels that the Irish lord chancellor had told him that the Banishment Act would not be fully enforced and that some regular clergy would be allowed to stay, especially those who were too old to be sent away.[4] However, a dispatch from the internuncio to

---

2   J. G. Simms, 'The bishops banishment Act 1697' in *Irish Historical Studies*, vol. 17 (1970), p. 185-99.
3   Ibid., passim.
4   Cathaldus Giblin, Catalogue of 'Material of Irish interest in the collection Nunziatura di Fiandra, Vatican Archives' in *Collectanea Hibernica*, no. 4 (1961), p. 72.

cardinal secretary-of-state Spada in Rome puts a somewhat different slant on the situation in that the internuncio records that Count Auersperg had seen a letter written by Lord Galway, one of the Irish lords justices, in which the latter gave assurances that moderation would be used in dealing with Catholics, that it was not intended to make any further change in Irish ecclesiastical affairs apart from the expulsion of the regular clergy and that this latter measure had been taken for grave reasons of state.[5]

This intervention by Austria, while it came too late to have any significant effect on the actual expulsions, must have had some effect in staying the hand of the Irish authorities with regard to taking action against those regulars who evaded the act or who dared to return to Ireland following transportation. In any event, the regulars soon began to filter back to such an extent that by the 1720s they were believed to be as numerous as they had been at any time since Charles II's reign.[6]

Although the Franciscans are on record as taking a decision to obey the banishment Act,[7] it appears that not alone did many of them remain in the country in the wake of the act, but they also seem to have maintained their organisation throughout the country reasonably intact. Otherwise, it would be difficult to explain how they continued to hold their provincial chapters regularly in Ireland, with the sole exception of those for 1699 and 1700, which were held in St. Anthony's College, Louvain. Significantly enough, the number of vocals present (i.e. persons entitled to vote at capitular elections) at chapters of the order in the early years of the century were: 1703: 64; 1706: 62; 1709: 62; and 1714: 63.[8]

Originally the Dublin Franciscans had their convent and chapel in Francis Street in the city liberties. Towards the end of Charles II's reign a Fr Barnewall erected a large chapel for the order there.[9] Following the Banishment Act the Franciscans handed over this fine church—for most of the eighteenth century the largest in the city—to the secular clergy, who never returned it. But it appears that from early in the seventeenth century the Franciscans also had a small convent in Cook Street, Dublin, located in a backhouse at the rear of a house with the sign 'Adam and Eve', which was probably an inn. Since entrance to this backhouse was by

---

5   Ibid., p. 66.
6   Gilbert Library, Dublin MS 28. In the 1720s there were around 650 regular clergy in Ireland; see Hugh Fenning, *The undoing of the friars of Ireland* (Louvain, 1972), p. 201.
7   H. Fenning, op. cit., p. 62.
8   John T. Gilbert, *History of the city of Dublin* (Dublin, 1854-9), vol. 2, p. 306.
9   Nicholas Donnelly (ed.), *State and condition of the R.C. chapels in Dublin . . . 1749* (Egerton MS 1772) (Dublin, 1904), p. 15.

way of 'Adam and Eve's', this led to the little convent itself being called 'Adam and Eve's'.[10]

Following the handing over of the chapel and convent in Francis Street to the secular clergy, the Franciscan house in Cook Street became the only one of the order in the city. Early in the eighteenth century a member of the community, Francis Walsh, converted what was probably a disused warehouse on the same Cook Street location into a chapel[11] which continued to be known as 'Adam and Eve's', as indeed have succeeding churches on the same site, including the present one, been known.

According to himself Sylvester Lloyd joined the Irish Mission presumably at the Cook Street convent, in 1713,[12] having, as recalled in Chapter 1, served a probationary period as a novice at Saint Isidore's College, Rome. In the bill of the middle chapter of the Irish province held on 10 May 1716 at the place of refuge of the Kilconnell, County Galway, community, it is recorded that Sylvester Lloyd was appointed a preacher and confessor of the laity with eleven others. The guardian elected for the Dublin convent on that occasion was Fr John Segrave. In the bill for the provincial chapter held on 16 October 1717 at the place of refuge of the Dublin community (presumably in Cook Street), Lloyd is recorded as having been elected guardian of the Dublin convent. At the Provincial chapter held in Dublin on 3 September 1720 Lloyd was elected a definitor for the province along with three others.[13] This means that he was one of

10 *Irish Builder*, vol. 33 (1891), p. 194. The location of the house in Cook Street named 'Adam and Eve' can be established with a degree of certainty by reference to memorials in the Registry of Deeds, Dublin and to Rocque's map of Dublin 1756, which was claimed to be meticulously drawn to scale. Rocque's map shows Adam and Eve's chapel to be located to the back of a small house, on the west side of which there was an entrance to Chapel Yard and the chapel. Two houses are shown in Chapel Yard just north of the chapel and these were no doubt the friary. A survey dated 4 May 1749 in connection with the setting of two pieces of ground to the Franciscans, in anticipation of rebuilding their chapel, shows that the small house mentioned was then owned by a John Williams (*Irish Builder*, vol. 33 (1891), p. 194.). A later memorial of a deed shows that Williams's house was called 'The Half Moon' (Registry of Deeds Ref. 150-566). A memorial of a deed dated 1743 (ref. 111-328) refers to the house 'Adam and Eve' and 'all that ground and *two houses*, outhouses, workhouses and yard now or of late in the tenure of Mr Forde'. In a later memorial (ref. 285-196) 'Adam and Eve' is termed 'a large brick house'. The two houses mentioned here appear to be the friary, the chapel itself being described apparently as 'outhouses, workhouses'. The friary, chapel and the house named 'Adam and Eve' would therefore appear to be all part of the same property. All this implies that the house named 'Adam and Eve' was the one next door to the 'Half Moon' and on the east side of it. A map dated 1791 (see copy of the *Irish Builder* for 1891, p. 165, in R.C.B. Library, Braemor Park, Dublin where the date 1791 is pencilled in) shows that by that date (1791) the Franciscans had acquired the Half Moon, and had extended their chapel, or at least the entrance to it, right into Cook Street. For a section of Rocque's map of Dublin see p. 79.
11 N. Donnelly, op. cit., p. 13.
12 Stuart Papers, RA SP(M) vol. 96/101, MFR 763.
13 Cathaldus Giblin, (ed.), *Liber Lovaniensis—a collection of Irish Franciscan Documents 1629-1717* (Dublin & London, 1956), passim.

3 St Isidore's College, Rome: view of aula

four assistants to the provincial in defining or deciding the affairs of the province. His name appears last on the list most probably because he was junior to the rest in years spent in the order. In a document dated August 1723 Lloyd is described as commissary (i.e. deputy) provincial.[14]

At the provincial chapter in Dublin on 23 July 1724 he was again elected guardian of the Dublin convent.[15] On this occasion he is described as emeritus professor of sacred theology. Fr Gregory Cleary states that Lloyd must have taught theology for a considerable number of years to be so described, unless this title was bestowed on him as an honorary degree—which was possible but not likely, according to Cleary. Cleary further speculates that Lloyd may have been teaching theology in Dublin to students of the order.[16] Lloyd does not figure in any official capacity in the order after 1724, probably because he had by then become too busy travelling abroad in various capacities, as subsequent chapters of this book will show. It might be remarked at this point, however, that in the case of a letter to the Pretender dated 9 July 1727 from the heads of the various religious orders in Ireland voicing their opposition to the catholic address to the king of July 1727, Lloyd, with the title of protonotary apostolic, attests the signatures to the letter.[17]

Various sources provide fleeting references to Lloyd during his time in the Cook Street friary. Easily the most traumatic event in which he was involved must have been that Sunday morning at the end of September 1716 when two of the galleries in the chapel collapsed, killing six people. A 1749 report on Dublin catholic chapels tells us that this event occurred while the congregation were waiting to hear a sermon from Fr Sylvester Lloyd.[18] The *Dublin Weekly Newsletter* reported:

> On Sunday last 30th two of the lofts in one of the Popish chapels in Cook Street fell, by which four persons were killed, viz James Farrell, a tailor; Mrs Brown in Cook Street, widow; Mrs Murphy in Patrick Street, widow; Mrs Delaney, mantua maker in Castle Street, besides a great many wounded, some of whom, they say, will not recover.[19]

14 C. Giblin, op. cit. in note 4, *Collectanea Hibernica*, no. 5 (1962), p. 107.
15 Anselm Faulkner (ed.), *Liber Dubliniensis—Chapter Documents of the Irish Franciscans 1719-1875)* (Killiney, 1978), p. I.
16 Gregory Cleary, 'Silvester Lloyd' in *Irish Book Lover*, vol. 16, no. 3, p. 69.
17 Stuart Papers, RA SP(M) vol. 112/27, MFR 770.
18 N. Donnelly, op. cit., p. 15.
19 *Dublin Weekly Newsletter*, 3 October 1716. The discrepancy in the number killed no doubt arises from two of those, said to have been injured in the *Dublin Weekly Newsletter* report, dying later.

Although Lloyd did not take up his first term as guardian of the Cook Street convent until a year later, it appears that the brunt of the task of soliciting funds for the rebuilding of the chapel fell on his shoulders. The following description of this chapel is from the 1749 report on catholic chapels in Dublin:

> The altar piece is a large painting of the Crucifixion and of the Assumption and Annunciation; behind the pulpit, which stands on the Epistle side, is a room for the preacher to rest in; there is a small altar under the pew gallery facing the great altar, which was raised at the expense of the friezemongers in High Street. There are two galleries, that on the Epistle side serves for a choir, and the other is full of pews and was built at the sole expense of one Major Stafford. Adjacent to the chapel is a house that lodges eight friars, with a closet to each chamber.[20]

Although the same report states that the chapel which Lloyd had built had since been 'repaired and altered by others', it appears that it was structurally the same chapel, and indeed quite a substantial and extensive building. The fact that the gallery provided by Major Stafford was 'full of pews' is an indication that this gallery was reserved for what was known as 'the better sort of people'. The chapel Lloyd built was rebuilt about 1751.[21] St Michael & John's chapel, with an entrance from Rosemary Lane, was adjacent to the Franciscan chapel, and when St Michael & John's transferred to Lower Exchange Street in 1815, the Rosemary Lane site was acquired by the Franciscans, who in 1832 opened their present church, which thus stands on the site of two eighteenth century chapels.

It will be seen from the report quoted above that the friary was adjacent to the chapel. Rocque's map of Dublin published in 1756 shows two houses beside the chapel in the lane called Chapel Yard, and it can be assumed that one of these, or perhaps both was the original friary. In 1756, Donnelly tells us, the Franciscans acquired a house (No. 5) in Merchants Quay, which they fitted up as a convent,[22] where they have remained ever since, acquiring in addition several adjacent houses over the years.

Another traumatic event for the Franciscans during Lloyd's time in Cook Street happened on Sunday morning 5 June 1718 when the friary

20 N. Donnelly, op. cit., p. 15.
21 *Irish Builder*, vol. 33 (1891), p. 194.
22 N. Donnelly, op. cit., p. 36.

was raided by the authorities and two priests were arrested. They were subsequently sentenced to transportation.[23] Lloyd was guardian of the convent at this time, but presumably he was able to make good his escape or he would doubtless have shared the same fate as the two arrested. It may indeed be the case that he had already at this date taken up residence in the house known as Adam & Eve's.

Records survive of the trials of two Franciscan priests in Dublin on 7 November 1718 and it seems likely that these were the same two who were arrested on 5 June of that year. Tried on the same day as the two Franciscans were two secular priests, one Jesuit, and one Augustinian. The prosecution in all cases depended on the evidence of Garzia, the priest-hunter. It will suffice to include here the record of the trial of one of the Franciscans, Francis Moor, alias Morrey:

> The third trial was that of Francis Moor . . . He [Garzia] said that he became acquainted with him about fourteen months ago and that he very well knew him to be a Franciscan friar, and to have celebrated Mass very often in Cook Street and for the nuns of the Duchess of Tyrconnell [Poor Clares, North King Street] . . . Being asked by the court if he had anything to say for himself, he [Francis Moor] said that there was one Denis Ryan in Court, who locked and unlocked the chapel door in Cook Street, could make oath that he [Francis Moor] did not celebrate Mass in the said chapel for fifteen months before.

However, Ryan under cross-examination 'did not rightly behave himself' and was ordered to be put into the dock. Francis Moor was thereupon found guilty, 'having officiated contrary to law'.[24] Shortly afterwards Edmond Byrne, archbishop of Dublin, was put on trial for taking on himself the title of archbishop, but there was almost certainly an intervention by some foreign power in his favour with the result that

---

23 Feargal Grannell, 'The strange story of Dr Sylvester Lloyd O.F.M.' Lecture given in the Old Ground Hotel, Ennis as reported in *The Clare Champion* of 15 January 1972. Whether the friars were in fact transported is not clear. Presumably it was the same incident which *Pue's Occurrences* reported in their issue of 7 June 1718: 'Last Sunday morning about two of the clock the High Sheriffs of this city, by order from the Government, seized six or seven of the Romish priests, and left them in prison; but on what account we do not yet know. And last night they were admitted to bail.' According to Fr Grannell's lecture (as reported in *Clare Champion*) six Franciscans were arrested on this occasion, but it seems to me that six priests in all were arrested, only two of whom were Franciscans. The second Franciscan tried on 7 November 1718 was Fr Jones, alias White.

24 Nicholas Donnelly, *Short histories of Dublin parishes* (Dublin, issued in parts, various dates), part 6, pp. 40-42.

Garzia did not come forward to give evidence against him and he walked free.[25]

In 1722 Lloyd was one of many priests appearing in a report on priests in Dublin at that time, compiled in Spanish by Garzia, and presented to the authorities. According to the Protestant Archbishop Synge, Garzia arrived in the country about 1716. He had been a priest in Spain or Portugal but had fallen foul of the catholic authorities there.[26] He continued to officiate as a priest for some time after coming to Dublin and so acquired a detailed knowledge of the priests in the city. This was to prove invaluable to him when he conformed to the established church and adopted the unlovely trade of priest-catcher. His report dated 2 February 1722 provides a valuable insight into how the catholic clergy were organised at that time. The portion dealing with Cook Street is of course of particular interest:

> In Cook Street one [?] chapel.
> Paul Murphy in his chapel in Chapel lane, a secular priest.
> Father O'Hero [O'Hara?], a secular priest.
> Francis [sic] Lloyd, a Franciscan friar in the sign of Adam & Eve.
> Fr Fitzgerald, a Franciscan friar, Fr Walker and four more in the same chapel which belongs to the Franciscan friars.
> Two [priests] in the house of Capt. Jaret in the same Cook Street.
> One [priest] in the high chapel in the same Cook Street.[27]

The chapel in Chapel Lane above appears to have been St Audoen's; Paul Murphy is evidently a mistake for Simon Murphy who was parish priest of St Audoen's in the 1720s. As to why Lloyd was living outside his friary in the house named Adam & Eve, it may be that the post of definitor in the Irish province, which he occupied at this time, entitled him to do so. The Fr Walker is probably Ambrose O'Callaghan, later to be bishop of Ferns, who is known to have used the soubriquet Walker. The high chapel referred to is apparently St Michael & John's, the entrance to which was from Rosemary Lane, which connected Cook Street with Merchants Quay.

The report on the state of Popery 1731 for the parish of St Michael returned two popish masshouses, with about five priests to each mass-

25 *Dublin Intelligence*, 14 November 1719.
26 Gilbert Library, Dublin MS 28, p. 155 - letter dated 6 March 1720 from Edward Synge, archbishop of Tuam to archbishop of Canterbury.
27 Kevin McGrath, 'John Garzia, a noted priest-catcher and his activities 1717-1723', *Irish Ecclesiastical Record*, vol. 72 (July-December 1949), p. 512.

house, but the wardens and minister making the return were unaware that one of the masshouses belonged to the Franciscans, their report going on to say, inter alia, that they knew of no friary in the parish.[28]

Early in the century when the various orders were trying to rehabilitate themselves in the city, accommodation was generally poor. By the 1720s, however, all religious orders had acquired substantial houses in which they could make some attempt at practising the rule of the order. In this the houses of the orders in Dublin and the larger cities differed from those in rural areas, where as a rule the convent consisted of no more than one or two thatched houses where the living of a normal community life was difficult of achievement.[29]

It will be seen that the 1749 report on the Dublin chapels noted that the Franciscans in Cook Street had a convent containing eight friars, with a closet (cell?) to each chamber. But even in the 1720s when reactivation of the penal laws was always lurking in the background, accommodation in Cook Street must have been reasonable. From Garzia's report, dated February 1722, we note that there were six friars living in the convent at that time, with Lloyd living nearby in the house named Adam & Eve. In a mood of despondency in 1728 at not having been promoted to a bishopric, Lloyd speaks of praying for the Pretender in his cell,[30] indicating that cells were provided at that time for the friars in Cook Street. There may not, however, have been a cell for each friar; the situation may have been somewhat like that of the Dominicans in Bridge Street where a 1734 report stated that 'half the community lacks cells'.

But even though in Dublin there could be little excuse for not living according to the rule, the fact of the matter was that the majority of regulars chose to observe their rule in a half-hearted manner or not to observe it at all by living outside their convents. Fr John Kent's report of 1742, which will be dealt with more fully in a later chapter, is far from edifying on this point. He tells us that the religious did not observe their

---

28 *Report on the state of Popery in Ireland, 1731*, reprinted in *Archivium Hibernicum*, vol. 4 (1915), p. 140.
29 It is well to remember that there were some remarkable exceptions. For instance, *A report from the lords' committee appointed to enquire into the present state of popery, relating particularly to counties Galway and Mayo and Galway City* (Dublin, 1731) states: 'It is also remarked that at Kilconnel [County Galway] the masshouse is a very good building where visitations and chapters are said to be held; the friary there is a very good house, rebuilt about three years ago; and that the friary of Ballinakill [County Mayo] is a large building wherein there are several ecclesiastics of the Franciscan order, and a splendid chapel belonging to the friary, and two lay brothers, in whose names the abbey lands are held, and who beg about the country for that society' (King's Inns Library, Dublin Ref. N.I. 26).
30 Stuart Papers, RA SP(M) vol. 96/101, MFR 763.

rules and constitutions even in those particulars which lay well within their power. In Dublin, where there were convents of every order, many religious lived outside them, loafing about with their friends, drinking and talking in taverns until midnight. Even those resident in the city convents did not recite the divine office in common. While readily admitting that there were many learned and excellent friars, he insisted that there were a far greater number of useless, ignorant idlers.[31] Likewise, Fr Myles Macdonnell in a report to the Pretender in April 1745 maintained that 'the grand city of Dublin' was encumbered with a superfluous number of regular and secular clergy . . . 'who either do idle their time there in alehouses etc., or for their bad lives and conversations have been driven from their respective abodes, and hence to get an easy livelihood either fall into that horrible vice of clandestine marriages or other illegal and shameful practices.'[32] Was Sylvester Lloyd one of those friars who lived a far from monastic life outside their convents? Garzia's report (1722) shows that at that time Lloyd was living outside his convent, albeit only a stone's throw away. Later in 1724, when he was making a bid to be archbishop of Dublin, it was said of him that while he made many friends by his charm of speech and pleasant manner, he did not show signs of holiness and gravity. Reading between the lines here we get an impression of a bon vivant, convivial friar, who may have been no stranger to the taverns and the alehouses.

It is fitting to dwell for a moment at this point on the kind of environment around Cook Street in which Sylvester Lloyd and his confréres had perforce to eke out a quite precarious existence.

Cook Street today is a dead street. All that is left in the matter of housing accommodation are a dozen or so working-class houses at one end and part of a block of corporation flats at the other. It is a place for parking cars, a short-cut to somewhere, a non-street. It occasionally comes to life when the congregation filters out the back door of Adam and Eve's church on a Sunday morning, or the children come out to play at the national school nearby.

And yet in the eighteenth century this area teemed with human life and activity. In Cook Street itself Rocque's map of 1756 shows about eighty houses, and the position would have been much the same early in the century and before, for this area was already fully built upon in the second half of the seventeenth century. There were a further 140 houses,

---

31 H. Fenning, op. cit., pp. 147-8.
32 Stuart Papers, RA SP(M) vol. 264/105, MFR 838. The fact that priests did not wear clerical dress made unpriestly behaviour that much easier.

approximately, in the lanes leading off Cook Street—in Rosemary Lane, Skipper's Lane, Michael's Lane, Cock Hill, Burrow's Court, Schoolhouse Lane, Audoen's Arch, Swan Alley, Farrell's Court and Newhall Market— making a total of about 220 houses in all for the area. At an average of fourteen persons per house—and this is a conservative figure for in 1798 the average number of persons per house for this area was sixteen[33]—the population can be computed at around 3,000. As to the religious make-up of the area during Lloyd's time in the friary in Cook Street, catholics and protestants were about evenly divided. This was at a time (*c.*1720) when the city as a whole was about two-thirds protestant and only about one-third catholic.[34]

Houses at this period were not numbered and so the best way to identify a particular house was by a sign. A random selection of signs of houses in Cook Street, culled from the Registry of Deeds, Dublin indicates that several were carrying on a business of some sort. The Ormond Arms, Black Bull, Black Moor's Head, Rose & Crown, Red Lion Prince Eugene and Adam and Eve's were probably inns or taverns, the Ship Tavern obviously so, while the business carried on in the Baker's Arms, Butchers' Arms, Frying Pan and Malthouse is reasonably clear. But the Half Moon, Blew Ball, Mansion House, Two Black Posts and The Struggler do not give much of a clue as to the kind of business transacted, if any, for it was not unknown for private houses also to boast a sign. It was probably a street largely of inns and eating houses, for a line from a contemporary poem has it that 'Cook Street echoes to hot mutton pies'.[35]

As well as being grossly over-crowded, like much of the rest of the city, the atmosphere was gravely polluted because of the prevalence of coal fires. Sanitation was primitive, the streets and lanes were befouled with animal and human excrement, and during periods of heavy rain the floods swept down from High Street, Michael's Lane, Schoolhouse Lane and Audoen's Arch, driving before them the filth of those streets. A local poet and teacher of Mathematics, Laurence Whyte, who lived most of his life in Rosemary Lane, in a piece of doggerel on *the fatigues of a faithful curate* (evidently a curate from St Michael & John's chapel in Rosemary Lane)

33　James Whitelaw, *An essay on the population of Dublin, being the result of an actual survey taken in 1798* (Dublin, 1805), p. 35.
34　Patrick Fagan, 'The population of Dublin in the eighteenth century with particular reference to the proportions of protestants and catholics' in *Eighteenth century Ireland*, vol. 6 (1991), p. 131.
35　Morrough O'Connor, *The petition of Morrough O'Connor . . .* (Dublin, 1740), p. 21. Cook Street was originally the street of the Cooks. The Guild of Cooks had their hall there (Gilbert, History of Dublin, vol. 2, p. 295).

lists one of the chores of that curate as keeping the lane clean for the parishioners frequenting the chapel:

> ... two men in weekly pay I'm forced to keep
> the pavements of this filthy lane to sweep;
> the floods from High Street, Cook Street, Michael's Lane
> still drive *materials* for our work again.[36]

But an even greater nuisance in the curate's eyes was the unruly, drunken behaviour of some people living in the vicinity:

> Contiguous to our house some monsters dwell
> and yet they choose to steer their course to hell;
> this is the greatest nuisance of our lane,
> no jakes or horse dung can be so unclean.
> Vile oaths and curses are their morning prayer,
> each other's fame alternately they tear,
> perpetual mobbings and eternal din
> at every house, without doors and within.
> Like Bacchanalians they conclude the day
> which seldom ends without a bloody fray.[37]

Amid all this Hogarthian low-life revelry, debauchery and violence the little friary seemed incongruously sited. But the uncongenial milieu afforded its own protection. It would be an easy matter to get lost in the crowd, to achieve an anonymity and, during the periodic cracks-down by the authorities, to lie low in safe houses in the labyrinth of mean streets and festering alleyways.

This is an appropriate place to deal with a claim that Lloyd was the author of the lengthy preface to the *Memoirs of the Marquis of Clanrickarde*, published in London in 1723. The claim surfaced in modern times in an article by S. O. Casaide in the *Irish Book Lover* for January-February 1928,[38] where the source for the claim was given as Canon W. P. Burke, author of *Irish priests in penal times*, who, according to O Casaide, was 'the

---

36 Laurence Whyte, *Original poems on various subjects*, (Dublin, 1740), p. 176. Intriguingly, one of the subscribers was 'Revd Dr S. L. ——'. Could this be Whyte's near neighbour for some years, Sylvester Lloyd?
37 Ibid., p. 176.
38 S. Ó Casaide, 'The anonymous prefacer, 1722' in the *Irish Book Lover*, vol. 16, no. 1 (1928), pp. 10-12.

greatest authority on the Ireland of the Penal Days', and who had informed O Casaide some time before that the author of the Preface was Sylvester Lloyd. This preface is chiefly notable for its attack on Dermot O'Connor's translation of Keating's *Foras Feasa ar Eirinn*. Burke's claim that Lloyd was the author must always have been highly questionable, more particularly as the prefacer himself in a letter to the London *Post Boy* in January 1723, without disclosing his name, claimed that he had 'in foreign universities taken all the degrees in the civil law and resided in one of our inns of court these last twelve years'.[39] This latter claim would be manifestly untrue of Lloyd. It now appears to be beyond doubt that the author of the preface was not Lloyd but Thomas O'Sullivane, an Irish scholar living in London.[40]

This is also as good a place as any to dispose of another *canard* with regard to Lloyd, to wit, that at some stage in his career he conformed to the established church. This revelation is to be found in volume 19, page 307 of the (British) Catholic Record Society publications, where Lloyd is dubbed an 'apostate', and where the source for this very serious allegation is given as John Kirk's manuscript biographies of English Catholics. It is significant, however, that when Kirk's biographies were published in book form in 1909, with J.H. Pollen and Edwin Burton as editors, this allegation was omitted.[41]

Alone amongst the Irish Catholic bishops of the first half of the eighteenth century, Sylvester Lloyd's life is quite transparent from 1713 until his death in 1747. We can trace his movements, almost year by year, throughout that period, and from 1725 onwards there is extant a relatively extensive correspondence from him. His life is such an open book from 1713 onwards that it would have been quite impossible for him to have conformed to the established church without such an incredible *volte face* being noted and commented upon by his contemporaries.

---

39 Ibid., p. 11.
40 Alan Harrison, *Ag Cruinniú Meala* , (Baile Átha Cliath, 1988), p. 86.
41 J. H. Pollen & Edwin Burton (eds.), *John Kirk's biographies of English Catholics* (London, 1909).

4

THE QUEST FOR A MITRE BEGINS

The Popery Bill of 1723 was arguably the most stringent measure against the catholic religion ever propounded by the Irish Parliament. When the lord lieutenant, the duke of Grafton, addressed the 1723 session of the parliament he put it to the members that they should make further provision for strengthening the protestant interest and particularly for preventing popish priests from eluding the laws, 'it being too notorious that the number of such is of late greatly increased'.[1] On the recommendation of the lord lieutenant the parliament set up a committee which proposed a number of resolutions directed against catholics, and on the basis of these resolutions a bill was introduced in the 1723-24 session under which, *inter alia*, no registered catholic priest, under the penalty of high treason, could say Mass in the kingdom except those who had taken the oath of abjuration. It also provided that all unregistered priests, as well as bishops and regular clergy, should depart the country before 25 March 1724 on pain of high treason[2]—the 25 March being New Year's Day under the old Julian calendar then in operation in Ireland. The bill was duly passed in mid-November 1723, but like all bills of the Irish parliament it required the consent of the British privy council before it could become law, and there was thus an interim period in which action might be taken by the catholics towards negativing the bill.

It is no harm to give some thought to how the Irish parliament saw the situation and the particular reasons which motivated them in framing the bill. The protestant establishment ever since the defeat of King James had taken particular exception to the regular clergy, who, as well as being the 'Pope's dragoons' were to a man loyal to the Pretender. Although the

---

1 Quoted in Thomas Wright, *History of Ireland from the earliest period to the present time* (London, 1854), vol. 3, p. 309.
2 Cornelius Nary, *The case of the Roman Catholics of Ireland*, in Hugh Reily, *Genuine History of Ireland* (Dublin 1762), p. 127.

regulars had been banned from the country under the Act of 1698, they had in the intervening quarter of a century re-established themselves to such an extent that their numbers by the 1720s were approaching those of the secular clergy. The Dublin government would, it appears, have been prepared to wear a situation where the regulars were kept out and the seculars could go quietly and unobtrusively about their business.

The fact that there was to be a complete *volte face* a couple of years later in 1726, when the pendulum of parliamentary opinion swung back in favour of a measure of toleration for catholics, suggests that there was a substantial measure of opposition within parliament to the 1723 bill. Certainly, two prominent churchmen, who were members of the House of Lords, are on record as being opposed to the bill. Archbishop Edward Synge of Tuam, in a letter dated 13 December 1723 to Archbishop Wake of Canterbury, had this to say:

> A most rigorous bill against Popery had its rise in the House of Commons, but has been a little moderated in the Council [i.e. the Irish Privy Council]. However it still remains such as I cannot give my consent to . . . If any Papist or Popish priest will not solemnly on oath renounce the Pretender, and also the Pope's power of deposing princes or absolving subjects from their allegiance, let him leave the Kingdom or be dealt with as a traitor. But if such a one is ready to do all this and further to give security to the government for his good and loyal behaviour I must own I cannot come into a law to put him to death (under the name indeed of high treason but in reality only for adhering to an erroneous religion and worshipping God according to it).[3]

Likewise Archbishop William King of Dublin expressed his opposition to the bill in a letter dated 2 December 1723 to Mr Edward Southwell,

> I can by no means come into this bill. I think it in itself barbarous and, if I mistake not, at this time unseasonable. There are in my opinion more gentle and effectual ways to root out Popery, but not being for the present profit of the landlords, they will not hear of them. If this act pass, I am well assured that it will never be executed and that we shall have the scandal of a barbarous law without any benefit from it.[4]

3 Gilbert Library, Dublin, Ms 28, Letter no. 77.
4 National Library of Ireland Ms 2056.

The bill was sprung upon a catholic clergy who were gravely disunited, particularly in Dublin, because of an ongoing feud between the secular and regular clergy. The feud basically was due to too many priests being financially dependent on a laity who were too poor to support both wings. Government policy of tolerating the seculars, while affording scant quarter to the regulars, was also calculated to keep the two sides at each other's throats.

The seculars indeed blamed the regulars for drawing the wrath of the government on all priests through flooding the country with hordes of mendicant friars, who were not needed and who were a burden on the catholic laity. Many seculars would have agreed with Cornelius Nary when in his pamphlet *The case of the Roman Catholics of Ireland* he put the question to the parliament: 'Must the civil and quiet priests who have lived this many years in the country, be destroyed for the indiscretion of other priests whose coming they knew nothing of, nor, if they had, was it in their power to prevent.'[5] The fact of the matter was that there were far too many catholic clergy in the country, and Rome itself was soon to admit this and to introduce drastic measures to bring the situation under control.

It must also be said that the tempers of the Irish legislators were not improved, to say the least of it, by two ships putting into harbour in Ireland, probably in Dublin, while the parliament was still in session and landing quite publicly seventeen friars, who had brought with them trunks full of religious books. The friars were promptly lodged in prison and the parliament could put forward their foolhardy exploit as a proximate reason for the enactment of the bill.[6]

Catholic reaction to the bill took three main forms. Firstly, the catholic clergy brought the provisions of the bill to the attention of nuncio Spinelli in Brussels. Spinelli lost no time in requesting papal representatives in catholic countries to implore their respective governments to use their good offices to have the bill negatived.[7] The pope, following receipt of a report from Spinelli, interceded with the various catholic powers to come to the defence of the Irish as resolutely and as speedily as possible.[8] Secondly, the catholic controversialist and activist, Fr Cornelius Nary,

---

5 Cornelius Nary, op. cit., p. 132. It can be said in mitigation of Nary's apparently selfish and unworthy remark that he probably had in mind the specific instance of the landing of seventeen friars in Ireland at his time.
6 Hugh Fenning, *The undoing of the friars of Ireland* (Louvain, 1972) p. 95.
7 Cathaldus Giblin, 'Catalogue of material of Irish interest in the collection Nunziatura di Fiandra, Vatican Archives', *Collectanea Hibernica*, no. 14 (1971), p. 38.
8 Ibid., p. 39.

published in 1724 the pamphlet already mentioned *The case of the Roman Catholics of Ireland*, arguing cogently against the bill. Thirdly, Sylvester Lloyd travelled to Paris late in 1723 with a view to getting the French court to make representations to the British authorities to have the bill quashed.

Some sources claim that Lloyd undertook this mission at the behest of 'the Irish clergy'. Considering the tension that had existed for many years between the secular and regular clergy in Ireland, it might appear at first sight unlikely that a largely secular hierarchy would want a regular to represent them on such a mission. On the other hand, Lloyd appears at this time to have been *persona grata* with a large section of the hierarchy, largely it appears because of his translation of the Montpellier catechism. This catechism, as noted in Chapter 2, was widely used in some dioceses, and Archbishop Byrne of Dublin had organised in its favour highly laudatory opinions from three groups of theologians when it came under the scrutiny of Rome. But whatever the *bona fides* of his mandate from the hierarchy, it is easy to see that Lloyd would be, at the very least, the choice of the regular clergy for such a mission, for he was by this time a prominent figure among the Irish Franciscans, who accounted for about half of the regular clergy in Ireland.

Although Lloyd was later to claim a deal of success for his endeavours in Paris towards having the bill quashed, Sir Patrick Lawless, writing from Paris, to the Pretender on 30 May 1724, was highly dismissive of Lloyd's efforts. Having referred to the delicate position in which France found herself—at peace with Britain and not wanting, at least not openly, to be seen to be espousing the cause of Irish catholics in case the British should seek to exact a *quid pro quo* for French protestants in the shape of the re-establishment of the Edict of Nantes—Lawless continues: 'It is, I say, highly injurious on this account that Father Lloyd should have sent accounts to Rome and all over Europe that by his means and solicitation in France, Ireland was delivered.' Lawless goes on to claim for himself the honour of having scuttled the bill, in that he had persuaded the Marquis de Pozzobueno, the Spanish diplomat, to make successful representations in London to have the bill dropped. Lawless maintained that Lloyd played no role in the suppression of the bill other than that of bringing it to notice in France.[9]

Sir Patrick Lawless belonged to the Lawless family of Talbot's Inch, near Kilkenny city. He served in King James's army and was taken

9 Stuart Papers, RA SP(M) vol. 74/108, MFR 753.

4 Manuscript of poem in Irish on Sylvester Lloyd's return to Ireland c.1723

prisoner at Aughrim. With his family's estate forfeited, he went to Spain where he had a highly successful career as a soldier, a diplomat and finally as governor of Majorca.

While all those mentioned could claim some input into the campaign to have the bill dropped, the principal credit must go to Vatican diplomacy, operating through the catholic courts in Europe. The 1723-4 parliamentary session ended with the bill apparently dropped, but it will be seen later that it became a live issue again during the next (1725-6) session.

It appears to have been following Lloyd's return to Ireland at this time that a poem in Irish was written in his honour. Since it appears only in Tadhg Ó Neachtain's Commonplace Book, now in the National Library, Dublin,[10] it is thought to have been written by Ó Neachtain, who was a schoolteacher living in South Earl Street, Dublin in St Catherine's parish. I have translated the poem into English and included it as Appendix A to this chapter.

Lloyd must have returned to Ireland towards the end of 1723 or the beginning of 1724 for, following the death of Archbishop Byrne of Dublin in February 1724, he was among the first to throw his hat in the ring in an unseemly scramble for the vacant archbishopric. He may have judged, incorrectly as it turned out, that the question of the orthodoxy of his translation of the Montpellier catechism had been satisfactorily settled by the judgments handed down by three sets of Irish theologians on his translation. The part he had played, or imagined he had played, in the quashing of the 1723 bill, could also be used to advantage in advancing his case for promotion as archbishop of Dublin. That he organised in a short space of time country-wide support for his candidacy is evident from Sir Patrick Lawless's letter already mentioned:

> This Father Lloyd has sent over hither [to Paris] one Father Bermingham to solicit this important dignity for him, and made use of subscriptions from home, mostly signed by people living outside the jurisdiction of Dublin, who consequently have no right to postulate, such are Lord Caher and Lord Dunboyne, whose estates are in Munster, Mr Poor [sic] Daly, Mr Denis Meagher and others who have not a foot of ground in that diocese, in order to engage some other credulous people, especially the Burgesses of Dublin, into his measures, for very few were simple enough to believe Father Lloyd or his emissaries; people went about in his name spreading rumours all over the city that he was the man that had lately delivered the country from the storm that hung over their heads,

10 National Library of Ireland Ms G 132, p. 103-4.

though 'tis notorious that he never as yet was even apprised, nor is he to this day, of the measures taken that really diverted that storm, and yet on the strength of the impression that noise made on credulous peoples' minds, he employed his emissaries in the extremity of the provinces of Connaught and Ulster, to get postulations for him, founded on this supposed important service, as appears by the testimonies of Dr Carbery Kelly, Bishop of Elphin and Dr Edward Kelly, Bishop of Clonfert, and others who set forth in his favour that by the speedy measures he took near his Most Christian Majesty [Louis XV], he saved the Kingdom from the heavy blow that was just ready to destroy the Roman Catholic religion in it. He also, as I am informed, got a letter signed by several people to Mr Dillon [i.e. Gen. Arthur Dillon], and writ in a very artful manner to engage him to favour him in his pretension, but never dared address himself to me, for he knows that I am better informed than anyone else here both of his character and of the groundless merit he attributes to himself, and that I am not to be imposed upon. It is manifestly against the spirit of the Church to solicit such dignities, and directly opposite to the constant practice of all ages to prefer new converts to the first employments in it, nay, such as come into it by a very different door than Father Lloyd entered by.[11]

Lawless stated in the same letter that he was speaking out as a native of the 'jurisdiction' of Dublin, and that he had been 'informed from very good hands that there were about twelve different factions that divide the nobility and clergy in such a manner on that head as not to be reconciled if any of them gets the better'. Although there was a lengthy and unseemly tussle on the question of the appointment of a vicar capitular and an archbishop in Dublin at this time,[12] Lawless's claim that about twelve factions were involved is doubtless an exaggeration.

11   Stuart Papers, RA SP(M) vol. 74/108 MFR 753. When Lawless states that he is a native of the 'jurisdiction' of Dublin, he is evidently referring to the province of Dublin and not the diocese, for, as explained in page 50, Lawless was a native of Kilkenny. As to the identity of Fr Bermingham mentioned in Lawless's letter, he may have been the Fr Bermingham mentioned in the Government list of 1697 (see *Irish Builder*, vol. 34 (1892), 174ff) as 'sometimes in St Paul's parish and sometimes in Cook Street'. This Fr Bermingham was probably one and the same as the Francis Bermingham appearing in 'A list of personnel of the Irish Franciscan province in 1700'—Cathaldus Giblin (ed.) in *Collectanea Hibernica*, no. 8 (1965), p. 52—who surfaces again as a confessor for religious in the Cook Street convent in 1729, and who died prior to the provincial chapter held in September 1733—see Anselm Faulkiner, 'Liber Dubliniensis' (Killiney, 1978), pp. 23 and 29.
12   For further information on the wrangling over the appointment of an archbishop and vicar capitular in Dublin at this time see Patrick Fagan, *Dublin's turbulent priest: Cornelius Nary 1658-1738*, (Dublin, 1991), Chapter 9.

Lloyd's purpose in sending Fr Bermingham to Paris on his behalf was no doubt to get the ear of the Pretender's agent there, General Arthur Dillon of Dillon's Regiment, so that Dillon could use his influence to prevail on the Pretender, who lived in Rome, to nominate Lloyd to the pope as the new archbishop of Dublin.

In the meantime Lloyd's bid for the archbishopric had been brought to the attention of nuncio Spinelli. Writing to the cardinals in Rome on 24 March 1724 Spinelli pointed out that there were many trying to get possession of the see of Dublin, and prominent amongst these was Sylvester Lloyd, a Franciscan, 'who has charm of speech but has also many other qualities which render him unsuitable for promotion to Dublin; first of all, his father was a protestant minister and he himself was born into the protestant religion; secondly, he was the author of the English version of the Montpellier catechism, and, although he knew the work had been condemned by the Holy See, he had the second part of the catechism published despite the papal prohibition;[13] he was not in a position to state anything about other candidates but when he had investigated the truth of the reports made to him, he would write again; he would do his best to find out about the doctrine, prudence and modes of life of those priests who are contending for the archbishopric, so that the Holy See will be able to choose the candidate who would be of most benefit to the disturbed and afflicted Irish dioceses.

In a further dispatch to Rome dated 7 April 1724 Spinelli again referred to Lloyd's candidacy. Two gentlemen, noted for their learning, standing and holiness, have now told him that Lloyd was completely unsuitable for promotion to Dublin, even though many would support him for the position; that Lloyd's protestant father was not ashamed to have two wives at the same time; that Lloyd, having killed an adversary in war, cast aside his protestant religion and joined the Hieronymites in Portugal; that some time later he became a Franciscan and, having done scarcely six months probation in that order at St Isidore's College, Rome, he was sent to Ireland where he made many friends by his charm of speech and pleasant manner, but that he did not, however, show signs of holiness and gravity which would merit his promotion to Dublin. As this is the testimony of two outstanding gentlemen, Spinelli does not hesitate to place it before the cardinals; he would let the cardinals know about the qualities of the other candidates as soon as he got definite information concerning them.[14]

13 C. Giblin, op. cit., no. 11 (1968), p. 76. This was a misunderstanding on Spinelli's part—see Chapter 2.
14 Ibid., p. 76.

The Quest for a Mitre Begins

Again on 9 June 1724, in a despatch to Rome, Spinelli, while noting that there were some in Dublin who accused Lloyd of being the instigator of all the trouble there, stressed firstly the necessity of having an archbishop appointed as soon as possible, and, secondly, that he did not consider Lloyd in any way a suitable choice, however much he might wish to procure that dignity.[15]

With regard to the speculation that Lloyd was 'the instigator of all the trouble', it has to be said that he could have had no direct part in the disturbance which took place at this time within the Dublin diocesan chapter, since Lloyd as a regular was not, and could not be, a member of the chapter. It is possible, of course, that he could have engineered trouble from outside the chapter, since he was by all accounts a personable, convincing and knowledgeable man of great charm. The fact that the chapter could not agree on a vicar capitular to manage the affairs of the diocese pending the appointment of an archbishop, nor upon the names which should be sent to Rome and from which the new archbiship might be selected, Lloyd would have seen as advantageous to his candidacy, since he might in that situation hope to see himself emerge as a compromise appointment.

On the question of Lloyd's securing the Pretender's nomination for the archbishopric, it appears from the Stuart Papers that he was not in the running at all. The Pretender gave very serious consideration to the nomination of Bernard Dunne, who was originally from the diocese or province of Dublin but had been a curé in Paris for some time. However, the Pretender had reluctantly to come to the conclusion that 'it was in the present circumstances found by no means desirable to send into the capital of that country [Dublin] any person from France, however qualified he was for the highest dignities.'[16] In the end the Pretender's nomination went to the bishop of Kildare, Edward Murphy, who was duly appointed archbishop of Dublin by the pope. Dunne was appointed bishop of Kildare in place of Murphy. Had the Pretender nominated Lloyd for Dublin it seems probable, in view of Spinelli's deep-felt opposition, that the pope would not have agreed.

It seems likely that, when Lloyd was in Paris in 1723 in connection with the Popery Bill of that year, he visited General Dillon and discussed with him how he might be useful to the Pretender. Self-seeking man that he undoubtedly was, it seems that he saw his role of being useful to the

15   Ibid., p. 78.
16   Stuart Papers, RA SP(M) vol. 76/72, MFR 754.

Pretender as a means of advancing his case for nomination to a bishopric. If so, it was a highly dangerous game he had gotten himself into, since some of the reports he provided for the use of the Pretender's court contained information of such delicacy that in the event of discovery by the Irish authorities, a gory encounter with the hangman in Stephen's Green would have been his fate.

The first of these reports is unsigned and undated and was conveyed by General Dillon to the Pretender with a covering letter dated 15 January 1725 in which Dillon states:

> I enclose under this cover an extract of a letter I received by a sure hand lately come from Ireland. The writer is a person who wishes very well to farmer's [i.e. code for Pretender] cause, though not having the honour of being known to him, and one who made it his business to know the country thoroughly, so as to be able to render a just account of it for farmer's use on a proper occasion.[17]

It later becomes reasonably clear that this anonymous report was written by Lloyd when he states in a much longer report[18] submitted at the beginning of 1726: 'I did from Dublin about twelve months ago furnish Mr Dillon with some reflections on this subject.' These two reports, which are of some value in providing information on the state of the country in the 1720s, are appended to this chapter as Appendices B and C respectively.

Meanwhile, the irrepressible Lloyd had been back again on the Continent during the autumn of 1725. The execution of a number of protestants at Thorn in the catholic kingdom of Poland earlier that year had led to threats of the re-introduction of the 1723 Popery Bill, in the parliamentary session starting in autumn 1725, by the more extreme members of the Irish parliament and the possibility of a new persecution began to loom large.[19] In these circumstances it appears that two Irish Franciscans made their way to the Continent to plead the cause of the Irish catholics, Ambrose O'Callaghan to Vienna to enlist the good offices of the Austrian emperor and Sylvester Lloyd to Paris to plead the cause at the court of France.

17 Ibid., vol. 79/49, MFR 755.
18 Ibid., vol. 90/70, MFR 760.
19 C. Giblin, op. cit., no. 11 (1968), p. 80. Ten protestants were executed in Poland in December 1724 for their part in an attack on and the desecration of a Jesuit college at Thorn. In addition, as a general punishment, protestant churches and schools were closed down. (See Ragnhild Hatton, *George I, elector and king*, London 1978, p. 274.)

The Quest for a Mitre Begins

We find that when nuncio Spinelli came to report to Cardinal Paolucci in Rome on 30 November 1725 on Lloyd's part in this business, he is full of praise for him and gone are the strictures with which he damned Lloyd's bid to be archbishop of Dublin only eighteen months earlier. Maintaining that Lloyd was a man of great spirit and particularly well-versed in matters connected with the present situation, Spinelli tells how Lloyd had come directly from England to visit him in Brussels and how he had given Lloyd a letter of introduction to the nuncio in Paris. When Lloyd had completed his business satisfactorily at Paris, where the court decided to send a strong letter to King George I, he came back to Brussels to find out what Spinelli thought of his plan of going personally to Hanover (where King George was at that time) to press even more forcefully the pleas to be put forward by the French ambassador. However, as Spinelli had an idea that King George was to leave Hanover shortly, and as he felt Lloyd would be easily discovered and would, as a result, do more harm than good to the business he had in hand, he advised him to remain at Brussels for the time being.[20]

Such is nuncio Spinelli's account of Lloyd's part in this affair. However, another account of diplomatic moves at this time at the court of France, in which there is no mention of Lloyd, is available from the correspondence of Abbé James Dunne, an Irishman who was then a curé in Boin, near Chartres, and was later bishop of Ossory.[21] According to a letter dated 10 September 1725 from Dunne to the Pretender, four members of the hierarchy—Archbishop Butler of Cashel, Archbishop MacMahon of Armagh, Archbishop Murphy of Dublin and Bishop Dunne of Kildare—had a conference, presumably in Dublin, on what action should be taken on the threatened reactivation of the 1723 Popery Bill. 'They foresaw' says Dunne 'it would not become their sovereign [i.e. the Pretender] to address to the Emperor considering the injurious and repeated wrongs and crying injustices done by that house to our royal family. 'Tis therefore they had application made another way to his Imperial Majesty.' This latter apparently refers to the selection by the bishops of Ambrose O'Callaghan as their agent to go to Vienna but there is no reference to Lloyd as their agent in France. Dunne goes on: 'As delays are dangerous on such occasions, I consulted some of those at the helm here and the man of my cloth, who has the greatest share of the

---

20 Ibid., p. 80.
21 Richard Hayes, *Biographical dictionary of Irishmen in France*, (Dublin, 1949), p. 77.

administration, told me he expected no such misfortune [i.e. a reintroduction of the 1723 bill] could happen in this juncture.'[22]

In a letter dated 22 October 1725 Abbé Dunne, having received a report of the lord lieutenant's speech at the opening of the current parliamentary session asking the members 'to consider what were the best methods for securing themselves from the mischiefs to be apprehended from the increase in the number of Papists', further reports to Hay, the Pretender's secretary of state:

> I have made it my business to inform this [French] Court also to the full of the designs of our implaccable Cromwellian enemies, who . . . make it a cloak of religion to defeat the King's [Pretender's] friends at a time they enter into the most sacred engagements with Roman Catholic princes abroad. I have been promised by the chief ministers here that they'd be vigilant and one particularly who is of my cloth and has great influence on M. Walpole will be, I hope, useful if things are pushed to the extremity we fear they shall be by our enemies at home.[23]

When the possibility of a reintroduction of the 1723 bill had eventually blown over, Abbé Dunne sends on 8 July 1726 a final report in the matter to Hay:

> As I remained six weeks with M. de Frejus soliciting the affairs of our Irish Roman Catholics, I thought it my duty to inform you of the account I have of a brief sent by the Pope to the King of France, and delivered some days ago, of which I have a copy. It is a letter of thanks for the services rendered to Irish Catholics in staving off the impending blow, which was near reaching them, if M. de Frejus had not so opportunely interfered. . . . I must however entreat your lordship to inform the King [Pretender] that the Bishop of Frejus ordered me to write from him to the catholics of Ireland to behave so as to give no umbrage to the present government, else he could not be useful to us upon a like occasion. I represented to his Lordship that our people acted *apertamente* [openly] to the usurpers and never swore allegiance to any of them because they thought in conscience they could not. His Lordship answered me that his intention was not to advise them to swerve from the loyalty they owed to their sovereign

22 Stuart Papers, RA SP(M) vol. 86/5, MFR 758.
23 Ibid., vol. 87/9, MFR 759.

[Pretender] but that he thought it not inconsistent with our tenets to live quietly under a government that protected them, and await favourable opportunities without undertaking anything that may bring a persecution on them from the government until they could find themselves in a situation to assert right.[24]

The person referred to above as 'a man of my cloth' and 'M. de Frejus' (i.e. bishop of Frejus) was André de Fleury, later to be cardinal and effective prime minister of France. Further recognition of de Fleury's critical part in this business is contained in a letter dated 2 March 1726 from secretary of state Cardinal Spinola to nuncio Spinelli, from which it is clear that the authorities in Rome gave much of the credit for quashing the bill to the intervention of de Fleury with Horatio Walpole, British minister at the court of France and brother of Robert Walpole, prime minister of Britain.[25]

Despite the fact that Abbé Dunne completely ignores the part played by Lloyd at the French court in regard to the reactivation of the 1723 bill, there can be no doubt but that Lloyd did play an important role, for have we not already seen the testimony of Spinelli in that regard? But whether Lloyd undertook his mission to France at the behest of the Irish hierarchy is debatable; it is quite possible that he had no other mandate than that of the regular clergy.

In 1725 General Dillon was replaced as the Pretender's agent in Paris by Colonel Daniel O'Brien. Since O'Brien was to figure as a correspondent of Lloyd over many years, it is appropriate at this point to include a thumb-nail sketch of his career. The son of Morrough O'Brien from Carrigogunnell, County Limerick, who had risen to the rank of general in the French army, Daniel O'Brien was born at Perpignan in the Pyrenèes Orientales departement of France in 1683. Following in his father's footsteps, he rose to the rank of colonel in the French Army. He served as the Pretender's unofficial ambassador to the French court from 1725 until 1747 and was deeply involved in the various Jacobite plots and intrigues over those years. He also served as a link-man with Irish Jacobites such as Lloyd; the latter rarely wrote direct to the Pretender but tended to funnel his communications through O'Brien. In 1747 the Pretender brought O'Brien to Rome where he installed him as his secretary of state and created him earl of Lismore. He retired from the Pretender's service in 1758 and died the following year.[26]

24 Ibid., vol. 95/67, MFR 763.
25 C. Giblin, op. cit., no. 14 (1971), p. 40.
26 R. Hayes, op. cit., p. 214.

Meanwhile Lloyd's quest for a mitre continued. When Bishop Donagh MacCarthy of Cork died early in 1726 he was not shy in putting himself forward for the vacancy. In the course of a letter to Colonel O'Brien dated 24 March 1726 he wrote:

> I told you in my last that the bishop of Cork was lately dead and that my friends would have me succeed him, if you think it proper, for I leave it entirely to you. The recommendations in my favour are in the hands of one Father O'Madden in St Isidore's at Rome. I shall be impatient till I hear from you.[27]

But apparently his friends had let him down for on 17 July 1726 we find Hay, the Pretender's secretary of state, writing to Col. O'Brien:

> I sent to know of Father O'Madden, the guardian of St Isidore's, if he had received any postulations to the bishopric of Cork in Mr Lloyd's favour, to which he made me answer that he had not. Neither has Father McLaughlin presented any, so that I reckon his correspondents have not served him well, having perhaps their views directed elsewhere, which it's fit I think you should inform him of, since the King has delayed deciding in that affair for some time, and is himself well inclined towards Mr Lloyd for the bishopric of Cork.[28]

August 1726 was to find Lloyd at Douai in North East France, for the purpose of delivering a near kinsman of the duke of Ormond, Lord Cahir's eldest son, to the English college there.[29] From Douai he wrote rather philosophically to Hay, who had recently been created earl of Inverness by the Pretender:

> Col. O'Brien has done me the honour to communicate to me the contents of the letter your Excellency was so good to write him on the subject of the vacant bishopric of Cork, and his Majesty's gracious intentions with regard to me. I shall never be able to express the just

---

27 Stuart Papers, RA SP(M) vol. 93/82, MFR 761.
28 Ibid., vol. 95/104. MFR 763. The Fr McLaughlin may be Mark MacGlaghlin who died before September 1733—see Anselm Faulkiner (ed.), *Liber Dubliniensis* (Kilkenny, 1978).
29 It is not clear from Lloyd's letter whether he was delivering Lord Cahir's son (James Butler) to the English College at Douai or to the Irish College there. However, the diaries of the English College in fact record the arrival in August 1726 of Butler at that college, accompanied by Lloyd. (See *The Douai College Diaries*, printed in vol. 28 of *Publications of the Catholic Record Society*, (London, 1928), p. 132.)

and dutiful sense I have of his Majesty's great goodness: but shall never cease to pray that God may bless and prosper him in all his undertakings, that he may overcome his enemies, that he may triumph in the throne of his ancestors, and that he may never be without an Inverness to assist him in his counsels. These, my Lord, shall be my constant prayers, let my station in life be what it will. And I beg your Excellency will do me the justice to believe that I shall at all times be better pleased with his Majesty's good opinion of me than with the highest dignity in the Church. If his Majesty in his great wisdom thinks that it may be for the honour of God and his service, I shall receive it from his regal hands with joy and thankfulness. If otherwise, I am but dust and ashes, and shall pray for him in my cell with as much fervour as if he had placed me upon a throne and put a mitre upon my head. As to any postulations or recommendations from Ireland, I can only say that I thought there had been some in Father O'Madden's hands. I believe I was some years ago recommended by many of the prelates and nobility of our country for the archbishopric of Dublin, and I have not since that time forfeited their esteem. This, my Lord, is all I can at present say. . . . If it were even proper for me to move in my own favour, I can do nothing at present being at this distance from my friends. I must therefore take the liberty to throw myself entirely upon your Excellency's goodness and beg your protection at least so far as that I may not suffer in his Majesty's opinion for want of new recommendations on this occasion. I know but too well what some of my countrymen are capable of, when their pretensions are crossed, and I tremble for the consequences, so that I had much rather my name were never made use of than that I should be made the butt of their malice. [He goes on to give some personal details of his early life which have already been mentioned in Chapter I] I most humbly beg your Excellency's pardon for this tedious letter and if what I have here sincerely (but perhaps with too much freedom) said to your Excellency should not be enough to remove any impressions my enemies may have made, I most sincerely refer myself to what the Nuncio in Brussels shall say of me. He has our royal master's interests very much at heart, he knows the affairs of our country and will, I am sure, without favour or affection inform your Excellency of the truth.[30]

---

30 Stuart Papers, RA SP(M) Vol. 96/101, MFR 763.

For want of the necessary postulations in Lloyd's favour then, the Pretender was obliged to pass him over and give his nomination to Thaddeus MacCarthy, who was appointed bishop of Cork by the Pope. However, the Pretender's estimate of Lloyd was such that it was only a matter of time until he would find it possible to accommodate him with a bishopric.

Meanwhile it was no harm to keep up the pressure and leave no stone (or vacant bishopric) unturned, as in the course of a letter to O'Brien dated Dublin, 5 January 1727:

> I am infinitely obliged to you for the honour you did me in sending my letter to 275 [the Pretender] whose good opinion is dearer to me that all the dignities in the world. As for vacancies there are a great many: Ross in the County of Cork, Kilmore, Down & Connor and Derry in the North. I leave all to yourself.[31]

With all these vacancies around, promotion could not be much longer delayed!

Appendix A: *On the return of Father Sylvester Lloyd from France to Ireland*[32]

1. Welcome to the Land of Flann,[33] dear Lloyd from Edmunds' plains,[34] scion of the warriors of the territory of Corc,[35] eminent, fortunate advocate.

---

31 Ibid., vol. 101/67, MFR 765.
32 What is believed to be the only manuscript copy of this poem is included in National Library of Ireland MS G 132. An tAthair Cuthbert Mág Craith edited the poem and included it in the anthology *Dán na mBráthar Mionúr* (Dublin, 1967), pp. 280-2.
33 Land of Flann: Ireland.
34 In the second line of the first stanza of the original poem occurs a phrase which I read as 'a chláir Eumainn'. However, in his *Dán na mBráthar Mionúr* Cuthbert Mág Craith rendered this phrase as 'a chléir chumainn'—the 'h' in 'chumainn' in italics to indicate that it is not in the original. Accepting that what Ó Neachtain wrote was 'a chláir Eumainn', there is then a problem as to what this phrase means. The obvious interpretation is that it is a place-name, but there are a number of objections to this. Firstly, when 'clár is used with a proper name to form a place-name, (e.g. Clár Cruachan, Clár Daire), the initial letter of 'clár' should be a capital. Secondly, it has not been the practice to use the plural 'cláir' in such place-names. Thirdly, I have searched in vain for 'Cláir Eumainn' as a place-name. Admittedly, there is the possibility that what Ó Neachtain had in mind was not a place-name as such, but the estate of some landlord with a Christian name Edward or Edmund—Edmund Butler, Lord Dunboyne, would fill the bill here—in which case the translation 'from the plains of Edward/Edmund' would be quite acceptable.
35 'Críche Cuirc': the territory of Corc, a Munster king of the fifth century. According to *Onomasticon Goedelica* 'Críche Cuirc' was generally understood to mean North Munster or the counties of Clare, Limerick and Tipperary.

2. Thou tree bearing the fruit of the great love of God, noble prop of the faith, yet to be fierce in spirit is not your disposition, oh gentle friend, who never deserved reproach.

3. Thou strong delegate against the foreigners' laws, travelling over the rough seas, suffering the persecution and the hatred of the English, to save your country and your friends.[36]

4. Dear companion of the true faith, Ireland's darling and her honour, godly favourite of the savants and the elders, discreet confidant of the gentry.

5. Thou pledge of the Irish, guarding his flock, preserving them and minding them; like an angry wolf sweeping away sin, dear countenance of love.

6. Thou thirst-preventing well of wisdom, dear philosopher of the professors, faithful theologian of the Son of God, you who were humbled so you could be exalted.

7. Thou godly student of obedience, bright star of the Friars Minor, dear child of Francis of the miracles, dear fount of gentleness.

8. In France great was your charge as a delegate from the gentry of Ireland, a delegate who procured a hearing from the king of France, and affection, love and respect from the nobles.

9. May you have indulgence from God as a result, supplicator and intercessor for Ireland; night and day continually may saints and angels guard you.

10. May St Anthony of Padua[37] protect you and shelter you, dear love, until you reach the Fortress of the Son of God in the company of Holy Mary and the angels.

11. But, for fear of making orphans of us, may it be long until you reach your King in the Kingdom of Heaven; God save you, my love!

12. O love of the poets and love of every saint, O love for whom every good man would provide every luxury; O love of Ireland who freed her from every sorrow, O love of the Irish, a hundred welcomes to you.

13. Awaiting you are every churchman and authority, all the gentry and nobility, every territory, every clan, old and young; awaiting you is their welcome, their talk, their music, their strength; forever their gentle love, O Lloyd, is yours.

14. Yours forever their hearts without lie or guile, dear father of the weak

---

36 This verse refers to Lloyd's visit to France in 1723 to seek support for the quashing of the 1723 Popery Bill.
37 Anthony of Padua, a Franciscan saint.

and alms-seeking orphans; may the blessing of Jesus shelter you from the persecution of the English; night and day hundreds of welcomes for you—15.—to this land of Fiacha and of Art,[38] thou knowledgeable historian, who was conducted by Almighty God over the waves to mist-enshrouded Ireland, which awaits good men to rescue her. Hail!

Appendix B: *Stuart papers—British Library Ref. MFR 755, Vols. 79, No. 49*

Extract of a letter from Dublin writ to Dutton [Arthur Dillon], by a person of credit and well-versed in the state of his country, for farmer's [Pretender's] use.

Sir,

I have spent this last summer in the western parts of this kingdom, where I had frequent opportunities of seeing multitudes of your friends, who long for nothing so much as to have it in their power to convince you of their readiness to serve you. There are none absolutely against you but such as have got illegal fortunes, which they are sure to lose if you gain the law suit. Those for you may be reduced to three classes.

The first are of those who are in your own way of thinking as to God and man, and who never deviated from it.

The 2nd is of those who lately were of the same opinion but have altered by fear or interest.

The third are those who differ from you in one point but who, out of principle of justice or resentment, are now the most forward and loud in their declarations for you.

The first are infinitely the greatest number and such as you may entirely depend upon. If you will give me leave to except some few, perhaps not absolutely in the whole, whose possessions are the right of some persons in your circumstances, and whose avarice stifles the sentiments of virtue, but they are men of such mean character, that they are worth nobody's while to mind them.

As to the 2nd class of men who have changed their way of thinking, they are numerous and of the most powerful in this kingdom. A great deal is to be expected from them, and I dare confidently say that they are rather willinger to serve you than any of those mentioned in the first class, as it is certainly

---

38   Land of Fiacha and Art: Poetic name for Ireland.

more in their power so to do, being men of fortune, qualified by the laws to possess what implements may be necessary for you, and as they are old natives, they still retain the affections of the people. I can firmly assure you from my own knowledge of several amongst them, they are more impatient than any to see you; the consciousness of their failure, together with the impossibility, as the case now stands, of retrieving it otherwise than by supporting your claim, adds a spur to their friendship and makes them more earnest to serve you than ever.

I come now to the third class, you have truly in it several persons of true honour, at the head of whom I'll place the old Earl,[39] who continued always very steadfast to you, and will remain your friend to his dying days. These are men of interest, capable to lead a great part of the multitude. The rest are guided by the hope of having better usage from you in point of trade, which they all follow. They are very zealous to drink your health and indiscreet enough to babble a great deal, which though useful in some measure to keep up sinking spirits, yet certainly do more hurt than good, for by this indiscretion they alarm your enemies, and give handles by their folly for oppressing your real friends, and making new rules to disable them from ever serving you. Though I should not advise to depend on the humour of this latter sort, animated at present against Wood's coin, if not set to work in such a temper, yet there will remain a twain not to be despised. On the whole I can assure you of ten that will join you for one that will appear against you, which I think is a fair chance. When you find a proper time for it, and whenever you please to give a call, I shall be ready to wait on you and explain the particulars for and against you by name and dwelling.

Appendix C: *Stuart Papers—British Library Ref. MFR 760, Vol. 90, No. 70*

An account of the present state of Ireland by Father Lloyd, received enclosed in Col. O'Brien's letter of February the 4th 1726

---

[39] The 'old earl' was probably John Bourke, ninth earl of Clanrickard, who had been a colonel in the army of James II and had been taken prisoner at Aughrim. He was attainted and his estates were forfeited, but he regained them in the early years of Queen Anne's reign. In fact he had already died, aged eighty-two, when Lloyd wrote his report, but Lloyd must not have known that. (See Lodge, *The Peerage of Ireland*, vol. I, p. 139). The fact that this report is not as clear and grammatical as Lloyd's reports and letters usually are, may be due to Dillon's amanuensis not having copied the original accurately.

Sir,

I have in obedience to your commands made the following observations upon the present state of Ireland with regard to the King's [Pretender's] interests. I did from Dublin about twelve months ago furnish Mr. Dillon with some reflections on this subject which were, I believe, more exact and just than anything I can say in my present hurry. If they were laid before His Majesty in the manner I wrote them I must for some things refer myself to that paper. However, Sir, I shall to the best of my memory and judgment give you my sentiments and shall be at all times rejoiced to find any opportunity of sacrificing my life and liberty to His Majesty's [Pretender's] service.

All of the places of trust and profit in Ireland are in the hands of His Majesty's enemies, or at least of such as appear to be his enemies, though I do not doubt but some amongst them would prove friends in case of trial. We must however at present consider them as enemies.

The standing army, consisting of twelve thousand effective men, all on the Irish Establishment though not all at this time in the Kingdom, are commanded by His Majesty's enemies, except the Royal Scotch, commonly called Orkneys, who are to a man, officers and soldiers, the King's friends, and have been therefore quartered and continued in Ireland ever since the insurrection in Scotland. The private men in all the other regiments are mostly friends and would, in case there were a stand made, recruit His Majesty's army in time of trial.

The nobility, gentry, clergy and people of Ireland are with regard to religion and government to be considered as follows.

First, the established religion is the Protestant and takes into its civil and national communion and protection all those who are not Catholics. It is hard to say exactly at this time how this society stands with regard to the King's interest or whether His Majesty has most friends or enemies amongst them. But 'tis my opinion that he gains every day and that the numbers are for him, especially since the late attempts made upon Ireland by the copper patent [*in margin*; A Patent to one Wood to coin brass farthings for Ireland] and the act of Navigation.

A great many of the nobility and gentry are, and always were, his professed friends, and so are a great majority of the Bishops and inferior clergy. And their hearts turn every day more and on account of the partiality shown by the Government in promoting English men only to bishoprics and benefices. The Bishop of Bristol's[40] late promotion to the see of Armagh hath given great offence to all the clergy of Irish birth.

The civil employments being in like manner given only to English men causes great heart burnings among the great men and may in time have a good effect. The late removal of Lord Midleton, als. Brodrick,[41] from being Chancellor and of sending Mr West, an Englishman, to fill that place has angered the whole Brodrick faction, which was the most Whiggish and powerful in the Kingdom. Their resentment has shown itself with violence in this session of Parliament wherein they have opposed the Court in everything; and my letters from Ireland say they have baffled Lord Carteret[42] in all his demands. So that if a moderate way of speaking with regard to property and restitution could be but politically observed by some of the King's friends as well abroad as at home, and any room given to think that Ireland should, in case of a restoration, be at greater liberty with regard to its national government and foreign trade than it now is, I don't doubt but His Majesty would find the good effects out on the day of trial.

The common people likewise and soldiers of the Protestant religion have had their cause of disgust by an Order directed some time ago to Lord Shannon, General of the forces, for purging (as they call it) the army of all the Irish and putting English men in their places,[43] for though this was not thoroughly executed in all the regiments yet the distinction and preference gave disgust to all those of Irish growth. This circumstance might be also improved for His Majesty's service in case it were thought proper that anything should be ever undertaken and a party assembled which could cover deserters.

The great and powerful body of men among the Protestants who are best able and most willing to serve His Majesty are they who to preserve their estates or acquire new ones changed from the Catholic to the Protestant religion. These men did indeed change their language but not

40 The bishop of Bristol was Hugh Boulter who was appointed archbishop of Armagh in 1724. As one of the lords justices, who effectively governed the country in the absence of the Lord Lieutenant, he was to play a leading role in the Irish administration until his death in 1742 (see *Dictionary of National Biography*).
41 Alan Brodrick, Lord Midleton, had filled a variety of posts in Ireland—solicitor-general (1695), speaker of the house of commons (1713), lord chancellor (1714). But his opposition to Wood's halfpence was to make him so obnoxious to the lord lieutenant, Lord Carteret, that it was necessary for him to resign as lord chancellor in 1725, when he was succeeded by the Englishman, Richard West (see *Dictionary of National Biography*).
42 Lord Carteret, despite his treatment by the Irish house of commons, was to return for a further term as lord lieutenant in 1727.
43 It is of interest that Irish protestants (as well as Irish catholics) were debarred from serving in the British army, although Lloyd notes that the order was not fully executed in all regiments. However, the purpose in debarring protestants was to prevent the further diminution of the protestant population in Ireland.

their manner of thinking; however free they made with God, I am sure they did not forsake their King. They are the most eager and impatient to serve him of all his subjects, for besides their affection for His Majesty's person, they cannot as the laws now stand return to the Profession of what their consciences still dictate, without a *Praemunire*.[44] They must make their children be really what they themselves are but in appearance, and they despair of ever easing their minds and saving their estates but by a restoration.

This makes them willing and the situation they are in makes them able. They are in possession of their fortunes. They are well-mounted and armed. They are many of them in both houses of Parliament, many in the army and many in Commissions of the Peace and other employments all over the Kingdom. Their followers, or clans, as being old natives, are vastly superior in numbers to the Old English Protestants, as they are called, who are still looked upon but as aliens and strangers by the common people. And they are demonstrably, for these reasons, better able to serve their King than the English Protestants are, though their estates may be otherwise greater.

This the Government is so well convinced of and alarmed at, that they have in this present session of Parliament set a law on foot which has already passed the House of Commons to prevent, as they term it, the Occasional Conformity of Papists and whereby they intend to disable all converts from the Popish to the protestant religion from bearing any employments, civil or military, from sitting in Parliament, pleading at the bar etc till after seven years of probation from the date of their conversion, during which time they are to receive the Sacrament according to the rites of the Protestant Church three times every year and produce a certificate from their respective curates of having so done. Otherwise they are to be reputed papists and Recusants.

What is all this for but to discourage their becoming Protestants? It was found by experience that the penal laws made against Catholics were so far from strengthening the Protestant interest that they rather put the sword into the hands of the Government's enemies. This law, though it should not pass in England, will add to their resentments and make them every day more and more impatient to restore the king.

And I think I may with confidence assure you, Sir, that even among the English and Old Protestants, the King's interest is at this day equal, if not

---

44 Praemunire: a writ charging the sheriff of a county to summon a person accused of asserting or maintaining papal jurisdiction. The legal basis for it was the pre-Reformation Statute of Praemunire in the reign of Richard II.

superior, to the Usurper's. The North of Ireland, called Ulster, is indeed mostly inhabited by Scotch, and those the most rigid Presbyterians, yet I am assured that the better half of them are the King's friends. The town of Derry, which was the first which opposed his royal father, is at this day in such a way of thinking that the Government hath not been able for some years past to get either a Whiggish Mayor or Sheriffs elected to that Corporation. The chief of the Protestant gentry all over the North are His Majesty's friends. If it be thought necessary or proper I will from Ireland furnish you with a list of their names, estates or interests as well in the North as in the other parts of the Kingdom.

In the meantime let us further consider—

That the Roman Catholic religion, notwithstanding all the pains taken to abolish it, is that which is most universally professed. And is, I am positive, in regard to numbers in the proportion of seven to one to all other sects in the kingdom.[45] A great many of the nobility and gentry are still Catholics and have considerable estates and interests. Most of the dealers and rich tradesmen are Catholics and I am of opinion that Dublin alone would furnish the King with ten thousand able-bodied young men, apprentices and journeymen to several trades, weavers, tailors, shoemakers etc, a great many of them descended of good families, whose estates have been forfeited and are therefore very impatient of their sufferings and would be ready on the first notice to sacrifice themselves for the king. The rest of the great towns, as Cork, Waterford, Kilkenny[46] etc, are to be considered in proportion. Those men are not indeed suffered to carry arms, yet are not altogether strangers to the use of them having war and a restoration always in their minds, and being in the towns accustomed to certain exercises whereby youth are prepared for war.

45 Lloyd's statement that there were then (1725) in Ireland seven catholics for every one protestant (that is, that only 12.1/2% of the population were protestant) is quite inaccurate. In fact the protestant share of the population in 1725 was 20-25%. A census carried out by the hearth money collectors for 1732-33 (see *Abstract of the number of Protestant and Popish families*, Dublin, 1736) shows that there were three protestant *families* for every eight catholic ones, that is, that 72.7% of families were catholic. But when allowance is made for the higher number of persons per catholic family and deficiencies in the returns, the catholic proportion of total population would be something in the range 75-80%, and the protestant proportion 20-25%. The first census to give a break-down on a religious basis, that of 1836, showed the catholic proportion as 81%.

46 The inclusion of Kilkenny, with Cork and Waterford, as the great towns in Ireland after Dublin may appear surprising and might imply that Lloyd had some personal knowledge of Kilkenny. However, figures for 1726 in Arthur Dobbs, *Essay on trade and improvement of Ireland* (Dublin, 1731), part 2, p. 6, show that the number of houses in Kilkenny was greater than in Waterford, Galway or Belfast. But the number of houses in Limerick (not mentioned by Lloyd) was some 50% higher than in Kilkenny.

You may, Sir, from these observations see that His Majesty's interest is not so low in Ireland but that a great deal may be expected from us in case His Majesty's service require it. We should at least be able to employ twelve thousand of the usurper's best troops which would be no small service while His Majesty's friends made a push elsewhere.

A few Irish officers of good conduct sent beforehand into the respective parts of the kingdom, whereof they are natives, would soon make an universal commotion and the King would find as many men as he had arms to give them. Nothing would be more easy than to surprise the Barracks and Castle of Dublin where there are ordinarily but one regiment of Horse and two of foot, and where there are arms and ammunition for several thousands of his Majesty's friends.

In case of an insurrection I am of opinion that the River of Waterford would, for several reasons, be the best place for landing arms, ammunition etc. *First*, because it is an open and safe entrance and has a large communication by the River Suir to the town of Waterford seven miles from the sea, and to the town of Ross, about the same distance by the rivers Nore and Barrow. The coast is for above forty miles without other fortification than the small fort of Duncannon wherein are a company of men. This place might be easily surprised and, though it should not, cannot hinder the landing of men or arms.

The River is about sixty miles from Dublin and forty from Cork. The counties of Waterford, Kilkenny and Wexford meet here. The country of both sides is full of the King's friends and the main succours [reinforcements] that may be reasonably expected from Dublin have nothing in their way to hinder them from flocking to the standard. The enemy's troops are quartered mostly upon the Western coast from Cork to Sligo and are at a great distance. The country about this place, especially the counties of Waterford and Wexford, are naturally fortified with mountains and bogs where the King's forces might with safety wait the coming of their friends from all the other parts of the Kingdom. Two day's march would from this place carry them to Dublin, or into the centre of the Kingdom where they might from every side expect succours and hinder the joining of the Usurper's army.

The River is within twenty or five and twenty leagues of the South coasts of Wales and of the River of Bristol, so that there might be an easy communication between his Majesty's friends in the West of England, and those in Ireland.

If Waterford should not be thought the most proper place, there are in the counties of Cork, Kerry and Clare several harbours and the country of every side inhabited by the King's friends. There are from Galway northwards as far as Carlingford also several good harbours. But as these places are very remote the enemy could join with ease and hinder the country from coming in. If Waterford should not be pitched upon I would recommend the counties of Galway and Mayo because most of the great estates in that part of the Kingdom are either in the hands of Catholics or such as have turned Protestant within these twenty years past and are, as above mentioned, the best able and most willing to serve His Majesty. All the common people are Catholics and you may in some places ride twenty miles before you meet the house of a Protestant or man disaffected to the King. There is nothing in their way to hinder their march to Athlone, a fortified place on the river Shannon and the most important post of the Kingdom, though but slightly garrisoned. This is the place where the enemy will endeavour to form their camp, if not prevented. A rising in the county Galway and about Waterford at the same time cannot miss having a good effect because the forces may march directly to one another and cut off the enemy from meeting. All these things I most humbly submit to better judgments. But as it may be for His Majesty's service to know what persons of weight and good sense might be depended on or entrusted beforehand with a design of this nature, I shall sincerely give you my opinion.

Amongst His Majesty's friends of the Protestant religion there are a great many who drink his health every day and will, I am sure, fight for him on occasion, but I should not be for trusting many of them with so important a secret. However, if His Majesty has not other reasons against it, I should in the first place for the province of Leinster propose the Earls of Anglesey[47] and Grenade[48] for the secret, and among the clergy Vesey, bishop of Ossory,[49] a creature of the Duke of Ormond and a very worthy man.

---

47 Arthur Annesley, fifth earl of Anglesey, in place at the time of Lloyd's report, was a brother of James, the third earl, who had married in 1699 Lady Catherine Darnley, natural daughter of James II. She divorced him in 1701 on grounds of cruelty. However, the marriage was indicative of Jacobite tendencies in the Annesley family which were apparently shared by the fifth earl (see Burke's *Extinct and dormant peerages* (London, 1881)).
48 Grenade should probably read Granard. (It has to be remembered that Lloyd wrote these names in a numerical code and mistakes may have been made in deciphering.) Arthur Forbes, second earl of Granard (1656-1734) had commanded a regiment in the army of William III, but was deprived of it and was imprisoned in the Tower of London for a time. He had previously served under Turenne in the French army. It would not be too surprising to find that he was a Jacobite sympathiser. (see Burke's *Peerage and Baronetage*, 105th edition).
49 The bishop of Ossory in question was Sir Thomas Vesey. From being chaplain to the duke of Ormond he was, through the influence of Ormond, advanced in succession to the bishoprics of Killaloe and Ossory. As a creature of Ormond he could be expected to support Ormond's defection to the Pretender in 1715 (see *D.N.B.*).

For the province of Munster the Earl of Bari[50] and Sir Richard Cox,[51] formerly Chancellor of Ireland and a creature of the duke of Ormond, turned out on that account. Among the clergy the Bishop of Cork.[52]

For the province of Ulster Lord Charlemont[53] and Mr Brownlo,[54] commonly called the great [Blank]. All the Protestant clergy except the bishops, who are mostly made by this Government, are the King's friends.

For the Province of Connaught Lord Athenry[55] and Lord Mayo,[56] both converts. The bishops are of late creation but the inferior clergy are general friends. A great deal is to be expected from this province, being the most Catholic in the kingdom.

There are great numbers of Roman Catholics who are men of sense and great loyalty in most of the counties of the Kingdom. If it be thought necessary I shall be able to furnish you with a list of their names.

This, Sir, is the truest state of Ireland that I can at present think of. I have some materials and memoirs at home[57] that may be of use. If you think it for His Majesty's service I will with the approbation of some of his best friends send you a further plan from Dublin. I beg, Sir, you will

50 I have failed to discover any Lord Bari. What is intended no doubt is Barrymore. The holder of that title at the time of Lloyd's report was James Barry (1667-1748), a British army general and a privy councillor. From 1710-1747 he was a Tory member of the British house of commons, while he was simultaneously a member of the Irish house of lords, where with other lords on one occasion he made an unsuccessful bid to have the accounts of the nation laid before the house. Despite all this, Lloyd was correct in listing him as a supporter of the Pretender, for he was later to be an active Jacobite (see Eveline Cruikshanks's article on him in Romney Sedgwick, *The house of commons 1715-1754* (London, 1970).

51 Sir Richard Cox had filled several Government posts—lord chancellor (1703), lord justice (several times) and chief justice of the queen's bench (1711). His removal from the latter post on the fall of the Tories on the death of Queen Anne may have pushed him in the direction of the Pretender (see *D.N.B.*).

52 The bishop of Cork in question was Peter Browne. When provost of Trinity College, Dublin he had refused to participate in an oath to King William. He also provoked controversy by questioning the appropriateness of drinking to 'the glorious and immortal memory'. He was commemorated in a protestant oath of the time with the words 'a fart for the bishop of Cork' (see *D.N.B.*).

53 James Caulfield, second Viscount Charlemont, was MP. for Charlemont from 1703 to 1727 (See Burke's *Peerage & Baronetage* 105th edn.).

54 The Brownlows were county Armagh landlords who held the Armagh and later the Lurgan seat in the Irish house of commons.

55 Francis Bermingham, 14th Lord Athenry, married Lady Mary Nugent, daughter of the catholic earl of Westmeath. His involvement in the hounding of O'Gara, catholic archbishop of Tuam, in the early 1730s does not mark him out as in any way accommodating to his former co-religionists (see *The complete peerage*, 1982, vol. I, col. 294).

56 Theobald Bourke, Viscount Mayo, had conformed to the established church in 1709 but some of his children were reared as catholics. One of his daughters was educated by the Dominican Sisters at their convent in Channel Row, Dublin (see NLI, Pos. 3787).

57 This indicates that Lloyd compiled the report while on the continent, probably when he visited Paris in the autumn of 1725.

assure yourself that I would freely lay down my life to restore His Majesty and that I am with the greatest respect your most obedient, humble servant.

5

THE QUESTION OF AN OATH

The formulation of an oath acceptable to catholics who were prepared to accept the reality of the Hanoverian succession and to renounce the Pretender, was first mooted in 1722 by Edward Synge, archbishop of Tuam, in a letter to Archbishop Wake of Canterbury. Synge enclosed with his letter a draft of the oath he had in mind. In the course of the letter he set out the reason for the proposed oath:

> And some there are who think it hard to require an Oath [i.e. the Oath of Abjuration] from them, which even an honest Papist, who desires to be faithful to the present Government, cannot in conscience take. . . . To obviate all these pretences, and for the relief of all Papists that are sincere and honest, and the detection of those that are not, I have often thought that an Oath might be framed against which they can have no manner of pretence, except they will openly profess themselves not to be subjects to King George but to the Pretender and the Pope. . . . A Papist, whose interest as well as duty obliges him to be faithful to the King, positively told me that, if I could draw up the form of an Oath of Fidelity, that should be free from those objections which he made, and I have above mentioned, he would propose it to as many of his persuasion as he could; and was content that all who refused it should be treated as rebels.[1]

The idea of an oath for catholics was later taken up by Archbishop Synge's son, also named Edward, who was later to be successively bishop of Clonfert, Cloyne, Ferns and Elphin. Edward Synge, fils, reproduced almost verbatim his father's draft oath in a pamphlet published in 1726 in the course of a controversy with Radcliffe, vicar of Naas, which arose out

---

1   Gilbert Library, Dublin ms 28, 174 ff.

of Synge's proposal for a degree of toleration for catholics which he made in a sermon before members of the Irish house of commons in October 1725.[2] The Synges were not the only Church of Ireland clergy who at this time advocated toleration for catholics. Theophilus Bolton, bishop of Elphin and later archbishop of Cashel, went even further than the Synges with a proposal for 600 catholic priests with one resident bishop, the priests to be educated in Trinity College, Dublin.[3] When it is remembered that both Archbishop Synge and Bishop Bolton were members of the same house of lords which passed the iniquitous 1723 Popery Bill, initiated in the Commons, the degree of disagreement amongst the protestant legislators is evident.

We have seen in Chapter 4 how the catholics succeeded eventually in having the 1723 bill negatived in London. When the Synges reactivated the proposal for an oath for catholics during 1726, there appears to have been a degree of consultation with some of the catholic clergy at that point, for Bishop Nicolson of Derry, writing to Archbishop Wake of Canterbury, remarked:

> The archbishop of Tuam said he had met with a great many Popish priests, who profess their readiness to abjure all manner of power in the Pope to absolve them from their allegiance; which they are ready to swear in the most binding and solemn manner to King George. But they pointed to an expression or two in the Oath of Abjuration which they thought might be omitted without hazard to the Government. And his Grace [of Tuam] seemed to intimate his own intention shortly to give the House [of Lords] his reasons for agreeing in the same opinion.[4]

Of the catholic priests whom Synge is said to have contacted one was almost certainly Cornelius Nary, parish priest of St Michan's, Dublin and a doctor of both canon and civil law. Nary himself later drafted a form of oath, and the main difference between it and Synge's is that Nary's oath does not contain any renunciation of the Pretender, while it does swear allegiance to King George. The forms of oath proposed by Synge and Nary are set out in Appendices A and B to this chapter.

There can be said to have been two main planks to Synge's oath—

---

2   Edward Synge, *Sermon preached in St Andrew's Church, Dublin before the honourable house of commons, 23 October 1725* (Dublin, 1725), passim.
3   Gilbert Library, Dublin MS 27, p. 380.
4   Ibid., p. 380.

(a) the swearing of allegiance to King George and the renouncing of the Pretender and (b) the rejection of the pope's supposed powers to depose princes and to dispense their subjects from their allegiance. The first of these was largely a political matter. Many catholics were of opinion that the Pretender's cause was by then irretrievably lost and saw little point in continuing to ignore the reality of the Hanoverian succession. As to the second, the French Church had under the Gallican articles of 1682 rejected the pope's deposing and dispensing powers, and it was difficult for Irish secular priests, educated mainly at the Irish College in Paris and at other Irish colleges in France, not to come under the influence of Gallican principles, and many, like Cornelius Nary, were vocal in their opposition to the papal pretensions concerned.

The regular clergy, on the other hand, were, if we except two small Capuchin houses at Bar-sur-Aube and Vassy,[5] educated in other countries besides France, i.e. in Irish colleges in Italy, Portugal, Flanders and Austria. They were the Pope's dragoons, ultramontane to the quick and fervent in their defence of his deposing and dispensing powers. In tandem with this exaggerated loyalty to the pope, the vast majority of the Regulars were imbued with an equally exaggerated loyalty to the Pretender. To such people the idea of an oath which offended against both these loyalties was anathema, and to none was it more repugnant than to Sylvester Lloyd. No doubt he campaigned privately against the proposed oath, but it was scarcely feasible for him to do anything publicly since that would leave him open to retaliatory measures by the authorities in the form of imprisonment and possible transportation as a member of the regular clergy.

In his dispatches to Col. O'Brien in Paris and to the Pretender's secretary of state in Rome, Lloyd kept the Pretender informed about events in Ireland. His on-the-spot commentary is an invaluable source of information, although it is regrettable that a long letter by Lloyd in the spring of 1726 on the subject of the oath cannot now be traced in the Stuart Papers. It is apparent from Lloyd's letters that the treatment of the catholic population by the authorities could oscillate wildly over a short period between the opposite poles of persecution and toleration. For instance, on 24 March 1726 Lloyd writes to O'Brien:

> Our Lord Lieutenant is just going off and we are assured he is to be sent forthwith to your Court [France]. He has been shamefully

---

5 I am ignoring the Irish Franciscan college at Boulay in Lorraine since Lorraine did not become part of France until 1766.

The Question of an Oath

baffled here and though our parliament has sent him an address of thanks, I believe he looks upon it as a banter.

It is impossible to tell how much the catholics are enraged at the attempts made upon them lately by the Protestants, and though Miller [King George] put a stop to it, yet the desire of revenge is so great that they would do anything when desperate. We are full of war. We are in hopes 'tis inevitable. The people of Dublin are transported at the thought, but I shall do all that is possible to keep the spirit alive. Many scandalous things have been written from abroad about the affair in Rome, the blame in the most malicious sense laid at the King. I have cured all my acquaintances of their prejudices and shall do all I can to disabuse others; the malice of people is unaccountable. I beg if you have any instructions to give me on this head that you will do it as soon as possible by post directed according to my last letter.[6]

But by 1 June the tune has changed completely when he reported to Hay, the Pretender's secretary of state:

As to affairs of religion the catholics are treated of late with extraordinary mildness. The judges in their circuits everywhere recommended moderation to the magistrates, as they did in the most earnest manner good behaviour and fidelity to the catholics. Your Grace may easily judge from what spring we have this change. The Oath of Allegiance is no longer talked of.

I sent Col. O'Brien a copy of what was intended for us by the last parliament. I hope we shall be able to disabuse some deluded people with regard to their notions on that head, or any other that may be to the prejudice of his Majesty's [Pretender's] undoubted right to our allegiance.

I shall from time to time give Col. O'Brien a faithful account of all that shall happen here. And if I can be serviceable in any other way I shall be at all times ready to sacrifice my life with pleasure for his Majesty's service . . .[7]

In the first of the two foregoing extracts 'the many scandalous things' is undoubtedly a reference to the Pretender's alleged adultery with the wife

---

6 Stuart Papers, RA SP(M) vol. 93/82, MFR 761. Lord Carteret, the retiring lord lieutenant, did not become ambassador to France as suggested by Lloyd. In fact he returned to Ireland in the autumn of 1727 for a further term as lord lieutenant.
7 Ibid., vol 94/54, MFR 762.

of his secretary of state, John Hay, earl of Inverness. The situation was serious enough for the Pretender's wife, Clementina, to leave him temporarily for a convent and for the pope to cut the Pretender's pension, although the pope's action derived as much from the education of the two princes largely by Protestants in the Pretender's entourage. Their education appears to have affected the two princes differently, for, while Charles Edward ('Bonnie Prince Charlie') later became a protestant, his brother, Henry, was to become a cardinal. The adultery crisis was solved by the removal of the Hays to Spain, upon which Clementina found it possible to return to the Pretender.[8]

In the second extract above, when Lloyd speaks of the 'spring' from which the new lenity of the administration towards the catholics derived, he is evidently alluding to a rumoured European war in which Britain would be involved. In such a situation the Pretender and his cohorts would be weighing in on the side of Britain's enemies with invasion of Britain as a goal, and the Irish administration would see a need for cosseting the catholics with a view to countering their Jacobite sympathies. However, once hostilities were begun and there was a possibility of Irish catholic involvement in the Pretender's invasion plans, it was to be expected that the attitude of the administration would change and, instead of lenity, catholics could expect a considerable degree of repression.

Pace Lloyd's assertion above that the oath of allegiance was no longer talked of, it is evident as we have already noted from Archbishop Synge's correspondence that the latter still had at least the intention of reactivating the question of an oath during 1726. 'What was intended for us by the last parliament' is apparently a reference to the reactivation of the 1723 Popery Bill, Lloyd's argument being that this was the kind of thing catholics could expect from the government and anyone who thought that a special oath for catholics could be realised was only deluding himself.

The reaction of the Pretender to the idea of Irish catholics swearing an oath of allegiance to King George was predictable. His secretary of state, John Hay, advised on 29 May 1726:

> The only answer which can be made to Mr Lloyd's long letter ... is that the King [i.e. Pretender] never can give his consent to his subjects in Ireland taking any oaths which can hinder them from

---

8   Peggy Miller, *James*, (London, 1971), passim.

The Question of an Oath

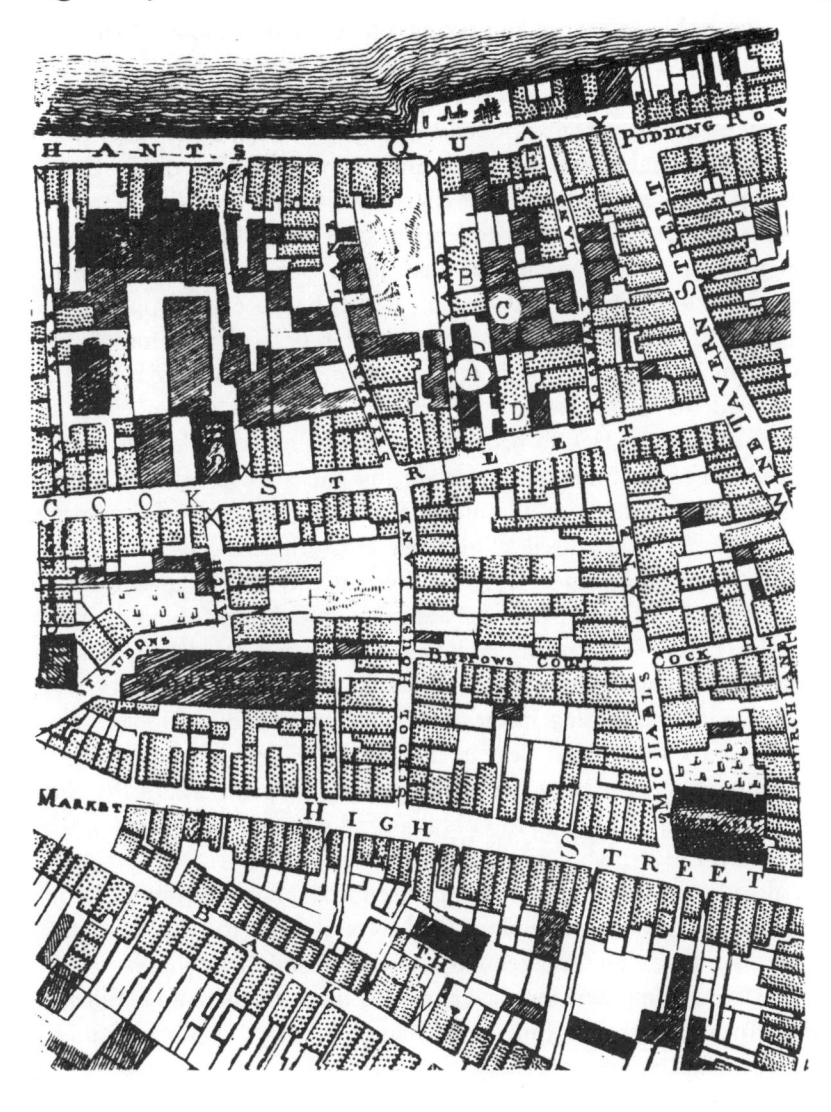

5 Enlarged portion of Rocque's map of Dublin (1756) showing A: Franciscan chapel; B: Franciscan friary; C: SS Michael & John's chapel; D: suggested location in Cook Street of house named Adam & Eve; E: No. 5 Merchants Quay which the Franciscans acquired in 1756.

coming to his assistance and taking a forward part in his service when we shall have occasion to call upon them.[9]

The rumours of war, mentioned by Lloyd, prompt some brief résumé of the international situation at this time. While the War of the Spanish Succession had been brought to a conclusion by the Peace of Utrecht in 1713, friction between Britain and Spain over West Indies trade and the British presence in Gibraltar had continued. Some changes in alliances had also emerged. France and Britain, which had been an opposite sides in the War of the Spanish Succession, had more recently found themselves on the same side in a war against Spain, France having been drawn in on the side of Britain because of a bid by the Spanish king, Philip V (a grandson of Louis XIV), to become regent of France. Relations between Britain and France remained good during the 1720s, but the Austrian Emperor, who had been an ally of Britain during the War of the Spanish Succession, now recognised a need to curb Britain's power and was showing an unhealthy interest in the Pretender's plans to invade Britain. What had once been the Spanish Netherlands had been ceded to Austria under the Peace of Utrecht, and this meant that Austria was now a maritime power with ambitions for trade with the East Indies which conflicted with the trading interests of Britain and Holland.

While there was a great deal of massing of troops and marching and counter-marching, the only real conflict was in Spain, where the Spaniards early in 1727 laid siege to Gibraltar and suffered heavy losses, while casualties on the British side were light.

As already indicated, rumours of an approaching war raised Jacobite hopes, and in Ireland people like Lloyd were at hand to rally the faithful, and to give them an exaggerated notion of the possibilities of their delivery from their serfdom as a result of a forthcoming European conflict. In his letter of 1 June already quoted, Lloyd is already gung-ho with great expectations:

> I have since my landing in this kingdom seen multitudes of his Majesty's friends, as well protestant as catholic. It is impossible to express the impatience they are in to do him service. The rumour we have of an approaching war has made many, whom I never believed sincerely in his interest, declare themselves in the most honest and resolute manner. Let the matter be as it will, our enemies here are in

9   Stuart Papers, RA SP(M) vol. 94/48, MFR 762.

the greatest consternation. Four regiments of foot have been shipped off for the West of England. General McCartney is come over hither and 'tis said the remaining part of our troops are to form a camp near Athlone.[10]

But *Faulkner's Dublin Postboy* was more specific when it reported that, at his Majesty's express command, General McCartney went for Ireland on 11 May to ship off six battalions of foot in transport ships for Spain, in order to prevent the designs of the king of Spain upon Portmahon (in Minorca) and Gibraltar.[11] With the country virtually placed on a war footing, the government's mood of lenity reported in Lloyd's letter of 1 June quickly changed to one of repression of catholics. Spurred on no doubt by their high expectations that deliverance was near, the catholic mob demonstrated openly on the streets of Dublin and the summer of 1726 turned out to be a particularly violent one in the capital. The authorities feared that what catholics had in mind was not simply rioting, but open rebellion and the murder of protestants. It was rumoured that, in order to facilitate the murder of protestants, catholic houses in Dublin were being marked with a special sign. Tadhg Ó Neachtain, son of Séan Ó Neachtain, the poet, in an item in his Commonplace Book for June 1726 dismissed such rumours in satirical vein:

> It was imputed to the Irish of Dublin that in a sermon in one of their churches the public were told to rise up and cut the throats of the English and to slay everyone of them . . . Cork, Kinsale and other places in the country were not without the same kind of fiction, so that every Englishman was cleaning his gun and equipping to defend himself from the bloody, wild, barbarous Irish, as the English themselves said. The Irish were in a fine state at that time to murder the English, the Irishman having only a stick to counter a man with a sword, a gun, a pistol and bullets.[12]

The authorities, however, were taking no chances. They decided on a show of strength, and, according to one source, 'an armed force was marched in hostile array through the streets of the metropolis, and an unresisting multitude of either sex and every age were fired upon and put to flight'.[13] Despite this, however, the Pretender's birthday on 10 June

10 Ibid., vol. 94/54, MFR 762.
11 *Faulkner's Dublin Postboy*, 18 May 1726.
12 National Library of Ireland MS G 132, p. 92. Tadhg Ó Neachtain's comments are in Irish; the translation into English is mine.
13 Matthew O'Connor, *History of the Irish catholics* (Dublin, 1813) p. 196.

was celebrated with perhaps more than usual fervour in St Stephen's Green. On the evening of that day a great mob gathered in the Green, and 'expecting something, which not happening as expected, . . . they fell to toss dead dogs and cats about'. Lord Abercorn, who lived nearby, spoke to them from a window of his house, asking them to disperse. But their reply was to shower his lordship's house with stones, brickbats and dead creatures. They then got so completely out of control that the main guard had to be called to deal with them, and the rioting did not cease until 'a great number were desperately wounded and taken prisoner'.[14]

From a further letter written by Lloyd to Col. O'Brien about this time it will be seen that there was a real expectation of a Jacobite incursion into Ireland. Lloyd at all events was decidedly hopeful of such an incursion:

> I have been lately in Munster where you have many friends and very impatient to see you. You may assure yourself that I will miss no opportunity that I can with prudence lay hold of to promote your interest. One thing you may depend on that whenever you think proper to commence your suit, you will not want witnesses to prove your title, so impatient are all your old neighbours to see you restored to your rights. Arms and officers are all that we want. I shall make use of all means that art and providence can suggest to dispose our friends in Dublin to do their duty if any army should be intended. We must endeavour to seize the Banque [Barrack?] of Dublin, the small port of Waterford and other places if matters be discreetly managed. There will be no impossibility in this.

In the same letter Lloyd reported that:

> A ship with four and twenty guns and a great quantity of arms and commanded by one Doyle, an Irishman, has been lately seized at a place called Killybegs, a harbour in the north of this Kingdom, on suspicion that he came with an evil design on our coast. The captain was brought thither under a strong guard and is actually a prisoner in the Castle. I am told he says he is bound from Holland to the West Indies and only just into Ireland to take in provisions. What the end of this affair will be I can't tell but we are in a great fright.[15]

---

14 *Dublin Intelligence*, 11 June 1726.
15 Stuart Papers, RA SP (M) vol. 114/137, MFR 771.

Further evidence of a possible Jacobite invasion was provided by the *Dublin Intelligence* of 11 June 1726:

> There are reports in Town that a ship was taken in Waterford, that had a great deal of arms and ammunition on board, said to be for the Pretender's servants.[16]

Throughout the year the government had been active in suppressing recruitment for the Pretender's cause. In January 1726 it was reported from Cork that 'the Mayflower of London was lately seized near that place [Cork] for transporting men for the Pretender or some other foreign service who are called Wild Geese, fifty or sixty of them are apprehended and committed to gaol.'[17] On 7 May the *Dublin Intelligence* stated that:

> Notwithstanding several fellows have been apprehended as adherents of the Pretender, and are liable to the law, we are informed that many others are constantly plying about the city for lusty fellows under the notion of recruiting the Irish regiments in France etc. Tho' 'tis done with all secrecy possible, many of the recruiters passing under the notion of French merchants, yet not of the common appearance and behaviour of those gentlemen who are really such.[18]

The same newspaper in its edition of 11 June noted that:

> On Wednesday last the men apprehended on suspicion of being enlisted for the Pretender, were examined before one of the Judges of the King's Bench, and it appearing they were criminal, were committed to Newgate and laid in irons; the other two turning evidence for the King and discovering their intrigues, were only kept in custody of the Tipstaff of the King's Bench in order to appear for the prosecution of the rest.[19]

Presumably it was one of these men, Moses Nowland, who was executed in Stephen's Green early in July 1726. Again the *Dublin Intelligence* reported:

---

16   *Dublin Intelligence*, 11 June 1726.
17   *Dublin Postman*, 24 January 1726.
18   *Dublin Intelligence*, 7 May 1726.
19   Ibid., 11 June 1726.

Wednesday last, Moses Nowland, condemned for enlisting men with a traitorous design for the service of the Pretender, was brought from Newgate accompanied by a troop of Horse Guards to St Stephen's Green and there pursuant to his sentence was executed, his bowels being burned, his head cut off etc.[20]

But it has to be said that there does not appear to have been any general or indiscriminate persecution of catholics at this time, as witness the following excerpt from a letter from Stephen MacEgan, then bishop of Clonmacnoise, to the Pretender's secretary of state: 'The opening of letters in the Post Office here [Dublin] has been much practised these four months, but, as I never traffic in politics, was safe.'[21]

Later that year in a letter dated 19 November, Lloyd was to disclose to Col. O'Brien in Paris full details of the military strengths of all barracks and outposts throughout the country. Some 108 cities, towns, villages and outposts throughout the four provinces are named, with the number of companies of foot soldiers and troops of horse-soldiers stationed in each. The list furnished by Lloyd showed that there were then 212 companies of foot and 37 troops of horse stationed in Ireland. Munster must have been regarded as by far the most vulnerable to attack since it had far more than its fair share of troops at 40% of total. Leinster followed with 25%, then Connaught with 18.5%. Ulster, predictably, because of its geographical situation and its protestant majority, must have been regarded as least in need of protection with only 16.5% of total. Dublin was, naturally, the most heavily protected city in the country with thirty companies of foot (three regiments) but only three troops of horse. Limerick was not far behind with twenty-two companies of foot. Galway had sixteen foot companies, Cork fourteen, Waterford seven and Derry six.

In his covering letter to O'Brien Lloyd had this to say:

> If anything more be required, I am ready to give all possible satisfaction. I remember that you did me the honour when you saw me last to desire that I would give you some account of our military establishments in this Kingdom, which is, as it were, a nursery of war for Great Britain. It was some time before I could inform myself exactly, and that was the reason you did not hear from me sooner on the subject. I hope the following account will answer your expectation.

20 Ibid., 9 July 1726.
21 Stuart Papers RA SP(M) vol. 96/52, MFR 763.

Our quota of men to be quartered in the Kingdom in time of peace is twelve thousand. We look upon ourselves to be injured when any of those are removed into England and paid out of our treasury. We have at present in the Kingdom four regiments of horse, six of dragoons and twenty regiments of foot, which are all quartered in very convenient barracks in different parts of the Kingdom. . . If anything further occur to me that may be of any amusement or diversion to you, I will be sure to acquaint you with it. We look upon war as a thing inevitable.[22]

It is rather incongruous that all this information should have been supplied by a Franciscan monk who, if the laws had been applied, should have been behind bars awaiting transportation. That he was in a position to acquire such information could only have derived from having friends in the right places, but no doubt his military experience in his youth was also a help.

In a letter to O'Brien on 5 January 1727 Lloyd had some further information on the military situation to impart:

We are here in the greatest hurry on account of a rumour that Gibraltar is besieged. The winds having been contrary for some time, kept off our pacquets so that we had yesterday four or five [pacquets] together. Several principal officers are landed in order, as 'tis said, to raise four new regiments, and ship off four more for the Straights [of Gilbraltar]. If there should be a war, all our troops will be sent off, and we shall be left trusting to our militia.[23]

But in the spring of 1727 international tensions eased, the siege of Gibraltar was lifted and, with the fading prospects of a European war, Jacobite hopes for an invasion of Britain or Ireland also faded.

Lloyd also reported in his letter of 5 January above that the duke of Newcastle was expected to be the new lord lieutenant (this proved to be incorrect: Lord Carteret was to return for a second term in autumn 1727), that the lord chancellor had lately died, and that the chief justice of the common pleas, an Englishman, was expected to replace him. It was expected that the consequent vacancy for a chief justice would also be filled by an Englishman. He goes on: 'These promotions of Englishmen are very offensive to our lawyers of Irish birth who think they have as much merit with the present government as any Englishman alive.' The

22 Ibid., vol. 99/29, MFR 764.
23 Ibid., vol. 101/67, MFR 765.

churchmen 'were no less disgusted on their side' because it was expected that the vacant archbishopric of Cashel would also be filled by an Englishman.

When Lloyd next communicated with O'Brien on 15 July 1727 he had some sensational news to convey. Earlier that month there had been a meeting of prominent catholics in the Lion Inn in Werburgh Street, Dublin, under the chairmanship of Thomas Nugent, earl of Westmeath (commonly known as Lord Delvin), when an address of loyalty to the new King George II was drawn up and signed. The text of the address is given in Appendix C. Before coming to the throne in June 1727 George II had shown signs of liberality and toleration, and it was felt that an address of loyalty to him might in time bear dividends in the form of some easement of the penal laws. In reporting the matter to Col. O'Brien, Lloyd represented the address, which he of course resolutely opposed, as the culmination of the campaign for a catholic oath which had been in train for some years. Here is his letter:

> [That] I have not heard from you this great while is no small uneasement to me. You can't forget that I near two years ago [stated] there were overtures made to bring the catholics of this kingdom to take a certain Oath of allegiance to the present government and you must remember that I last summer sent you a sermon that was preached before the House of Commons with an answer and a reply or a vindication wherein this scheme was laid open. And I again last spring gave you an answer of a pamphlet written by a catholic lawyer of this city in defence of the whole scheme. And I don't know whether you or your friends took any notice of these things but I am to tell you now that the affair has broke out, that the Lord Delvin whom you must have known in Paris is lately come from London into this kingdom and has with unspeakable and incredible success in ten days time brought most of the catholic nobility and gentry now in this town to sign an Address to King George II, the strongest argument made use of to prevail on such as were slow or made any objection to it, was that it was recommended to be done by the great man that is at the helm of your affairs. In a word, Sir, he has prevailed, the Address is signed and the Lord Delvin himself in person is to present it to the new king. You may imagine this affair makes a noise here and it is incredible with what passion it is carried on by the laity. The Council here has been consulted about it and I have with much difficulty procured a copy of it which I here send to you and is, you may depend upon it, word for word with the original.

[*The Address follows—see Appendix C.*]

This, sir, is the Address you will soon hear about from other hands. It is to go off from hence in a day or two. It is signed by the Earl of Carlingford, Earl of Westmeath, Earl of Fingal, Lord Trimbleston, Lord—[24] and about twenty of the chief of the Commons in and about this town in their own names and in the names of others who have not been as yet consulted. I got the copy but just now and can scarce be the last to give you this account which will, I am sure, surprise you. You shall hear from me again soon.

In margin: I hope you will make allowances for the hurry I am in. No clergyman was consulted in this affair.[25]

With regard to the matters mentioned in preceding letter, the sermon preached before the Irish house of commons was given by Edward Synge, fils; the reply to the sermon was from the pen of Stephen Radcliffe, vicar of Naas, and this was followed by the 'vindication' of his proposals by Synge, in which he set out the form of a proposed oath for catholics. These matters have already been referred to earlier in this chapter. The pamphlet 'written by a catholic lawyer', which was in the nature of an intervention in the controversy between Synge and Radcliffe, is believed to have been the work of Fr Cornelius Nary in collaboration with a catholic lawyer.[26] 'The gentleman that is at the helm of your affairs' was Cardinal de Fleury, chief minister of France. As to whether de Fleury, as claimed, supported the address, such a position would scarcely be in line with how de Fleury believed Irish catholics should conduct themselves as reported by Abbé James Dunne in his letter of 8 July 1726, already quoted in Chapter 4.

It is evident from Lloyd's words 'it is incredible with what passion it is carried on by the laity' that the vast majority of the catholic laity in Dublin favoured the Address. The clergy, Lloyd says, were not consulted; this was probably because it was anticipated that they would be mostly against the Address. It is interesting that this pattern was repeated in 1759 in the case of a catholic address to the lord lieutenant and in 1761 in the

---

24 The name after Lord Trimbleston is not clear, but it is a short name and it is probably Lord Delvin. The practice of referring to the earl of Westmeath as Lord Delvin, when this was properly the courtesy title of the earl's eldest son, must have led to confusion at times. However, in the case of the Address, if, as appears likely, father and son both signed it, it is to be expected that they used their proper titles.
25 Stuart Papers, RA SP(M) vol. 108/80, MFR 768.
26 Anon., *A letter to the Revd. Stephen Radcliffe . . . on the subject of his letter and reply to Mr Synge's sermon and vindication* (Dublin, 1727). For a discussion of the authorship of this pamphlet see P. Fagan, op. cit. note 12, Chapter 4.

case of a similar address to king George III on his accession, when strong laity support for these addresses was counterbalanced by strong clerical opposition to them. That opposition, on all these occasions, had its genesis for the most part in the influence exercised on the Irish church by the Pretender through his right of nomination of Irish bishops.

The earl of Westmeath (at the time in question Thomas Nugent) appears to have been generally known throughout the eighteenth century as Lord Delvin, although this is a courtesy title which properly belongs to the eldest son of the earl of Westmeath. Thomas Nugent was a colonel in the Jacobite army at the siege of Limerick and was one of the hostages handed over to the Williamites as an earnest of the good faith of the Jacobite side. In accordance with the Articles of Limerick Nugent retained his extensive estates in Westmeath, Cavan and Meath. He died in 1752 at the age of ninety-six, outliving his son by a few months. He was succeeded briefly by a brother, and then by a nephew, who conformed to the Established Church.[27]

On the question of the subsequent fate of the Address, the historian, Francis Plowden, claimed:

> It was presented to the Lords Justices by Lord Delvin and several reputable Catholic gentlemen, but it was received with silent contempt. The Lords Justices, who were humbly entreated to submit it to his Majesty, never condescended to make an answer to those who presented it, nor has it been known to this day whether it reached the hands of the Sovereign.[28]

Pace Plowden, there is ample evidence that the Address was in fact presented to the King. It may well be that the Lords Justices received the catholic deputation in the frosty manner outlined and did not bother to transmit the Address to the lord lieutenant, Lord Carteret, then in London. But a copy *was* brought to London, apparently by Lord Delvin, and delivered to Carteret, who presented it to the king. The *Dublin Journal* makes this much abundantly clear. Its issue for 5-8 August 1727 states 'The Address of the Roman Catholics of Ireland, being presented to his Majesty, by his Excellency, Lord Carteret, was graciously received, as it was inserted in this paper on the 29th past'. Again, in its issue of 29 August—2 September 1727, the same journal printed the following

---

27 *Dictionary of National Biography* (London, 1895).
28 Francis Plowden, *An historical review of the state of Ireland* (Egerton, 1803) vol. I, p. 262.

'extract of a letter from his Excellency, Lord Carteret, to a noble peer in Ireland, occasioned by the Address of the Roman Catholics of that Kingdom to his Majesty':

> His Excellency, after having expressed the obligations he was under to his Lordship and the other Roman Catholic peers for their good opinion of him, proceeds to acquaint his Lordship that the King received the Address very graciously and had commanded him to assure his Lordship that his Majesty desired nothing more than to make all his subjects easy and happy under his Government.

It should be remembered that Lord Delvin, or, to give him his proper title, the earl of Westmeath, was an absentee from his Irish estates living in London, and so was in a favourable position to have access to Lord Carteret. The tone of Carteret's letter and the attitude of the king, it has to be conceded, was surprisingly conciliatory.

That Lloyd was the prime mover in organising opposition to the Address is clear from a letter dated 19 March 1728 from Fr Francis Stuart, provincial of the Irish Franciscans, to the Pretender.

> I beg leave in my name and the name of the order committed to my charge to express my abhorrence of the late undutiful behaviour of some few, who against the laws of God and these Kingdoms, transferred, as far as in them lay, what was your Majesty's undoubted right, to another. But, God's holy name be blessed, it ended in their confusion. I cannot here omit recommending to your Majesty's favour and protection Fr. Sylvester Lloyd, who undoubtedly opposed their wicked attempt and did by writing as well as declaiming against it, awaken the loyalty of your faithful subjects, and not only prevented many from following their wicked example laid before them, but in some measure rendered the whole project abortive. His behaviour in this affair having made him many powerful enemies and having reason to believe that they have stirred up some even of the most eminent of the clergy against him, who, perhaps conscious of their omission of duty, may be ready to misrepresent him abroad for their private ends, it is therefore that I most humbly beg your Majesty will not listen to their calumny, he being a man who has rendered great service to his country and has always behaved as becomes a good religious and fellow missionary. As will appear by the testimony of

unbiased prelates and others which I send to be laid before your Majesty and beg his further vindication.[29]

Lloyd certainly lost no time in getting his campaign under way, for within five days of his letter of 15 July above he was writing again to Col. O'Brien enclosing a number of queries on the address which had been circulated to the signatories and had the effect, Lloyd claimed, of one Lord and one commoner withdrawing their signatures.[30] The Queries as afterwards printed are included here as Appendix D. That those who opposed the address were far from agreed on the line to be taken is borne out by a letter from Bishop Stephen MacEgan to the Pretender in which he stated that the address was opposed by a vast many as soon as they heard of it, 'judging a Remonstrance of grievances with assurances of fidelity [to George II] to be more proper'.[31] It is certain that Lloyd and his fellow Jacobites would have been strongly opposed to giving any assurances of fidelity to King George. Indeed, it is significant that Lloyd, in forwarding the Queries on the Address to O'Brien, omitted Query 13 which asked whether 'an humble petition to the King, and a Remonstrance of our grievances . . . would not be much more proper on this critical occasion'. Surely, Lloyd's omission of this Query is an indication that he did not agree with it.

Some protestant comments upon the divisions among catholics over the address can be noted here. Archbishop William King of Dublin in a letter dated 29 August 1727 to Robert Southwell noted with some satisfaction:

> I did imagine that the Catholic Address would please, they are mightily divided about it here, the clergy are out of patience at it and have published reasons against it. . . It is right to make the best use of this address but to be sure it is not to be depended on. It must be a discouragement to the Pretender and his party.[32]

Primate Boulter remarked briefly that 'the address yesterday presented by some catholics occasions great heats and divisions among those of that religion here'.[33]

In his opposition to the address Lloyd was to find a powerful ally in the Vatican. The Brussels nuncio, Spinelli, on being made aware of the address,

---

29 Stuart Papers, RA SP(M), vol. 114/138, MFR 771.
30 Ibid., vol. 108/99, MFR 769.
31 Ibid., vol. 112/36, MFR 770.
32 National Library of Ireland MS 2056.
33 Hugh Boulter, *Letters* (Oxford, 1769), vol. I, p. 188.

wrote to secretary of state Lercari that even though many Irish catholics thought they should swear an oath of loyalty to the king who preceded the present monarch, provided they were granted freedom of conscience, none of them considered that it was permitted to them to swear at the same time that they were of opinion that the pope had no authority over the temporal jurisdiction of princes, an opinion that was to be found in the address in a somewhat mitigated form.[34] In its reply to Spinelli, Rome was to blow the address up out of all proportion by describing it as an oath of fidelity. It was intimated that the cardinal secretary of state was not yet in a position to give a precise answer concerning 'the oath taken by the Irish catholics to the present king of England'; that the pope had referred the matter to the Holy Office for detailed examination, and that he would then decide what should be done.[35]

Lloyd apparently about this time received a letter from the Pretender himself extolling him for his efforts, for in a reply to the Pretender dated 9 March 1728 he exudes obsequiousness:

> It is impossible to express the joy mixed with (if I may be allowed to say so) tenderness that brought the tears from my eyes which I felt on receipt of your Majesty's letter. It has next my duty to God ever since I came to any kind of knowledge in the world been my greatest study how to be of any service to your Majesty. And it is the greatest pleasure to me to find that my poor endeavours are approved of. I hope no consideration either of interest or fear shall ever make me depart from my duty.[36]

He then proceeds to give a progress report on the results of the address:

> Our Add—rs [Addressors], at least a great many of them who were brought into that scandalous affair without being let into the secret views of the first promoters of it, begin to be confounded and ashamed of the deed. Whether this proceeds from principle or considerations of guilt or rather from disappointment, I can't say. They promised themselves mountains from the present parliament and in reward of their great loyalty, but the thing was quite otherwise

---

34 Cathaldus Giblin, 'Catalogue of material of Irish interest in the collection Nunziatura di Fiandra, Vatican Archives' in *Collectanea Hibernica*, no. 5 (1962), p. 121.
35 Ibid., no. 14 (1971), p. 40.
36 Stuart Papers, RA SP(M) vol. 114/136, MFR 771.

understood than they expected. For the majority of members in the late election proved to be Tories who in their hearts were offended at them. And the old True Blue Party took it to have been a scheme set afoot by the Ministry and entered into by these few catholics in order to procure an English Act for repealing the Penal Laws made in this Kingdom against them, and so establish a Popish party here to make a kind of balance against that Protestant spirit which in the last Parliament made so obstinate a stand in assertion of their independence of the English parliament and against the patent granted to one Mr Wood, or rather to the Duchess of Munster [*recte* Kendal], for coining copper half pence for this Kingdom.

These reasons, or perhaps others which I can't penetrate, have hindered the Parliament having hitherto done anything for the Add—rs, for though they made a petition to the House of Commons for leave to take long leases, mortgages and perhaps lands etc. their petition at last reading was not only rejected but to their great confusion hissed with indignation out of the House, so that on the whole affair your Majesty has rather gained than lost by the lamentable step: for the rest of the Catholics are so rejoiced to have been out of the affair that it has served to renew their old spirit of loyalty and it has given an opportunity to your Majesty's faithful friends by letters and [one word illegible] to instruct and inform them in their duty—nay, to rouse up and open the eyes of others who were either lukewarm or of contrary sentiments.

As to your Majesty's interest among the Protestants I have pleasure to assure you, Sir, that besides the majority of Tories I already hinted at in the House of Commons, those they call Converts are almost to a man your friends, as are seven in ten of old Protestants, nay, great numbers of the very Presbyterians, especially those of the North who are mostly of Scotch descent, are as I am credibly informed, so zealous that the Government has not been able for some years past to procure the election of a Whiggish magistrate in any corporation of Ulster except Belfast. So that whenever your Majesty shall in your great wisdom think fit to assert your right in any of your Kingdoms, you may depend upon a considerable diversion of your enemy's troops in this country, which is in some measure their nursery of war.[37]

As background to Lloyd's letter above it should be pointed out that the Tories had not held power in the Irish parliament since 1714. The Tories

37 Ibid., vol. 114/136. MFR 771. 'Duchess of Munster' should read 'duchess of Kendal', the king's mistress.

had the reputation of being soft on catholics and sympathetic in varying degrees to the Pretender's cause. The Whigs on the other hand were as a general rule rabidly anti-catholic and resolutely committed to the Hanoverian succession. Catholic free-holders still had the vote in elections, but in truth it could be said that there was no election of any extent except for about 25% of the 300 seats in the Irish house of commons. The remaining seats were either in pocket boroughs in the gift of powerful (usually Whig) families, or in freeman boroughs with a very small number of freemen voters. In any event, it was highly unusual prior to the Octennial Act of 1767 to hold a general election except on the death of the monarch.

The Whig majority in parliament continued after the 1727 election, but it was a somewhat split majority with two powerful factions, one led by William Conolly and the other by Alan Brodrick, vying for the ear of the lord lieutenant as to which of them should be appointed 'undertaker' to put the government programme through parliament. In practice the terms Whig and Tory were not generally used in describing the parliamentary scene. Instead the 'undertakers' were called the 'court party', while the opposition, which could on occasion include some Whigs, was known as the Country or, increasingly as the 'patriot party'. The terms Whig and Tory had indeed begun to be used to an extent in a pejorative sense, as when Primate Boulter spoke of the 'Popish rabble [in Dublin] coming down to fight the Whig mob' on the Pretender's birthday.[38]

When Lloyd tells us that 'the majority of members in the late election proved to be Tories', he can only be referring to the minority of seats for which there was any real election. Boulter who was one of the lords justices in effective control of the country in the absence of the lord lieutenant, had his agents around the country watching the progress of the election, and it must have been clear to him that the catholic vote had been critical in the success of many Tory candidates. He perceived then the votes of catholic freeholders as giving catholics a voice in parliament indirectly through the Tories. This was something he was not prepared to stomach and later, in 1728, he was instrumental in having an act put through parliament depriving catholic freeholders of the vote. Lloyd's thesis that the Tory members suspected the Ministry of trying to manipulate emancipation for catholics so that there could be a popish party in parliament to set off against the Tory opposition seems a bit too Machiavellian to be taken seriously. That a catholic petition 'for leave to take long leases, mortgages

---

38 National Library of Ireland MS Pos. 3649, p. 208.

and perhaps lands etc.' was hissed out of the House was only to be expected from a house of commons with a large Whig majority.

As regards the last paragraph of Lloyd's letter of 9 March 1728, he was altogether too sanguine in his estimation of support for the Pretender amongst protestants. As events were to prove during the Jacobite rising in Scotland in 1745, there was precious little support amongst Irish catholics, let alone protestants, when the chips were really down. However, his view that converts from catholicism to the established church were almost to a man loyal to the Pretender, is one that was shared by the protestant Edward Synge, pére, then bishop of Raphoe in a letter dated 13 April 1715 to Archbishop Wake of Canterbury:

> . . . Irish converts to the protestant religion have by experience hitherto generally been found to be altogether insincere. . . If by any extraordinary charge and pains we should bring any great numbers of them outwardly to own the established church and religion, they would hereby become qualified by law to keep and use arms, as well as other protestants. And, if at any time the Pretender or the French King should make an attempt upon Ireland, the greatest part of our new converts would certainly return to Popery, and be able to give them great assistance upon the first appearance.[39]

In the spring of 1728 Lloyd had plans to publish a book, the subject of which we can only speculate about. Apparently he broached the matter of the book to Fr Michael MacDonogh, a Dominican then resident in Rome, who was later to be bishop of Kilmore but who at this time occupied a position of some influence as an intermediary between the pope and the Pretender. MacDonogh in turn wrote in the matter to Edgar, the Pretender's secretary, who, having put the proposal to the Pretender, set out the latter's reaction in a letter dated 19 May 1728 to MacDonogh:

> H.M. orders me to tell you that he has a very good opinion of Fr Lloyd's zeal and attachment to him. He is persuaded that his publishing of the book you mention may do good service. But H.M. leaves that matter entirely to Fr Lloyd himself, who can best foresee both the personal risks he may run by it and the inconveniences that may attend by giving the usurpers a new handle to persecute the Catholics in that country.[40]

39 Gilbert Library, Dublin MS 28, p. 23.
40 Stuart Papers, RA SP(M) vol. 116/48, MFR 772.

It is not possible to say whether Lloyd ever went ahead with the publication of the book. I have not been able to trace any book or pamphlet published under his own name, but he may of course have published one anonymously or under some pseudonym. As to the subject of the book it may have dealt with the then very topical subject of the address to the king and the question of an oath to the king; it apparently had some relevance to the Pretender's position since otherwise it is difficult to see why Lloyd should be seeking the Pretender's blessing to the project.

When Lloyd next reports to Col. O'Brien on 1 June 1728 he is in Douai in France, having spent, he says, much longer than he expected in London on his way to Flanders. While he was in London he had been keeping a watchful eye on Lord Delvin:

> I was detained at London much longer than I expected and therefore did not receive the honour of your letter until yesterday that I arrived here.
>
> The Lord Delvin is very obsequious to the English Court. He was about a fortnight ago introduced to the Elector and his Lady by the Duke of Richmond and was received, as the newspapers call it, very graciously. I watched him as narrowly as possible and could only find that he intended to give in a petition in the name of the Irish Catholics begging that they may have leave to purchase lands and to take long leases, inasmuch as their behaviour to the Government has always been peaceable, and that besides their late loyal address they are ready to give the Government all such further security for their fidelity and allegiance as shall be thought necessary. I did not see the petition but have it from very good hands that this is the substance of it, which is I think as injurious as it possibly can be because it not only confirms the late Address but tacitly surrenders the Articles of Limerick which are our sheet anchor and leaves us absolutely at the discretion of the Government for such Oaths and Tests as they shall think proper. I can assure you, Sir, and that by express commission from your friends, who are infinitely the greater number, that not one but the Addressors have given in to this new scheme. I can't yet positively say that he will give in his famous petition but this I know that he is very busy and has received remittances from his party in Ireland for carrying on the affair. It was whispered to me by one of his intimates that he had sent a copy of the intended petition to Paris to be approved there and to endeavour to have it recommended by the Cardinal from thence to the Government. You may soon find the

truth of this affair. The person he depends much upon at Paris for the low part of his intrigues is one Dr. Donlevy and one of his chief agents at London is Dr. Connell lately come from Paris with another profligate, a lame fellow called Harrold. He is despised and avoided by all honest men at London.

I doubt but you have seen what Mist says of him in his journal with regard to his reception at Court, and the great share he had in procuring the Popish Address.[41]

In the foregoing extract the Elector is of course King George II; in Jacobite eyes he was never anything more than elector of Hanover. Lloyd is a bit naive in speaking of the articles of Limerick as the catholics' sheet anchor, since the Articles had long ago been violated by the Irish administration, in particular by the Popery Act of 1704. In any event, Lloyd conveniently overlooks the fact that the Articles provided for an Oath of Allegiance to the British king, which he and his fellow Jacobites were not prepared to take. The articles of Limerick were by this time largely an anachronism, and, if some new accommodation could be arrived at by the catholics in return for some degree of toleration, this seemed a sensible step to many catholics. It should be noted that Lord Delvin was at this time endeavouring to get Cardinal de Fleury, chief minister of France, to use his good offices to have his (Delvin's) proposals accepted by the British, and by extension, by the Irish government. Lloyd's disparaging remarks about Donlevy, Connell and Harrold need not be taken too seriously; their only sin was that they were opponents of Lloyd. Andrew Donlevy was a provisor of the Irish College in Paris and later the compiler of a catechism in Irish. Harrold is probably John Herald, a Dublin priest, who is described in a postulation to Rome by the Dublin clergy in 1729 as doctor of theology and professor of sacred theology.[42] According to the priest-hunter, Garzia, he presided c.1721 at a clerical disputation on the supremacy of the pope and other matters in St Michan's chapel, Dublin.[43]

The success of the campaign instigated by Lloyd against the special oath for catholics and against the catholic address to the king was to sour the minds of many protestants, such as the Synges, and to cause them to

---

41 Ibid., vol. 116/152, MFR 772. The 'Mist' mentioned is apparently *Mist's Weekly Journal*, an anti-ministerial London journal with Jacobite leanings.
42 P. F. Moran (ed.), *Spicilegium Ossoriense* (Dublin, 1893), vol. 3, p. 136.
43 Kevin McGrath, 'Garzia, a noted priest-catcher' in *Irish Ecclesiastical Record*, vol 72 (July-Dec. 1949) p. 512. I have failed to discover any further information about Father Connell.

have second thoughts about their proposals for a measure of toleration for catholics. It was to cause the whole climate of opinion among protestants in regard to toleration to harden to such an extent that the Irish House of Lords were noting in December 1729 that 'several pretended Popish archbishops, bishops and their officiates had of late exercised ecclesiastical jurisdiction within the realm in defiance of the laws, and that the behaviour of Papists within the Kingdom had of late years been very insolent in building many public mass-houses and erecting convents of friars and nuns, and on many occasions insulting the protestants'.[44] Their lordships went on to resolve that the judges be directed to give in charge to the justices of the peace and all other magistrates more effectually to put the laws against popery in execution, particularly those against regulars and all persons exercising ecclesiastical jurisdiction. The lord lieutenant undertook to have their lordships' wishes carried out.

Edward Synge, fils, then bishop of Clonfert, must have been expressing the feelings of many protestants when he remarked in a sermon preached in Christchurch, Dublin on 23 October 1731:

> Now, in answer to this, 'tis allowed that such an Address was framed and I believe presented to his Majesty. And would to God, that it had really been, what 'tis most artfully styled, *The most humble address of the Roman Catholics of Ireland*. We might then hope that the deadly venom of Popish principles was at last destroyed: And that notwithstanding their other gross errors in religion, they were disposed to be and continue good subjects. But the truth is, and 'tis fit it should be known, that neither the body of the Roman Catholics of Ireland, nor the major part of them, concurred in or approved of this address. No! They were generally displeased at it: And of those who were displeased, some had not the prudence to conceal their dislike, but drew up and dispersed a most remarkable set of *Queries*, in which the Address itself, and the promoters of it, are very freely censured[45]. . .

The campaign by Lord Delvin, Cornelius Nary and their supporters for an oath of allegiance acceptable to catholics, in return for which there would be some easing of the penal laws, could be said to have foundered twixt the Scylla of Irish loyalty to the Pretender and the Charybdis of

---

44 TCD Library, press A 75, no. 157, *Resolutions of the Lords Spiritual and Temporal* (Dublin, 1729).
45 Edward Synge, *Sermon preached in Christ Church Cathedral, Dublin on Saturday 23 October 1731 . . . by Edward, Lord Bishop of Clonfert* (Dublin, 1732), p. 14.

Vatican intransigence in its adherence to the outmoded papal deposing and dispensing powers. The net result was to postpone by nearly fifty years catholic hopes for an easement of the penal laws. For it was not until 1774 that an oath acceptable to catholics was finally settled with the act of that year 'to permit his Majesty's subjects of whatever persuasion to testify their allegiance to him'. The oath prescribed under that act was arguably no improvement, from the catholic point of view, on the oath proposed by Archbishop Synge and his son in the 1720s. Yet it was subscribed to by the vast majority of catholics with a stake in the country either under the 1774 act itself or under the relief acts of 1778, 1782 and 1793.

Thus, the Irish clergy's and people's excessive loyalty to Pope and Pretender could be said to have had the effect of postponing by half a century the beginnings of the emancipation process. If catholics had been prepared to accept in 1726-8 what was eventually accepted in 1774, the path towards full emancipation could have been considerably shortened.

Appendix A: *Archbishop Synge's form of Oath of Fidelity*

I, A. B., do promise, testify and declare before God, that I am and will continue a true and faithful subject unto our Sovereign Lord King George; and that I will bear faith and allegiance to him as a good subject ought to do.

I do also profess, testify and declare before God that I hold myself bound in conscience to pay all that duty and allegiance unto our Sovereign Lord King George, which according to the Laws of God, and the present Constitutions of this realm now in force, is due to the King of Great Britain and Ireland in all matters and things which concern the lives, liberties and properties of the subjects of this land.

I do also promise and swear, that I will not at any time, directly or indirectly, by word or deed, encourage or assist any person or persons whatsoever in any design to deprive our Sovereign Lord King George of the crown or Supreme Authority which he now enjoys within the Kingdoms of Great Britain and Ireland, or either of them, or to set up a right or title to the same in any other person whatsoever; and that I will immediately discover every such design that is, or shall hereafter come to my knowledge; so that the same may, to the best of my power, be prevented, and the promoters thereof brought to punishment according to the laws now in force within this realm.

I do also profess and swear, that I do not believe the Pope, or Bishop of Rome, or any Council or Assembly of Bishops, or Ecclesiastical Persons, has or have any lawful power, in any case whatsoever, to depose Kings or Princes, or do deprive them of their authority, or any part of it; or to absolve their subjects from their allegiance; Neither do I believe that either he or they or any of them, have power to absolve me from that allegiance which I have now sworn to Our Sovereign Lord King George, or to dispense with any part of the Oath which I now take: Neither have I already taken, nor ever will accept of any such Dispensation.

I do also promise and swear, that I will not either directly or indirectly, by word or deed, attempt or endeavour to hinder or alter the Succession of the Crown of Great Britain or Ireland, as the same stands now limited to the heirs of the late Illustrious Sophia, Electress and Duchess Dowager of Hanover; but will to my power maintain and defend the same against all persons whatsoever, and particularly against the person pretending in the life of the late King James to be Prince of Wales, and since his death pretends to be King of England and Ireland, or of Great Britain by the name of James the Third, or of Scotland by the name of James the Eighth. And if I shall at any time know of any attempt or endeavour to defeat or alter the said Succession, I will with all speed make such discovery of the same, as that to the best of my power such attempt or endeavour may be rendered ineffectual, and the authors and promoters thereof punished according to the laws now in force.

And all this I do sincerely and faithfully profess, promise and swear, according to the ordinary sense of the words now read unto me, in the true faith of a Christian, without any secret collusion, equivocation, or mental reservation; and will in like manner honestly and sincerely to the best of my power perform what I have now sworn, and every part thereof; so help me God.

Appendix B: *Cornelius Nary's proposed form of oath*

I, A. B., do promise and swear to bear true faith and allegiance to his Majesty King George the Second, his heirs and successors, and that I will make known all treasons, traitorous conspiracies and plots, against his Person, Crown or Dignity, if any such shall come to my knowledge. I also profess that I detest and abhor from my heart as impious, scandalous and abominable to believe that it is lawful to murder or destroy, any Person or Persons whatsoever, for, or under pretence of being heretics; and also that base, unchristian principle that no faith is to be kept with heretics. I further declare that it is no Article of my Faith, that any person whatsoever has power to absolve me from my obligation to this Oath, or that the Pope hath power to depose Princes: And therefore I do promise and swear that I will not teach, preach, hold, maintain or abet any such doctrines or tenets, and that I will not accept of any Absolutions or Dispensations whatsoever with regard to this Oath, or any Part thereof. And all this I promise and swear upon the Faith of a Christian freely, readily and willingly, in the plain and ordinary sense of the words now read unto me, without any secret Collusion, Equivocation, Evasion or Mental Reservation whatsoever. So help me God.

Appendix C: *Catholic Address to the King, July 1727*

To the King's Most Excellent Majesty,
The most humble Address of the Roman Catholics of the Kingdom of Ireland.

Most Gracious Sovereign,

We Your Majesty's most loyal and dutiful subjects, the Roman Catholics of your Kingdom of Ireland, are truly grieved for the unspeakable loss that this nation, as well as Your Majesty's other Dominions, has sustained by the decease of our late most Gracious Sovereign, Your Royal Father; the goodness and lenity of whose Government we are deeply sensible of, which emboldens us thus in a most humble manner to approach Your Majesty's Most Sacred Person, to congratulate Your Majesty's happy accession to the Throne, and to crave leave to assure Your Majesty of our steady allegiance and most humble duty to Your Majesty's Person and Government. And we most humbly beseech Your Majesty to give us leave to affirm that our resolution of an inviolable duty and allegiance to Your Majesty proceeds not only from our inclination and the sincerity of our hearts, but also from a firm belief of its being a religious duty, which no power on earth can dispense with.

Appendix D: *A few queries seriously offered for the consideration of the Lords and gentlemen who lately signed an Address intended to be (and since presented to King George the Second) in behalf of the Roman Catholics of the Kingdom of Ireland.*

Q. I. Whether about twenty or thirty lords and gentlemen, without election or deputation from the Roman Catholics of Ireland, can in any sense be understood to be the Roman Catholics of Ireland?

Q. II. Whether at their meeting at the Lyon in Warburgh Street on the 8th day of July 1727, the proper parties concerned were all present, and time for full deliberation, or a full freedom of debate allowed to those that were?

Q. III. Whether the peremptory signing of an Address of this high nature at first reading, was not precipitate, passionate and presumptuous?

Q. IV. Whether any arguments were made use of to terrify the weak, or catch the unwary, which were anarchical, contrary to the fundamental laws of these realms, injurious to the sentiments of our Holy Mother, the Church, and dishonourable to the much-renowned Fidelity of an Irishman?

Q. V. Whether these words 'the goodness and lenity of whose Government we are deeply sensible of, which emboldens us thus in a most humble manner to approach etc.', do not wipe away our tears without removing the cause? And, whether they do not wipe away some men's scores? While they disarm our Mediators on all occasions and future times, when a sharp execution of the Laws still in force may make it as necessary as it is natural for us to complain?

Q. VI. Whether these words 'and we most humbly beseech Your Majesty to give us leave to affirm that our resolution of an inviolable duty and allegiance to Your Majesty proceeds not only from our inclination and the sincerity of our hearts', may not be understood to be vile and nauseous flattery?

Q. VII. Whether the continuation 'but also from a firm belief of its being a religious duty, which no power on earth can dispense', be not making a new Creed for the Roman Catholics of Ireland and arrogantly deciding of a question of right, which no conscience can affirm, because no understanding can reach?

Q. VIII. If duty and allegiance to King George II be a religious duty, his right and power which are their necessary correlatives, must be of course divine. Why then did not the Junto go generously and take the

Oath of Abjuration for all the Roman Catholics of Ireland, and so save Lord Delvin the trouble of going for England?

Q. IX. Though allegiance to the Lord's anointed may be perhaps a religious duty, with which no power on earth can dispense, yet since it is evident from our history that there may be Kings de facto and since Coke and other of our great lawyers say that allegiance is due to Kings de jure in their natural capacities; and since allegiance does in our language and laws signify something more than mere fidelity, which is reciprocal to mere protection, (We mean as the Flemings swear to their successive Governments, Spaniards, Germans, French, Dutch or English). Whether then, and in every such case, allegiance be a religious duty equally due to all Kings de facto, as well as de jure, and finally, in all cases, whether the Parliament be not a power on earth actually existing, that often has, and still can dispense with such duty?

Q. X. Whether such of the subscribers as were hurried into this affair, without seeing into the private views of the scheme, ought not to think it as just, as it will be undoubtedly honourable in them, to withdraw their names and acknowledge they were imposed upon?

Q. XI. Whether the Junto were not obliged to answer these and innumerable other queries to all Irishmen, before they presume to present their famous Address in the name of the whole Kingdom?

Q. XII. Whether if the Address must absolutely go, it ought not to be entitled *The humble address of us the Subscribers?*

Q. XIII. And last to be forthwith answered, whether an humble petition to the King, and a Remonstrance of our Grievances, notwithstanding the public faith given at Limerick, and our peaceable behaviour ever since that time, would not be much more proper on this critical occasion, and contribute more to our relief at a future Congress?

6

THE CONGRESS OF SOISSONS

As already pointed out in Chapter 5, the 1720s was a period when, although there was little in the way of actual fighting, there were tensions and frictions between various European countries which constantly threatened to erupt into war. The Peace of Utrecht (in reality a series of twelve treaties) which ended the War of the Spanish Succession in 1713, contained terms of peace which were almost guaranteed to breed further trouble. For example, the British presence in Gibraltar would be a constant irritant to Spain, while the Austrian presence in what had previously been the Spanish Netherlands, with a consequent outlet to the Atlantic, led to the setting up by Austria of the Ostend Company for the purpose of trade with the East Indies to the discomfiture of British and Dutch trading interests in that region.

Just before he died in June 1727 George I, who took an active interest in foreign affairs, had succeeded in settling the preliminaries of a treaty with Austria and Spain. The European Congress which opened at Soissons, an old cathedral town on the Aisne in north-east France, in June 1728, was a further step in the same direction. The Congress could be said to have been the culmination of the policies towards peace of the chief ministers of Britain and France, Robert Walpole and André de Fleury. De Fleury came very late to top statesmanship and a cardinal's hat—he was already seventy-five years old in 1728 and had been at the helm in France for only two years—and it is said that it was to convenience this old man that the Congress was held at Soissons within range of Paris. The purpose was to provide a forum within which the nations of Europe could discuss, and hopefully, settle differences, de Fleury being an early exponent of the notion of a League of Nations or a United Nations.

There was considerable disagreement among the participating states as to the issues which should be discussed by the congress: some like Britain and Austria wanted a very restricted agenda, while others such as Spain and Holland favoured a wide agenda. But we are here concerned primarily with only two of the possible issues for discussion—the efforts and hopes of the Pretender to be restored to the British throne, and the question of religious toleration and liberty of conscience in the various states. Two Irish Franciscans were involved in these two aspects: in the first case Ambrose O'Callaghan, later to be bishop of Ferns, held a watching brief for the Pretender, and, in the second case, Sylvester Lloyd was involved in the efforts of the Irish and English catholics to have the penal laws affecting them examined by the congress with a view to some relief being effected.

Lloyd claimed to be representing the Irish regular clergy as well as those who had opposed the Address to the King. It is significant that he did not claim to represent the Irish bishops, and it is understandable that that body would not want to have as their representative someone who had only recently been the cause of deep divisions in the church in Ireland through his organisation of the opposition to the Oath and the Address. Why the English catholics, many of whom would have been diametrically opposed to Lloyd on the question of the oath of allegiance to the king, should have chosen him as one of their representatives must be either a tribute to Lloyd's plausibility or an indication of how little the English really knew about him.

Lloyd was to find the English catholics just as disunited as those in Ireland, and for the same reason. Catholic disunity in England went back to 1716 when Bishop Stonor, vicar apostolic of the Midland District, aided by the English-born Strickland, later bishop of Namur, began his campaign for an oath of loyalty for catholics to George I. Of the four vicars apostolic in England and Wales, Stonor was the only one to favour such an oath, but admittedly he had substantial support amongst the catholic nobility and gentry. The possibility of religious toleration being put on the agenda of the Soissons Congress brought the question of an oath to the fore once more in England in 1728, because of its value as a bargaining counter if the negotiation of relief measures for Irish and English catholics became a reality.

We have already seen in the last chapter how, during his sojourn in London in May 1728, Lloyd was keeping a watchful eye on Lord Delvin. He reports to Col. O'Brien in the same letter, dated 1 June 1728, written in Douai, that he was also at this time involved in some high-level discussions with English catholics on the forthcoming congress:

> As to my present affair I am, as soon as we have here translated into Latin an abstract of the Penal Laws passed in England against the

Catholics, to go to Brussels to meet one Dr Umfreville, an English clergyman who is to go from thence to solicit that Court for recommendations to the Congress in favour of their cause. I was to be joined in commission with him to act in that affair but I declined it for some time until I had consulted my friends, and must therefore beg your advice. My reason for making difficulties to myself is that I have it upon a conference or two with the Duke of Norfolk and others of the chief Catholics from England that they do not expect to be relieved from any of the Penal Laws without being obliged to take the Oath of Allegiance at least as a test for their fidelity, and I must own to you that I found them all inclined to take it, if not perhaps something more if required. You are the best judge how far this may be for his Majesty's [Pretender's] interest. For my part I don't like it and will not have any hand in the affair till I have your opinion upon it. They depend upon me for drawing the state of their case in Latin to be sent to Vienna and Poland. I shall find means to avoid it if you think, as I already do, that it will be more to our master's interest that things should go on as they hitherto have done, than to tamper with the Government and be perhaps drawn into measures that may be destructive in the end. I have a commission from all the religious superiors in Ireland to act if need be at the Congress in their behalf and the behalf of the Non-Addressors. As I do not know how this affair may end or what consequences it may be attended with, so I again beg you will instruct me how I ought to behave. I take from home my Lord Caher's eldest son and shall go to Ypres in my way to Brussels where I shall expect your answer enclosed to the Abbess of the Irish Dames for I should be glad to know your sentiments before I see the Nuncio in Brussels from whom I am to receive credentials. In case I undertake the affairs of the English Catholics I beg you will let me know what you think of one Mr Ramsey now at Paris. They have thoughts of employing him.[1]

'Dr Umfreville' mentioned in the foregoing letter was the pseudonym of Charles Fell (1686-1763). Born in England of French extraction, Fell was reared in France. He was ordained in 1713 and took a doctorate from Paris University in 1716. Following his assignment to the English

---

1 Stuart Papers RA SP(M) vol. 116/152, MFR 772. There is some evidence that Bernard Dunne, bishop of Kildare, was selected by the primate to represent the Irish catholic interest at Soissons but he declined to move without the permission of the Pretender (see Stuart Papers vols. 112/89 and 136/116).

Mission, he spent most of his clerical career in London. His greatest achievement was his *Lives of the Saints* in four volumes, which not only got him into debt but also earned him a denunciation to Rome from Robert Witham, president of the English College, Douai, whose main criticism of the 'Lives' was that they contained few miracles.[2]

The Mr Ramsey mentioned was probably Andrew Ramsay (1686-1743). Born the son of a baker in Ayr in Scotland, Ramsay's early life had a curious similarity to Lloyd's (as set out in Chapter 1) in that he appears to have suffered a crisis of conscience while serving with the British Army in the Netherlands during the War of the Spanish Succession. He left the army in 1706 and in 1710 he was received into the catholic Church. He developed a friendship with Archbishop Fenelon of Cambrai, who wrote extensively on politics and was one of the foremost exponents of the mystical movement called Quietism. Under Fenelon's tutelage the young James Stuart, the Pretender, is said to have come under the spell of Quietism for a time. When Fenelon died in 1715 he left all his papers to Ramsay, who then went to Paris where he occupied himself in writing a Life of Fenelon. Subsequently he was tutor to the Pretender's children for a short period, but this did not prevent him from being chosen a member of the Royal Society, London or from receiving an LLD degree from Oxford University. Apart from his biography of Fenelon, Ramsay was the author of several works on politics, mythology and epic poetry. His *Apology for the free and accepted masons*, published in Dublin in 1738, had the distinction of being publicly burned in Rome.[3]

It will be seen from Lloyd's letter preceding that the penal laws were being translated into Latin for the benefit of Austria and Poland, two of the foremost catholic states to be represented at the congress. Presumably it was unnecessary to provide Latin translations for the other main catholic powers, France and Spain. On previous form Lloyd's attitude to an oath to George II should have been a foregone conclusion and he should not have needed any advice from O'Brien on that score. His problem appears to have been that he was torn between wanting to play an important role at the congress and adhering to his principles with regard to the oath.

Apparently the advice he got from O'Brien was not to take part in any discussions that might involve acceptance of an oath, for when he next wrote to O'Brien on 10 June from Ypres he had this to say:

2   John Kirk, *Biographies of English Catholics in the Eighteenth Century* (John H. Pollen & Edwin Burton eds.) (London, 1909), p. 78.
3   *Dictionary of National Biography* (London, 1895).

6 James Francis Edward Stuart, the Pretender, in 1745.

It is a great pleasure to me to find by the letter you did me the honour to write to me on the 4th instant that your judgment is the same as my own private opinion was before, that it will be much the safer and more honourable way for the Catholics as well of Ireland as of England not to make any application at the present Congress, for, besides what you very judiciously observe of the difficulties that are but too obvious as well with regard to the Court of France as in general with regard to the suffering any agent to move in affairs of that nature, I am sure that such application, though admitted, would produce no good effect, for suppose the best, and that the Government could be prevailed on to do something in our favour, we can't expect they will do it without obliging us to some test of allegiance to them, which must be not only prejudicial to our Master's right but dishonourable to our country and scandalous to our religion. It was for these reasons that I in London absolutely refused to be concerned in any scheme of the kind till I had first seen our Master's approbation of it. And the rather because I found plainly, as I had the honour to tell you before, that some of the Chiefs seemed to make no difficulty of taking any Oath of Allegiance, insisting strenuously that allegiance and fidelity are the same thing and both due to a king *de facto*. I know there are several of the clergy as well as the laity of better sentiments and I was glad to find the worthy President of Douai and his whole college in the same way of thinking.

They did intend when I left London to employ one Ramsey now at Paris as their agent, being as was given out a person very much in the esteem of the Cardinal. Lord Stafford was the man who recommended him and wrote into England that he had accepted of the commission. They had thoughts of employing one Southcott, a monk, jointly with him. You know the men to be sure and can best judge what may be expected from them. They promised to send an English clergyman called Umfreville after me to Brussels, there to concert proper measures with the Nuncio, but as I have not heard from him as yet so I hope they have thought fit to drop the project. I shall set out tomorrow from hence to Brussels and I shall from thence acquaint you with what may occur but am for my own part determined not to meddle directly or indirectly in the affair.

I believe I forgot to tell you in my last that I had last winter a most gracious letter from our Master on the subject of the unhappy Address and with it a short paper which I believe his Majesty intended should be communicated to his friends. It was with regard to a certain person's refusal to come to him to Avignon but as the account of his going over the Alps again came to my hands before his letter, so I thought it more proper not to make use of it till I heard how matters went at their meeting. The good news you do me the honour to give me has given me the greatest joy. The great God bless and prosper them and preserve a perpetual harmony between them.[4]

'The worthy President of Douai' was evidently the president of the English College at Douai, Robert Witham, and not the president of the Irish College there. He was Stonor's chief opponent on the question of an oath, and Lloyd would have recently met him when he visited the college with Lord Cahir's eldest son, who was resuming his studies there. 'The Cardinal' is presumably Cardinal de Fleury. Lord Stafford was the son of the Viscount Stafford who was executed in London in 1680 for his alleged part in the Titus Oates-invented Popish Plot.[5] 'Southcott, a monk' was Thomas Southcote, an English benedictine. He published a translation of part of Quesnel's *Nouveau Testament avec des Réflexions morales* but that was before Quesnel's work was condemned by the Holy Office in 1713. He was president of the general chapter of his order on several occasions between 1721 and 1737.[6]

The last paragraph of the above letter is a further reference to the Pretender's matrimonial troubles. On the death of George I in June 1727 the Pretender's hopes of a restoration revived and he rushed to France, where he hoped de Fleury might champion his cause. But de Fleury was unreceptive and, following a stay in Lorraine, the Pretender took up residence in the papal city of Avignon and asked his wife, Clementina, to join him there. She refused to do so, probably because John Hay and his wife (with whom the Pretender was said to have had a liaison) were back with the Pretender. Because of pressure on the pope by Britain, the Pretender was compelled to leave Avignon in January 1728 and went to Bologna in Italy. By this time the Hays had left him once more, and so a reconciliation with Clementina proved possible.[7]

By 23 June Lloyd has had a definite offer from the catholic body in England to act on their behalf at the congress with Southcott, and, clearly flattered by such a request and teetering on the brink of acceptance, writing from Brussels he again rather halfheartedly asks O'Brien for advice as to what he should do:

4   Stuart Papers, RA SP(M) vol. 117/34, MFR 772.
5   John J. Delaney & James Tobin, *Dictionary of catholic biography* (London, 1962).
6   John Kirk, op. cit., p. 215.
7   Peggy Miller, *James* (London, 1971), pp. 283-4.

I have nothing new to tell you from hence but that I this morning received a letter from the persons who are at London entrusted with the management of the affairs of the English Catholics wherein they gave me to understand that some of the Catholic lords, whom they do not name, have in imitation of the Duke of Norfolk kissed the Elector's hand. I dreaded something like this would be the consequence of what I hinted to you before. The persons that write to me say that this step was no more than an exterior decency but that they are still the same men *in fora conscientiae* and that they hope it may facilitate their applications at the Congress or elsewhere. They say they had good encouragement in the beginning from some great men but that they have been lately forbid by the same persons to make any public application either to the Congress or to any foreign power whatsoever. Notwithstanding which they have done me the honour to charge me with their affairs jointly with Mr Southcott of Paris.

My instructions are to write immediately to Mr Southcott and let him know that I am ready to meet him at such place as he shall think proper, there to concert proper measures with him for privately possessing the Plenopotentiaries of our grievances. Their advice is that we should place ourselves somewhere near Soissons where we may be at hand if a favourable opportunity should offer, to give in the states of our case and answer such objections as may be perhaps started against us. I do by this post write to Mr Southcott as they desired but shall never stir in anything without your advice. I don't doubt but you know Mr Southcott and that he will communicate this affair to you, for my correspondents tell me they have writ to him to the same purpose as to me, but if he should make a secret of it to you, I beg you will not make any mention of it as coming from me. And then be so good as to let me know your opinion for I hope you will do me the justice to believe that I will never directly or indirectly act in anything that may be so much as remotely against my Master's interest. I shall expect your answer directed to me at the P.O. in Brussels with impatience. If he should appoint a place of meeting I will from thence give you a faithful account of all that passes.

The Nuncio of this place tells me he has no instructions from His Holiness to move in any affair of this nature. And yet our friends in England positively say that the Pope has been consulted and has promised to recommend them to all Catholic princes. Perhaps the Nuncio of Paris knows something of the matter but these matters seem to me to be somewhat misled. I must therefore beg your sentiments of the whole affair because that, though I have no great hopes of any success in the undertaking, yet I would not be backward to show these gentlemen, who do me the honour to entrust me with their affairs, preferably to some of their own countrymen, that I would do anything consistent with my Master's interest to serve them.[8]

But efforts to put the religious question on the agenda of the congress met with little support even from the Vatican. Cardinal Spinola, in a dispatch dated 24 July 1728, informed nuncio Spinelli in Brussels that the course of action planned by the catholics of England and Ireland on the occasion of the proposed congress had been subjected to serious examination at Rome; it had been decided that the nuncio should make certain that the catholics in question refrained from doing anything impetuous or violent, as this could result in more harm than good for themselves and their religion; rather, the nuncio should advise them to direct their petitions to Cardinal de Fleury, and assure them that the pope would do all he could to procure the assistance of the French court for them and to interest all the other catholic powers in their welfare; but should the nuncio learn that the catholic clergy intended to take some kind of oath to 'the duke of Hanover' (George II), he was to see to it that no decision was taken until the matter had been examined at Rome and precise directions issued by the Holy See.[9]

Spinelli, in reply, expressed the view that Irish and English catholics would not do anything to cause alarm, or that they had any plan in mind to take an oath to the duke of Hanover. He complained that they had failed from the very beginning to put forward a well-digested plan and that there was such confusion and discord among them that they did not know exactly what to do. He mentioned that the vicar apostolic of the London area [Giffard] had written to him asking him to recommend the cause of the English catholics to the emperor, as they believed they had more to hope for from him, because of his protestant subjects in Germany, than from any other catholic prince. Spinelli considered, however, that there were no grounds for such hopes, since the minister of the emperor had never shown himself to be particularly interested in the welfare of the English and Irish catholics, the situation in Germany

8 Stuart Papers, RA SP(M) vol. 117/105, MFR 772.
9 Cathaldus Giblin, 'Catalogue of material of Irish interest in the collection Nunziatura di Fiandra, Vatican Archives' in *Collectanea Hibernica*, no. 14 (1971), p. 41.

differing greatly as regards religion from that in England; the religious freedom of the protestants in Germany was safeguarded by many treaties, while in England and Ireland there were no guarantees allowing catholics there to practise their religion. (Spinelli is here making the point that, since German protestants already enjoyed religious toleration, the necessary prerequisites did not exist for a trade-off in the matter of toleration between protestants in Germany and catholics in Britain and Ireland.) Spinelli had therefore advised the vicar apostolic to have recourse to de Fleury but to do so in moderate, decorous terms.[10]

Later in a Vatican dispatch of 2 October of the same year Spinola praised Spinelli for advising the English and Irish catholics to enter into consultation with the nuncio at Paris, so that he could guide them in whatever steps they intended to take at the congress; he was refraining from giving Spinelli any specific instructions in the matter as it was thought that questions of religion would not be discussed at the congress. Nonetheless, Spinola went on, the nuncio at Paris would be directed to keep a vigilant eye on events, with a view to blocking any move the protestants might make to gain the advantage, while in the meantime, as opportunity arises, Spinelli should keep in touch with the nuncio in Paris in regard to possible developments.[11]

Such Vatican prevarication stemmed in part from the fear that any concessions granted to Irish and English catholics would be counterbalanced by an oath involving not only allegiance to King George II but also renunciation of the pope's deposing and dispensing powers. There was also the consideration that any concessions in the matter of toleration gained for catholics in Britain and Ireland would almost certainly have to be matched by similar concessions to persecuted protestants in France and Poland. The opening of the can of worms of religious toleration could have a net overall result which might not from the Vatican's global point of view be, on balance, favourable to catholicism.

Given the Vatican's temporising stance, it is not surprising that Lloyd's ambition to play a part in the Soissons congress was to be thwarted. Indeed, the congress was little more than a month in being when he realised as much and sent from Brussels the following report dated 23 July 1728 to the Pretender:

---

10 Ibid., no. 9 (1966), p. 8.
11 Ibid., no. 14 (1971), p. 41.

May it please your Majesty,

I was in April last called for England by some friends in order to concert jointly with the English Catholics the proper measures for an application to the Congress for relief from the Penal Laws wherewith your Majesty' Catholic subjects in both Kingdoms are oppressed.

I was in the course of some meetings and debates not a little surprised to find dispositions in some of the leading men not at all consistent with their duty to your Majesty which made me, as far as I could in prudence, discourage the project and at length refuse absolutely to be concerned in it till I first saw your Majesty's approbation of it, for though they assured me that it had been communicated to your Majesty, yet I could not be persuaded the manner they intended to pursue it in, could produce anything better than perhaps a temptation to depart from their duty. And therefore excused myself from undertaking anything till I had first consulted the Nuncio in Brussels and other friends from whom I expected to know your Majesty's as well as his Holiness's sentiments. I told them that I would if they pleased go to Brussels and there wait for their instructions. They then intended to join Dr Umfreville, an English clergyman, with me in their commission, but he not being ready to set out, I insisted on going off before him to prepare matters at Brussels, which they consented to. So I immediately took shipping in the River and landed at Calais from whence I gave Col. O'Brien an exact account of all that was intended and of the consequences I foresaw would follow from their schemes if not seasonably prevented. I waited at Douay for his answer which confirmed me in my resolution of defeating the project if possible.

I therefore came directly hither and laid the affair in its true lights before the Nuncio. I told him that the dispositions I found some of the English Catholics on, together with what happened in Ireland with regard to the late infamous Address, gave me reason to fear that many of them would readily go into the government schemes provided the Government came into theirs; and since it could not be expected that the present jealous ministry would give us any privileges without extraordinary assurances on our side of allegiance or something worse, I therefore begged he would not readily come into any of their schemes till he knew on what bottom they were grounded.

I found him [Nuncio] zealously in your Majesty's interest and averse from everything that might be even remotely contrary to it. So I waited with impatience for further advices from my friends in

England and after some time, instead of Dr Umfreville's coming, received a long letter from Mr Adam Coleslogh (who was the person I was to receive my instructions from) with an account [from] which I but too plainly foresaw that the Duke of Norfolk and others had communicated their thoughts to Sir Robert Walpole, that he had given them fair promises, that the Duke had been drawn in to kiss the Elector's hand, and that some others were preparing to follow his example in order, as they thought, to facilitate what they had in hands, when Sir Robert all of a sudden sent them express orders at their peril not to apply either to the Congress or to any foreign power whatsoever.

My friend Mr Coleslogh owns they were thunderstruck at this and found they had been duped but still told me they were resolved to proceed in a private manner, and had by that post writ to Mr Southcott at Paris to join me in endeavouring privately to possess foreign princes and their ministers of the hardships we lay under in order that they should, as from themselves, mediate for us in case the religious grievances came into debate. I immediatly wrote to Mr Southcott to put him on his guard and at the same time signify to Mr Coleslogh that the steps taken in England had alarmed all honest men, that I knew many of the Catholic powers would be offended, that His Holiness would not recommend their case, that his Nuncio had refused to act, and that I myself was resolved not to meddle directly or indirectly. I in answer to this received several letters, wherein they endeavour to justify their proceedings and the sincerity of their intentions which may be as they say. But I must venture to tell your Majesty that I am convinced that Bishops Strickland and Stonor were again in the bottom of the affair by their private commissions, and that some great men whose understandings are not perhaps so clear as their hearts may be sincere were overreached by them, which they now see and are ashamed of.

I gave Col. O'Brien due notice of everything that came to my knowledge in this affair as well as the new game Lord Delvin is now playing at London for himself and his Addressing friends which I doubt not he [O'Brien] has faithfully communicated to your Majesty. I intend with the blessing of God to return to London in a few days and from thence to Dublin. And thought it my duty before I parted to give your Majesty this account and to beg leave to assure your Majesty that I shall at all times be ready to lay down my life for your service.

May the Almighty God bless and preserve your Majesty with the
Queen and Royal Issue shall be the constant prayer of
> Your Majesty's faithful subject and servant
>> Sylvester Lloyd

May it please your Majesty

Postscript

I hope my answer to your Majesty's gracious letter from Avignon went safe by the same bearer.[12]

It will be seen that Lloyd's report to the Pretender of the events of the previous three months, made with hindsight, has been somewhat tailored to show himself off in as good a light as possible to the Pretender. Bishop Thomas Strickland (c.1679-1740), mentioned in Lloyd's report, was born in Westmoreland but was brought up in France at St Germain, whither his parents had fled in 1689 following the Glorious Revolution of 1688. Following his education at the English College at Douai and ordination as a priest, he returned to England in 1712. He was proposed as coadjutor to Bishop Giffard, vicar apostolic of the London District, but was rejected on the score of youth. Later he incurred Jacobite wrath because of his advocacy of an oath of allegiance for catholics to George I. Around 1719, he settled in London and was active on a catholic committee which came to nothing. In 1727 he was appointed bishop of Namur in the Austrian Netherlands but does not appear to have attended too diligently to his episcopal duties, preferring instead to continue a life of intrigue. Shortly afterwards he was in Rome as an agent for the British government with the design of getting information on the Pretender. In the autumn of 1734 we find him in England, masquerading under the name of Mr Mosley and in the pay of the Emperor, on whose behalf he was endeavouring to bring England in on the side of the Emperor and against France in the War of the Polish Succession. But his efforts on that occasion were of no avail because of Walpole's opposition to such a move.[13]

John Stonor (1680-1756) had links with the English aristocracy in that his mother was a daughter of the eleventh earl of Shrewsbury. He too was educated at Douai and was ordained a priest in France in 1709. Having secured a doctorate, he was assigned to the English Mission in 1714 and two years later he was appointed a bishop and vicar apostolic of the Midland District. Shortly after, there was an intrigue, in which Strickland

12 Stuart Papers, RA SP(M) vol. 118/87, MFR 773.
13 *Dictionary of National Biography* (London, 1895).

was involved, to have him appointed vicar apostolic of the London district in place of the ageing Giffard, but the plans of the intriguers backfired. Like Strickland he considered that the best course for catholics was to accept the reality of the Hanoverian succession by an oath of allegiance to George I and hopefully thereby obtain a measure of toleration.[14]

Towards the end of July 1728 Lloyd embarked from the Continent for London once more, whence on 1 August he reported in the following quite enigmatic terms to Col. O'Brien:

> I was delayed eight days for a wind and came here three days ago where I found our friends divided into parties on account of the late steps taken by a certain great man. I gave my opinion freely on the whole affair and endeavoured to convince them that it was their true interest to drop all manner of applications at this time, but especially such as came recommended from a certain quarter which ought to be suspected. I can't say that all parties here are of my opinion but may venture to assure you that the greater party are. The gentleman in black, who was my correspondent at Paris, had endeavourd to do me some mischief here and that in the most base manner. I suppose he was not pleased that I differed in opinon with him or that I had the presumption to give my opinion at all in a matter wherein he had for some time given rules and dictated without contradiction. He has given his nephew, a great man here, an account that some things were known by a certain person at Paris relating to their Scheme which nobody could have discovered but one. I don't know what he means but I know very well that I never communicated anything to any soul at Paris but yourself, and from you I thought it was my duty not to conceal anything.
>
> It is whispered here that some people intend to apply to the G——t [Government] upon another footing which will turn them to as great ridicule as their first project did. Nothing shall be left undone to prevent them. The Lord D——n [Delvin] disappeared from home about ten days ago. It is now said for certain that he is gone to Soissons to pursue his old game. It is proper to have a sharp eye after him for his restless spirit will not stop at small things.
>
> I must now tell you that things here look better and better ever day, and that it is the opinion of the wisest people that the Chief Director of our Company will soon do his own business. His haughty

---

14   John Kirk, op. cit., p. 220.

behaviour to his under-directors and domestics is insupportable, nor is their resentment silent. His affectation of being thought wise and sagacious makes him often blab the counsels of his best friends to their private enemies in order to pass them as the products of his own brain, and by that means causes frequent broils and heats in his family. Such was the case last week when the Lord Scarborough and Mr Robert Walpole had hot words and so loud that the public heard them. It is however said that the former was obliged to submit which has at last decided that Mr Robt. is not only chief Minister but chief favourite.

I have to be sure heard of sixteen men-of-wars being lately put into commission and ordered to sea with all possible expedition. This gives great alarms to the trading people who can't be persuaded that they are intended only as guard-ships or to cruise upon the Tallymen who have perfidiously broken their treaties with us.

I am just upon returning home from whence you shall hear from me, having no more to add at present but to recommend myself to your good opinion and protection, who am your most faithful, humble servant.[15]

The 'Chief Director' mentioned in the foregoing is evidently George II. The 'certain great man' referred to is presumably Walpole, the chief (now prime) minister. 'The man in black' appears to be Thomas Southcote. Lloyd's exasperation with the English catholic scene has to be viewed in the context that numerically English catholics at that time were of little importance as compared with Irish catholics. Contemporary estimates put them at about 90,000 at the beginning of the century, and this figure had declined to about 63,000 by 1780.[16] This compares with a catholic population in Ireland which was approaching two millions in 1728. Any importance English catholics had at this time lay in their being top heavy with nobility and gentry.[17]

15 Stuart Papers, RA SP(M) vol. 118/134, MFR 773.
16 A letter to the pope in 1704 stated that there were 100,000 catholics in England, but in 1706 Dr Betham estimated the catholic population at 80,000 (see Basil Hemphill, *The early vicars apostolic in England*, London 1953, p. 102). My figure of 90,000 is the mean of these figures. Similarly, there are two figures for 1780 - 56,000 (Hemphill) and 69,316 (*New Catholic Encyclopedia*), giving a mean of 63,000.
17 K. H. Connell in *The population of Ireland 1750-1845* (Oxford, 1950) table 1, estimated that the population of Ireland in 1732 was 3.018m. as against the estimate of 2m. for 1732 in *Abstract of protestant and popish families* (Dublin, 1736) which was based on Hearth Money returns for 1732-3. Connell's estimate was based on the proposition that the Hearth Money returns were deficient to the extent of 50%. His views in this matter have been challenged by more recent writers, but it would seem prudent to allow for a 20% deficiency, giving a revised estimated population of 2.4m., composed of, say 1.9m. catholics and 0.5m. protestants.

Towards the end of the first paragraph Lloyd appears to be accusing O'Brien of having in a sense double-crossed him. Lord Delvin had indeed gone to Soissons, or somewhere near it, for his movements are charted in a letter dated 3 August 1728 from Thomas Southcote to the Pretender:

> I had since a letter of 6th August concerning the Catholics who are so divided that it is impossible to do them any good. Strickland, I am assured, was driven from hence [presumably Paris] by the Chevalier de Zinzendorf for talking too freely of obligations he pretended that family had to him, but Lord Delvin I think is still here, and finds too many of his own scandalous principles. However, I hope I have defeated his designs. I gave a memorial to the curate of S. Sulpice to keep him right and let the nuncio see all the consequences and tendencies of Lord Delvin's endeavours. All I can do is to keep [him] from doing mischief and that in the most general way I can.[18]

The congress of Soissons dragged on into 1731. Generally it proved unequal to the needs and expectations of the various states, although two treaties were concluded—that of Seville in 1729 between Britain, France and Spain, and that of Vienna in 1731 between Britain, Austria and Spain. The Austrian emperor's insistence on what became known as the 'pragmatic sanction' (that in the absence of a male successor, his daughter, Maria Theresa, should succeed him as Empress) proved highly unpalatable to various states, especially to France. When, under the Second Treaty of Vienna in 1731, Britain, in return for the dissolution of the Ostend Company by Austria, accepted the pragmatic sanction, France found herself isolated on this issue. It was an issue upon which in the next decade she was to go to war.

The curtain could be said to have been finally rung down on the ideals of Soissons when, in December 1731, the French administration in their instructions to their ambassador in London, stated that the reciprocal interests of Britain and France were separated by a distance so considerable that there was no longer a question of deliberating together upon the affairs of Europe.[19]

The congress's indifferent results were to an extent due to the plenipotentiaries of the different states not taking it seriously enough, and generally preferring to send deputies rather than attending meetings of the congress themselves. Cardinal de Fleury was the central figure of the

18 Stuart Papers, RA SP(M) vol. 119/134, MFR 773.
19 Arthur McCandles Wilson, *French foreign policy of Cardinal Fleury* (London, 1936), p. 239.

congress, and his old, temporising, cautious hand proved a bit of a deadweight in facing up to the real issues and in having decisions of substance taken. In a letter to the Pretender on 30 August 1728 Fr Ambrose O'Callaghan reported a prevalent view that 'no good was to be expected from Cardinal Fleury till be should be either frightened or threatened to be cashiered.' In the same letter O'Callaghan said it was the view of some influential people that de Fleury 'has it in his hands to oblige the World with a second Restoration'.[20]

While catholic hopes, that the congress might be used as a vehicle for some easement of the penal laws, were to be dashed, nevertheless, while the congress lasted, it appears to have operated as a restraining influence on the Irish administration in its treatment of catholics. In January 1730 we find Primate Boulter remarking in regard to a Popery Bill, partly for registering secular priests and partly for driving out the regulars, which in the event was rejected by the Irish house of commons: 'I must own it is better letting them [catholics] alone, whatever may otherwise be proper, till after the congress at Soissons is over.'[21]

It must have been a disappointed Lloyd who returned to Dublin in August 1728. However, although the Soissons venture had been a failure, it did no harm at all to his future prospects of promotion. He must have impressed the Pretender, and, what was perhaps more to the point, he had impressed the nuncio in Brussels. While in that city he had apparently renewed acquaintance with a nun of noble birth, Sister Mary Rosa Howard of Norfolk, whom he prevailed upon to write to the Pretender seeking from him a nomination to the vacant bishopric of Killaloe.[22]

Sister Howard's letter throws some further light on the termination of Lloyd's mission to Soissons. She says that Lloyd was sent over from Ireland for the Soissons congress 'on a subject that required deliberation and all things well examined', but that 'he stopped from acting till better satisfied with your Majesty's will and pleasure'. But it appears that the nuncio also had a hand in the termination of Lloyd's assignment, for Sister Howard comments that 'every particular was laid before our worthy nuncio Spinola [*recte* Spinelli] whose sentiments were so prudent and just that the conclusion was his [Lloyd's] return for the present'.

She goes on to stake Lloyd's claim to Killaloe with unremitting encomiums:

20   Stuart Papers, RA SP(M) vol. 119/135, MFR 773.
21   Hugh Boulter, *Letters*, vol. 1, (Dublin, 1769), p. 344.
22   Stuart Papers, RA SP(M) vol. 118/110, MFR 773.

> ... the merits of Mr Lloyd being very conspicuous, ... his Excellency [the nuncio] entering into the justice of the case, finding him learned, judicious, zealous, and soundly orthodox, and of a most exemplary life, thought him the most worthy to represent to his uncle, Cardinal Imperiali, last post, for that bishopric, which his Auditor this day assures me; with great encomiums on the character and merit of his person; telling me your Majesty's word alone was all he wanted.

This was not Sister Mary Rosa's first venture in bishop-making. She previously had had a hand in the appointment of Stephen MacEgan as bishop of Clonmacnoise in 1725.[23] She was a daughter of Bernard Howard, one of the younger sons of the third earl of Arundel. Her uncle, Phillip Howard, later cardinal, had re-established the English Dominican sisters in Brussels in the 1660s. Later three of Philip Howard's nieces, all daughters of Bernard Howard, joined this community, Mary Rosa being prioress from 1721 to 1724. An enthusiastic supporter of the Pretender, she turned the convent, which also operated a boarding-house, into a point of contact between the Pretender and English Jacobites.[24]

Subsequently, in March 1730 Sister Mary Rosa was to comment thus on the progress of her two protégés:

> I hear with great content that Mr Egen is much esteemed in his new bishoprick [Meath] on all respects, and how much coveted in Doublin by all the Catholic nobility. Mr Lloyd is no less commended where he is [Killaloe].[25]

She died in 1747 (the same year as Lloyd) at the age of seventy.

But to revert to her championing of Lloyd for the vacant bishopric of Killaloe. Cardinal Imperiali, protector of Ireland, was not as easily convinced of Lloyd's suitability for a mitre as was his nephew, the nuncio in Brussels. Lloyd's translation of the Montpellier catechism still rankled with Imperiali when he wrote in Italian in the following terms to the Pretender on 19 August 1728:

> Sacred Royal Majesty,
>   With respect to the bishopric of Killaloe, recently vacant, about which your Majesty had deigned to write to me, showing your

23 Ibid., vol. 81/36, MFR 756.
24 Peter Guilday, *The English catholic refugees on the continent 1558 to 1795* (London, 1914), p. 417.
25 Stuart Papers, RA SP(M) vol. 134/188, MFR 779.

inclination to nominate for it Father Sylvester Lloyd, the Franciscan, I must humbly represent to you how the said religious has against him the translation he made of the Catechism of Montpellier in which, although he corrected various errors, other errors crept in, for which reason it has been prohibited. I am led to understand that, on hearing of the prohibition, he publicly retracted from the pulpit, but there are no public documents in Rome to that effect. On the other hand I can tell your Majesty that the Nuncio in Flanders informed me many times of the worthy qualities of this subject. Furthermore, your Majesty may be so good as to notice on the enclosed page the substance of what the archbishop of Cashel wrote to the same nuncio about the said vacancy. Since the vacant diocese is in the province of Cashel, the contents of the archbishop's letter deserve much reflection. I shall await the further commands which your Majesty may deign to give me. Meanwhile, I remain with all respect, kissing your hands,
    Your Majesty's,
    most humble, devoted and obsequious servant,
    Giuseppe Renato Cardinal Imperiali.[26]

The grovelling, obsequious tone of this letter is an indication of the awe in which the Pretender, as the rightful king of Great Britain and Ireland, was held in the Vatican and of the very real say he had in the appointment of catholic bishops in Ireland. Within a couple of weeks Imperiali had relented, following confirmation from the Pretender that Lloyd had in 1725 publicly retracted his translation of the Montpellier catechism after he had heard of its condemnation by the Holy See. Imperiali added that he had now seen to the registration of this retraction in the Secretariat of the Index so as to close the mouths of all on this question.[27] The choice of Archbishop Butler, the metropolitan, as well as that of the priests and gentry of Killaloe, was thereupon disregarded, and the pope accepted the Pretender's nomination of Sylvester Lloyd as bishop of Killaloe.

The papal brief, in which Lloyd's name is given as Sylvester Ludovicus [Lewis] Lloyd, is dated 25 September 1728.[28] To meet papal misgivings it had been the practice since about 1714 for the Vatican to issue two briefs in respect of the appointment of Irish bishops—one for the bishop-elect in

26 Ibid., vol. 119/55, MFR 773. The letter of Archbishop Butler of Cashel, mentioned here, evidently recommended Denis Crowe for the vacant bishopric of Killaloe. I am indebted to Fr Hugh Fenning O.P. for the translation of Imperiali's letter.
27 Ibid., vol. 120/130, MFR 774.
28 Ibid., vol. 120/123, MFR 774.

which the nominating role of the Pretender was not mentioned, and one for the Pretender in which it was mentioned. When forwarding the latter brief to the Pretender, Imperiali stated that it had been thought well to send the first-mentioned brief to the agent in Rome of the Irish regular clergy, who would make it his business to direct it safely into Lloyd's hands.[29]

---

29   Ibid., vol. 120/163, MFR 774.

7

BISHOP OF KILLALOE

The diocese of Killaloe is one of the more extensive of the Irish dioceses. It comprises about four-fifths of county Clare, about one-third of County Tipperary, about one-sixth of County Offaly and a small part of County Limerick. While Kilfenora in north-west Clare is now administered by the bishop of Galway, in Lloyd's time it was a separate diocese. However, it had a non-resident bishop and there was an arrangement whereby the bishop of Killaloe administered (or was supposed to administer) this tiny diocese.[1] A long, straggling diocese, divided in two by the Shannon and Lough Derg, Killaloe is about one hundred miles across from Loop Head in Clare to Kinnity in Offaly.

When in 1728 the diocese became vacant on the death of Bishop Terlagh MacMahon, the front runner for the appointment appeared to be Denis Crowe (or MacEncroe), who had worked in the diocese for twenty-five years and was vicar-general and a doctor of theology. He was endorsed by a postulation dated 9 August 1728 signed by 33 of the foremost clergy of the diocese and supported by Archbishop Butler of Cashel as metropolitan.[2] There was a further postulation from 117 of the gentry of the diocese in favour of Crowe.[3] Judging by their surnames, these gentry appear to have come mainly from the Tipperary-Offaly end of the diocese, Denis Crowe being parish priest of Toomevara in Tipperary. There appears to have been virtually no local support for Lloyd, who could be said to have been imposed on the diocese by the Pretender. One anonymous writer later voiced his own discontent, and no doubt that of many others, when in the course of a letter dated November 1736 to the Pretender he complained:

1 Cathaldus Giblin, 'Catalogue of material of Irish interest in the collection Nunziatura di Fiandra, Vatican Archives', *Collectanea Hibernica*, no. 9 (1966), 56.
2 Stuart Papers, RA, SP(M) vol. 119/41, MFR 773.
3 Ibid., RA, SP(M) vol. 119/40, MFR 773.

> The clergy and gentry of the diocese of Killaloe postulated for Doctor Macrow, a gentleman of great merit, as did the clergy and gentry of Elphin postulate for Doctor Kelly, a most worthy gentleman. You took no notice of their postulations, but named two friars for the places.[4]

However, no record can be traced of any active opposition to Lloyd when he took up duty in the diocese in 1729. The ground had in any event been well prepared beforehand in directions which the Pretender gave to one of his underlings, Fr. Ingleton, on 2 October 1728.

> You'll acquaint the archbishop of Cashel, with many kind compliments from me, of the particular esteem I have for him and of the weight his opinion has with me especially in ecclesiastic matters, but that on the present vacancy in the diocese of Killaloe I have thought fit for weighty reasons to give my nomination for that see to Father Sylvester Lloyd, whose bulls I suppose are expended by what Cardinal Imperiali writes to me. I doubt not but by his behaviour towards the archbishop and the clergy he will now gain their esteem and goodwill in the new dignity he will be vested in, and that he will not less distinguish himself by his episcopal qualifications than he has already done by his great zeal for my interest.[5]

On the same date the Pretender wrote personally to Lloyd:

> It is long since Mr Birmingham sent me yours of 9 March and Fr. O'Brien here gave me since yours of 23 July, with the regular accounts Col. O'Brien sent of you, and not a little increase my desire of favouring you. But I always delayed expressing to you myself my satisfaction of your zealous conduct till I could join effect to words, and I can now tell you that the Pope has accepted of my nomination in your favour of the bishopric of Killaloe, and, as I understand, the

---

4 Hugh Fenning, 'Some problems of the Irish Mission' in *Collectanea Hinernica*, no. 8 (1965), p. 70. After giving some further examples of the Pretender's favouring friars, the anonymous letter continues: 'I heard the friars of the country often say that they did not doubt to have all the bishoprics there to themselves according as they became vacant, because they are sure of procuring such recommendations from great people that it will not be in your [Pretender's] power to refuse them. For while they are travelling from one country [i.e. county] to another for these recommendations, the secular clergy are at home minding the flock. And I really believe there are not three friars in that kingdom but expect a bishopric, their ambition is grown so intolerable.'

5 Stuart Papers, RA SP(M) vol. 121/8, MFR 774.

bulls should be e'er this expended and your Cardinal Protector has taken measures that you be no further liable to misrepresentations at Rome on account of your translation of the catechism of Montpellier. As this new dignity will enable you the more to be useful to religion and my service, I am persuaded you will make use of it with your usual prudent zeal for those ends; as you know how much peace and union amongst ourselves is necessary for both, I doubt not of your endeavour to promote harmony and concord amongst all that depend on you and over whom you may have any influence, and that you will give others the example by your behaviour towards the clergy and your worthy metropolitan, the archbishop of Cashel. If this cannot be sent safe to you, Col. O'Brien will transmit a copy or abstract of it, and I have nothing further to add at present but that I shall be glad you continue, as much you can with safety, your correspondence with him, and that my kindness for you is equal to the esteem I have long had of you.

And as a postscript the Pretender added:

Pray tell Fr. Stuart, your provincial, how kindly I take his loyal letter of 9 March. Your promotion is a proof of my regard for your order, which I am sure will always continue to deserve well of me.[6]

The Pretender's fears that the foregoing letter could 'not be sent safe' to Lloyd seems to imply that Lloyd at that date (October 1728) was in Ireland. It will be seen from Chapter 6 that the previous 1 August he had written from London, stating that he was 'just upon returning home'. It is not clear where or on what date Lloyd was consecrated bishop. It cannot be assumed at all that the consecration took place in Ireland for Lloyd loved travel and he was continually on the move. Indeed, when we next hear from him on 30 March 1729 he is at St Albans (a town some twenty miles north of London on the post road to Chester) on his way back to Ireland, having apparently come from the Continent. In this letter he regales Col. O'Brien with some London news and gossip:

I left London this morning and am on my way home. I have nothing to add to my former [letter] but everything is in a ferment here. They

---

6   Ibid., RA SP(M) vol. 121/9, MFR 774. Fr Francis Stuart, provincial of the Irish Franciscans mentioned here, was later to be bishop of Down & Connor. The Fr O'Brien mentioned was probably Fr William O'Brien who had recently joined St Isidore's College, Rome. See Stuart Papers, vol. 114/14, MFR 771.

say Mr Walpole and his party are labouring to give up Gibraltar etc. notwithstanding the late resolution of both Houses and 'tis believed they will certainly carry their point. If they do not, there will be war abroad, and if they do, there will, you can depend upon it, be something like war at home. You cannot imagine what a spirit there is up in the nation, and how fond all sorts of people are about holding that important spot of ground. I am not, I must own, of their opinion but do not, you may believe, differ with them. On the contrary I magnify the advantages of keeping it. No less than the honour and trade of England are at stake. I have not yet met a man from the innkeeper to his hostler that is not ready to spill his blood for Gilbraltar. God knows where this will end. You have to be sure heard of the civil war at Court. The duchess of Queensberry's disgrace is the most envied part of her life. The men visit her upon it. And the women wish themselves in her place. The duchess of Marlborough was heard to break out and say: 'Damn the saucy bitch. Fortune has thrown an opportunity in her way that I have been wishing for ever since the family came for England.'

I beg pardon for this dirty scrawl. I have not time to write it over. I will write at large from Dublin and you may be assured I will not neglect your affairs.[7]

At last, six months after his appointment as bishop, Lloyd was ready to buckle down to the job in hand. He took up residence in his diocese, probably in Ennis, where his successor, Patrick MacDonnogh, certainly lived. No doubt with his personal charm, his winning ways and his gregariousness, he soon won his way to the hearts of the clergy and laity and not least of his metropolitan, Archbishop Butler. However, in the late summer of that same year (1729) he found time to visit Dublin and to, believe it or not, attend a meeting of the Irish house of commons. How a catholic bishop, and a regular to boot, could have the entrée to that assembly is difficult to believe. The fact that this particular session met in the Blue Coat School in Queen Street, while the new parliament house

[7] Ibid., RA SP(M) vol. 126/87, MFR 776. The duchess of Queenberry's 'disgrace' was no disgrace to speak of. The public performance of John Gay's *Polly* had been forbidden by the Lord Chamberlain in December 1728. Gay thereupon decided to have the play printed and the duchess, a friend of Gay, was one of those who assisted in soliciting subscriptions towards the publication, which was an instant success. However, for her part in thus flouting authority the duchess was by official letter forbidden the court in February 1729. Swift commented: 'I would be contented with the worst ministry in Europe to live in a country which produces such a spirit as that girl's, and am sorry I was not acquainted with her. (See Swift Correspondence, Harold Williams Ed., vol. 3, p. 321).

was being built, may have made it that much easier of access.

He duly, in letter dated 25 September 1729, furnished Col. O'Brien with an account of what he saw:

> Our Parliament met the 23rd when a curiosity of seeing and hearing the debate of that great assembly brought me from the country where I constantly live. The Lord Lieutenant made them a short but very polite speech. He expressed his great joy at meeting them again, gave them great assurances of his Master's favour, recommended unanimity in the dispatch of business and besides the usual subsidies told them there were great deficiencies which must be made up. It is said that these amount to two hundred thousand pounds or more. Men talk variously of the manner of raising this sum. Some say by a land tax, others by a pole [sic] tax, but 'tis generally believed the Country members will not consent to either, and are for taxing it upon the officers and pensioners of this establishment, who live and spend their money in England. It is thought there will be great clashings about it, but we must yield for we are not (though it breaks our hearts) in a condition to dispute anything with our Masters.
>
> Yesterday the House met, when our great Speaker, Mr Conolly, was taken with fainting fits in the chair, was let blood and carried home. So that the House adjourned itself for some days. Our observators say that Conolly, who is a complete fox, and always has been a servant of the Court, fainted politically, foreseeing that he must either disoblige his old master or consent to the ruin of his country, where he has acquired a large stake. They say this morning that he is for surrendering the chair and that it will be filled by Sir Ralph Gore, a true blue. We are assured by the last pacquets that Dr. Hoadley, bishop of Ferns and brother of the famous Benjamin of Bangor, is made archbishop of Dublin. This gives unspeakable spleen to the clergy of Irish birth. And this is all I can at present tell you of public affairs.[8]

With regard to Lloyd's comments on this meeting of the Irish house of commons, the modus operandi of the Irish parliament has already been explained in Chapter 5. William Conolly had risen from humble beginnings to become one of Ireland's largest landowners, with a palatial

---

8   Ibid., RA SP(M) vol. 130/176, MFR 778. When Lloyd mentions 'country members' he has in mind those belonging to the country (later patriot) party, who were in the nature of an opposition to the ruling court party.

residence at Castletown, Celbridge. At the time Lloyd is writing about he had been the Government's chief undertaker in the house of commons for several years; in other words he undertook, as leader of the court party, to put the administration's programme through the commons. The fainting attack described by Lloyd was no sham, as some surmised, but the real thing. He was to die on 30 October 1729. As foreseen in Lloyd's letter, he was succeeded by Sir Ralph Gore as speaker. Gore also took over the leadership of the Court Party but he shared some other appointments previously held by Conolly with Marmaduke Coghill.

Lloyd in letter above goes on in suitably coded language to make a short reference to his work as bishop. When he speaks of 'rents' he seems to mean dues payable to the bishop by the laity and clergy:

> Everything goes, blessed be God, well with me in my new stewardship. No people are more willing to pay their rents but the markets are bad. All your relations wish you sincerely well and often drink your health. They long very much to see you. Pray, dear Sir, write to me.

But he had completed only two years of active ministry when misfortune overtook him in the shape of a disease of the eyes. It was an affliction that was to dog him with greater or lesser severity for the rest of his life. Archbishop Butler's letter in Latin dated 4 October 1731 to Montalto, administrator of the nunciature in Brussels, gives us the sorry details:

> To the great distress of his flock, Sylvester Lloyd, Bishop of Killaloe, has been stricken by a serious illness and is afflicted especially with an infirmity of the eyes. In an effort to find relief he has expended whatever little money he had on doctors and surgeons and has incurred heavy debts. He is in a pitiable condition and in need of immediate assistance. He has begun to improve somewhat and he can see a little but he has yet to bear heavy expenses and endure much suffering before he is completely cured. The pain he has borne by the hands of doctors and surgeons for four continuous months is beyond description, but he has endured all with extraordinary patience and has shown marvellous resignation to the will of God.

Butler states that he can attest personally to the truth of all he writes because he undertook a long journey to visit Lloyd, and returned full of admiration for him and thanking God for having given the afflicted bishop such wonderful consolation. Butler recommends that he and the Brussels nuncio work together to procure assistance for Lloyd and that they plead with the Holy See on his behalf to get help from the pope for him. Butler states that Lloyd contracted his infirmities because of his untiring labours in his diocese, and that since he arrived in it Lloyd had been working ceaselessly day and night, preaching, entreating, reproving, administering the sacraments and travelling through hilly, inaccessible districts and rugged, inhospitable places. Lloyd was very often hungry and thirsty and his life and liberty were frequently in danger. In Butler's opinion the very strenuous work done by Lloyd during the former Lent and after Easter was mainly responsible for his present illness, as he then confirmed thousands of men and women in places where the sacrament of Confirmation had not been given for a hundred years; he had then laboured without ceasing for two months from early morning until late evening and he did this even though he was a sick man who was suffering severe pain.[9]

But apart from Butler's vivid account of Lloyd's activities in his diocese in these early years of his ministry, there is very little hard information available as to how he ruled the diocese at this time. However, among the papers relating to the Meelick Franciscan friary, which was just outside the diocese of Killaloe in the south-east corner of County Galway, there is a letter which Lloyd wrote in 1731 in regard to the parish of Roscrea. The Meelick friars had for some time quested for alms in the Roscrea area and the decision of the provincial chapter to send a Fr Byrne as guardian to Roscrea conflicted with these questing rights. Fr Byrne duly arrived in Roscrea on the first Sunday in Lent 1730. He declared himself guardian of Roscrea and claimed that the right to quest for alms, belonging to the Franciscans, was his and not that of the friars of Meelick. Lloyd wrote from Dublin in January 1731 to Anthony McHugo, guardian of Meelick, in regard to this matter and a similar problem in regard to the town of Birr:

> My dear Sir, I received yours which was very welcome to me, not having received a syllable from you these two years. My constant indisposition hindered me from calling upon you at your own habitation, but I hope I shall have the pleasure before harvest. I think your late chapter did not use me well in sending the famous Mr Byrne to Roscrea. I have had a thousand complaints of him of late, and Mr

---

[9] Cathaldus Giblin, op. cit. no. 9 (1966), 24. It may seem strange that Butler had to undertake a long journey to visit Lloyd, seeing that they were in neighbouring dioceses. The explanation is that Butler lived outside his diocese, mainly at the family home at Kilcash in south Tipperary. The synopsis from the Latin is Fr. Giblin's.

Ryan knew very well what sort of man he was before he sent him, but the remedy is not yet out of my power. As to what regards your district about Birr, you know it is my business to support the possession of those I found possessed till better reasons are shown, and I really think a house that does so much good and honour to your order ought not to be starved to maintain reprobates that disgrace their order and character. I will write to Dr Carroll to forbid his preaching and begging anywhere in your districts about Birr.

All your friends are well. We often drink your health. Stephen is in the country. I am to meet him soon. Dr Dunne has published a second pastoral with quantations or explications of his first. Dr Fagan does not like it, and Morley is preparing to attack it. Others will join in the cry. *Error novissimus pejor priore.* Pray give my humble service to my worthy friends Messrs Madden, Locran and to the whole community. I am, my dear friend, your own Sylvester Lloyd.

Postscript: I long very much to see you. Pray let me know whether you still have a little book called *Usury Explained*. Direct me to the Harp in Pill Lane.[10]

As to who were trespassing on the territory of the Meelick Franciscans about the town of Birr, it seems the Dominicans from nearby Lorrha were the culprits, since the Dr Carroll mentioned is apparently Anthony Carroll of the Lorrha Dominicans. Since Lorrha is much nearer to Birr than Meelick, one would expect the Lorrha Dominicans to have a much better right to quest for alms there than the Meelick Franciscans. But as a Franciscan himself, Lloyd could be expected to support the Meelick friars in warding off encroachments on their territory. This episode serves to show that where questing for alms was concerned, the different friaries had their own well-defined territories, and infringements, especially by friars of a different order, could be vigorously resisted.

With regard to the persons mentioned in Lloyd's letter of January 1731 above, Mr (Fr) Ryan was minister provincial of the Irish Franciscans from 1730 to 1733. Stephen was probably Stephen MacEgan, the Dominican bishop of Meath who governed his diocese from Dublin, where he rented

10   Ibid., no. 16 (1973), 83. The Dr Carroll mentioned by Lloyd can be identified as Anthonius Carroll, listed as a member of the Lorrha community in the provincial's notes on Dominican convents 1734-35. (See PRONI, D. 1449/14). I note that Ignatius Murphy (op. cit. note 15, p. 104) believes that the Dr Carroll referred to here was Daniel Carroll P.P. of Nenagh, who, he says, 'was probably a Vicar-General'. However, the words 'I will write to Dr Carroll... to forbid *his* preaching and begging' points, I believe, to Anthony Carroll of the Lorrha Dominicans, who was also curate in the parish of Dorrha and as such would come directly under Lloyd's control.

lodgings from the Dominican nuns in Channel Row (now Brunswick Street). Lloyd later proposed MacEgan as archbishop of Dublin in 1734.[11] Dr Dunne was Bernard Dunne, who, as noted in chapter 4, was appointed bishop of Kildare in 1724. A pastoral letter issued by him in 1727, in which he appeared to question the pope's powers to depose princes and to absolve subjects from their allegiance, was the subject of a complaint to Rome by the Irish regular clergy, but the Vatican accepted that Dunne's views were orthodox.[12] As regards Dunne's second pastoral issued in 1731, *pace* Lloyd's view that 'the newest error was worse than the previous one', Dunne had succeeded in riding out the storm long before his death in August 1733.[13] The Dr Fagan, referred to in Lloyd's letter above, was Luke Fagan, then archbishop of Dublin and previously bishop of Meath. Martin Morley (or Marley) was a priest of the diocese of Meath. Lloyd's request to 'direct me to the *Harp* in Pill Lane' does not necessarily mean that he was staying there. He may have been merely using the *Harp* as an accommodation address.

Another side-light on Lloyd's episcopal ministry during 1731 is provided by an unfortunate interference by him in the affairs of the neighbouring diocese of Limerick. Fr James White, contemporary annalist of the Limerick diocese, supplies the details:

> The conduct of Rev. Matthew Gerane, coadjutor [curate] of St Mary's, being suspected, he was accused before the bishop, Dr O'Keeffe, and Mr John Flynn and Mr Darby Flannery appeared as witnesses against him; he thereupon quitted the parish and city, but meeting with Dr Loyd [*sic*] of Killaloe, of whose diocese he was a native, he was prevailed upon to return back to Limerick and vindicate his character, for which purport he put said John Flynn and Darby Flannery in the Protestant bishop's court for defamation; they did the like with him and put him in the bishop's court for adultery. The suit lasted with great scandal to religion for a long time. The bishop, Dr O'Keeffe, suspended Mr Matthew Gerane and in his place as Coadjutor of St Mary's parish he named in the month of August Rev. Michael MacMahon of the order of St Francis in place of Rev Matthew Gerane, who was expelled.[14]

The report on popery 1731, compiled by Church of Ireland ministers,

11 Stuart Papers, RA SP(M) vol. 167/186, MFR 795.
12 Ibid., RA SP(M) vol. 128/26, MFR 776.
13 Ibid., RA SP(M) vol. 144/152, MFR 784.
14 James White, *Annals of Limerick*, R.I.A. ms 24.D.21.

provides us with a statistical profile of the diocese of Killaloe as it was shortly after Lloyd went there as bishop.[15] According to the report there were then in the diocese 69 secular priests and two Regulars. However, it is generally believed that the report grossly understates the number of regular clergy and that in fact there were at that time as many as 20 such clergy in the diocese. The Church of Ireland ministers would have had great trouble in identifying these Regulars, since many of them were in the habit of moving around the country, putting in an appearance now and again at the convent to which they were reckoned to belong. There were Franciscan establishments at Ennis, Quin and Nenagh and a Dominican convent at Lorrha, Co. Tipperary.

According to the report there were seventy-two mass-houses (15 of which had been built since the first year of George I's reign, i.e. 1715) and three private chapels. The mass-houses can be assumed to have been nearly all thatched and looked for all the world like elongated thatched houses. For example in the union of Kilrush the mass-houses in the seven constituent parishes were said to be 'ordinary cabins and not lasting'. Inside, the mass-houses were low, damp, dark and uninviting, with possibly a little seating available for the 'better class of people'. In the parish of Killaloe there were two private chapels, one belonging to Francis MacNamara, Esq., and the other to Daniel MacNamara. In some cases the mass-house doubled up as a school on weekdays. There were some twenty Popish schools in the diocese, two of these in protestant houses and at first sight this might appear surprising, but seemingly it was not that unusual at this period. Indeed, the preamble to a bill, prepared in the early years of the century but never passed into law, claimed that 'great numbers of papists do continue to keep public schools and are entertained to teach children in private houses to the great detriment of the true protestant religion' and 'that most [Protestant] parishes in this Kingdom,

15 The Report on Popery 1731, in so far as it relates to the diocese of Killaloe, was printed in *Archivium Hibernicum*, vol. 2, pp 146-51. For information on the regular clergy in the diocese I am indebted to Ignatius Murphy, *The diocese of Killaloe in the Eighteenth Century* (Dublin, 1991). In regard to schools, I note that Father Murphy states (p. 248) that 'it was understood that the schoolmaster would teach the catechism as part of normal work'. No doubt such cosy arrangements were common, but they appear to have been far from universal. A contemporary Dublin pamphlet, (op. cit, Note 33, Chapter 2), referring to the laxity of parish priests in country parishes states:
'As to their flock's fine instruction they never take pains to teach 'em their Catechism, nor give one halfpenny to any schoolmaster to do that duty . . . so that scarce one in twenty know that there is a God at all, and a great many, even old men and women cannot repeat the Lord's Prayer or the Creed . . .' From this it appears that in the eighteenth century the schoolmaster generally expected to be paid for catechetical work and that otherwise it could remain unattended to.

except in cities or great towns, are either wholly destitute of [protestant] schools or privately entertain popish schoolmasters for want of due encouragement to protestants to keep schools'.[16] The purpose of the bill was to set up protestant parish schools throughout the country.

Although the Church of Ireland ministers were not required to give the names of priests, but rather the number of them, in fact in several cases the names of the priests are given. Not surprisingly, the name of Bishop Lloyd does not figure among them.

A chapel built in a back street in Ennis in 1735 may have been the first substantial catholic chapel in the Killaloe diocese. So substantial was it that it still stands and is now used as a community centre.[17] Although it was built during Lloyd's term as bishop, the credit for erecting it must probably go to others than Lloyd, since he was not resident in the diocese at that date, although he probably had a part in planning it. The 1731 Report on Popery, commenting on the country generally, noted that some masshouses 'appear to be large and pompous buildings, particularly one in Tipperary . . ., one in Mullingar, one in the parish of St Mary, Cork'.[18] The chapel opened in Ennis in 1735 may have been something of the same order, certainly with stone walls and probably a slated roof. Contemporary records show that many of the larger towns and cities could boast of substantial slated catholic chapels by the 1730s or 1740s.

By 1733 any pretence on Lloyd's part of administering his diocese had all but ceased. When in December 1738 the anonymous Paulus Benignus complained to the Congregation de Propaganda Fide, on behalf of the 'Zelanti' of Ireland, about, inter alia, the non-residence in their dioceses of certain Irish bishops, he said of Lloyd that in the space of five years he had not spent a month in his diocese, though he had several times toured England, Flanders, France and Germany, looking for money and pensions.[19] As a result of non-residence by bishops it was claimed that the lower clergy grew restless, the teaching of the catechism was neglected and the people were left defenceless before their adversaries. In Killaloe in particular the absence of the bishop was blamed for the apostacy of some priests including Lucius Macnamara, a Franciscan, who was later hanged at Tralee for sheep-stealing.

However, Lloyd's neglect of his diocese was not due primarily to the state of his health but to the following particular circumstances. On 3

---

16 National Library of Ireland microfilm Pos. 1946, p. 219.
17 Ignatius Murphy, op. cit., p. 61.
18 *Journals of the Irish house of lords*, vol. 3 (Dublin 1784), 604.
19 Hugh Fenning, 'John Kent's report on the state of the Irish Mission,' 1742, in *Archivium Hibernicum*, vol. 28, p. 59.

January 1732 John Hennessy, ex-parish priest of Doneraile, County Cork, appeared before Lord Doneraile and John Love, revenue collector in Mallow, and swore the following information:

> In the month of August or September 1729 he, this informant, was in company with Conor Keeffe, popish bishop of Limerick, Francis (sic) Lloyd, popish Bishop of Killaloe and Dr Stones, a Franciscan friar of the city of Dublin, at the house of Teigue MacCarthy, popish Bishop of Cork and Cloyne, when the said Keeffe and Lloyd delivered a letter to the said MacCarthy from Christopher Butler, popish Archbishop of Cashel, acquainting him that he had received a letter from the Pope's internuncio in Brussels; that the Pope had complied with the request of the Catholic archbishops and bishops of Ireland and that his Holiness had sent him an indulgence for ten years in order to raise a sum of money to be speedily applied to restore King James III to his right and put their present majesties and all the royal family to the sword. . . . That the money so raised from every parish, together with £5 from every parish priest, was to be paid to the bishop of each diocese; who swore said priests to a true account of what money they collected by virtue of the said bull.[20]

According to Hennessy the money raised in each diocese was to be handed over to the provincial agents who would send it abroad. The Munster agents were said to be Joseph Nagle, a Cork solicitor, and Sylvester Lloyd and their contact abroad was Nagle's brother, Francis, in Flanders. Hennessy further stated that Nagle and Lloyd were soon to go off from Dublin to Flanders with £1500 for the Pretender's use, a sum which had been collected as aforesaid.[21]

Raids on the houses of Joseph Nagle and Bishop MacCarthy disclosed papers in regard to a collection made to finance representations by lawyers in regard to certain anti-catholic legislation then before the Irish parliament.[22] The Irish parliamentary session of 1731-32 in fact passed five bills

20 *A Report from the Committee appointed to inspect the original papers seized in the houses of MacCarthy alias Rabah, a reputed popish titular bishop, and Joseph Nagle, a reputed popish solicitor* p. 5. The Dr Stones mentioned does not appear to have been a Franciscan, but rather a Dominican.
21 Ibid., p. 6.
22 Ibid., p. 2. There was nothing new about Irish catholics lobbying in London against legislation inimical to their interests. A London solicitor named Moloney, of Clare extraction, was active in petitioning the British privy council to block the bill to prevent the further growth of popery in 1703-4. A Dublin solicitor named Patt Brown is credited with having organised a successful lobby against the 'Castration' Bill of 1719. (See 'Letters & papers of James Cotter' in *Cork Historical & Archaeological Journal* vol. 68, p. 85.)

inimical to catholic interests, viz. (a) a bill closing loopholes in the law on the holding of arms by catholics, (b) an amendment of the law in relation to popish solicitors, (c) a bill for registering the popish clergy, (d) a bill for better putting into execution the laws for banishing popish regulars etc. and (e) a bill to annul and make void all marriages celebrated by popish priests and friars.[23] The first two of the foregoing bills were duly approved in London. The rejection of the other three by London, to some extent as a result of the representations mentioned (although there appears to have been pressure also from the Austrian emperor),[24] was no doubt seen as a slap in the face to the Dublin parliament, and the Hennessy disclosures provided an excuse for seeking out other means of making life uncomfortable for catholics. The upshot was that, following an examination of the affair by a committee of the Irish house of commons and a subsequent resolution of the house, the lord lieutenant issued a proclamation towards the end of 1733 requiring all magistrates to put the existing laws against popery in execution.

In regard to the reactivation of the laws which followed, Bishop Ambrose O'Callaghan of Ferns in a letter dated 20 March 1734 to Edgar, the Pretender's secretary, had this to say:

> Our post is so uncertain that I'm forced to give you new trouble by writing in brief what I writ already somewhat more at large viz. that we are in great fears of the storms lasting, which is the most terrible and shocking which has been since Oliver's days. The prints won't tell the half, but my general proposition, upon which you may depend, will give wherewithall to form a sad idea of our miseries.[25]

When the repression showed some signs of abating, Archbishop Butler of Cashel wrote a long letter dated 12 April 1734 to the nuncio in Brussels, of which the following are the more salient points. He states that he did not dare to write sooner because of the terror which gripped the country since December last; that nearly all letters coming out of the country and going into it are opened and brought to the government; and that all this disturbance had been caused by a poor priest from the county Cork, who, because of his scandalous life, had been dismissed by his bishop from a parish into which he had intruded himself. Butler pointed

---

23 National Library of Ireland microfilm, pos. 3651, p. 11.
24 Stuart Papers, RA SP(M) vol. 147/124 and 147/152, MFR 786.
25 Ibid., RA SP(M) vol. 169/21, MFR 796. Presumably O'Callaghan is here referring to Oliver Plunkett's days and not to Oliver Cromwell's.

out that there had been great difficulty in convincing the parliament that the money collected was not for the king (i.e. the Pretender), but that things were now beginning to ease somewhat and catholics were enjoying a little peace; however, the parliament was still in session and the clergy cannot find out what was being decided concerning them, so that they live in fear and are always on guard; most of the chapels had been closed for the past five weeks, and the lamentations of Jeremiah, which will be recited in the coming Holy Week, will be especially appropriate to the present situation.[26]

Meanwhile in London Stephen Dowdall, bishop-elect of Kildare, who had spent some years as chaplain of an embassy chapel in London decided to postpone his return to Ireland and 'stay some time at London to solicit some relief by means of the foreign ministers'. He goes on: 'I had recourse to them all but especially to those of France and Spain who exerted themselves with a zeal becoming them, and they have assured me we shall be connived at as hitherto,'[27] in other words that the persecution would soon be over and the laws against catholics would be left in abeyance as before.

So that the pope would have adequate information about the storm which had blown up against Irish catholics in the recent session of the Irish parliament, the Brussels nuncio, Valenti-Gonzaga, forwarded to Cardinal Firrao in Rome on 28 May 1734 a copy of Archbishop Butler's letter. At the same time he pointed out that the commotion had not yet completely died down; that like every misfortune the disturbance was taking much more time to pass away than it did to begin; that the fury of the persecution appeared to have abated somewhat and he hoped that the former quiet would be restored shortly.[28] The newspapers, however, are remarkably silent about any persecution of catholics during 1734, apart from the *St James Evening Post* of 12 February which mentions that in county Meath a person was fined £20 for harbouring an unregistered popish priest.

Such reactivation of the laws against the catholic clergy occurred periodically up to 1744, and during such periods it was the general practice for bishops to leave their usual places of abode and lie low, or go abroad, until the trouble had abated. Of the three bishops against whom Hennessy had sworn informations, O'Keeffe went to France for a year while MacCarthy left Cork and remained away for three years.[29] Lloyd

26 Cathaldus Giblin, op. cit. no. 9 (1966), p. 40.
27 Stuart Papers, RA SP(M) vol. 169/183, MFR 796.
28 Cathaldus Gilbin, op. cit. no. 9 (1966), p. 39.
29 Ignatius Murphy, op. cit. p. 64.

probably lay low in Dublin, where it is known he sometimes found accommodation with the Poor Clares (a Franciscan order) in North King Street. But he was soon on the move again, for he next comes to our notice in London in February 1735.[30] From there he moved to Flanders and did not return to Ireland until January 1736.

The ever-present threat of a crack-down by the authorities resulted in contingency plans by the Dominican nuns of Channel Row, Dublin to open a house of refuge for themselves in Brussels. A submission to this effect to the archduchess, Maria Elizabeth, sister of the Emperor Charles VI and governess of the Austrian Netherlands, was made in March 1733 by eight members of the Irish hierarchy—the archbishops of Armagh and Dublin and six bishops (all regulars), including Sylvester Lloyd. The archduchess submitted the project to the emperor, who duly approved it. However, the Dublin Dominican nuns later refused financial support towards setting up the refuge on the grounds that they would only make use of it if forced into exile by persecution at home. The refuge was later set up without their help, largely by the efforts of one of their number, Julia Browne, who had left the Dublin convent some years before. She is believed to have been a daughter of Sir John Browne, third baronet, of the Neale, County Mayo, who was a captain in King James's army and was taken prisoner at the seige of Derry. A member of this family was later in the century ennobled as earl of Altamont. The refuge was not a success and, because of financial difficulties, had to close down in 1740.[31] It will be seen later, in Chapter 8, how Lloyd fell foul of Julia Browne; it may have been because he did not lend his support to the refuge when it got into difficulties.

When in 1732 the English historian, Thomas Carte, arrived in Ireland for the purpose of researching his biography of the first duke of Ormond, one of Carte's Irish friends, Francis MacNamara of Moreisk, county Clare, referred him to 'Mr Sylvester Lloyd of the county of Clare', as a man deeply versed in the history of the country. MacNamara goes on to describe Lloyd as the Mr Lloyd whom Carte, who was known to be a Jacobite sympathiser, had met in Paris in the company of Mr Bowning, Matt Fitzgerald and others. This meeting presumably took place either in 1723 or 1725 when Lloyd was in Paris in connection with the 1723 popery bill. MacNamara hoped that Lloyd would go to Dublin to meet Carte, for, he concludes, 'there is no man in this kingdom, without exception, so clever, Swift excepted.'

30   Stuart Papers, RA Sp(M) vol. 178/24. MFR 800.
31   Hugh Fenning, *The Irish Dominican province 1698-1798* (Dublin, 1990) pp. 158-63.

Subsequently, in the course of a long letter to Carte, dated 6 October 1732, written in a place named Rehill, Lloyd states:

> I am so thoroughly convinced of the integrity of your heart and abilities for the useful work you have undertaken, that it grieves me beyond expression that the loss of my sight disables me from waiting on you and giving you all the assistance in my power in your enquiries into the truth of the history of that unhappy country, particularly that which regards the troubles that preceded and followed the fatal year 'Forty-one'; but I shall freely do all in my power at this distance by directing you to such as may make authenticated discoveries to you of many things that have been hid or been concealed, either because of the peevishness of the times ever since, or for complaisance to a certain name and family, which prevailed, or rather reigned in that kingdom, from the Restoration to the year Anne dy'd.[32]

By referring Carte to various important sources and to persons with special knowledge of the 1641-51 period, Lloyd proved to be very useful to Carte in his researches, but it was a debt which Carte left unacknowledged in his monumental life of Ormond. Rehill, where Lloyd was when he wrote to Carte, would appear to be in the parishes of Shanrahan and Tubrid in south Tipperary. It formed part of the estate of Lord Cahir, with whom, as already noted, Lloyd was on friendly terms.

MacNamara's throw-away, ill-considered remark about Lloyd's learning should not be taken at its face value. There were several, besides Swift, in Ireland at that time who were not inferior in learning to Lloyd, for example, Cornelius Nary, Archbishop Edward Synge, William Dunkin, Anthony Raymond, Dermot O'Connor and James Arbuckle. That Lloyd had some reputation as a historian is evident from Tadhg Ó Neachtain's address of welcome to him (see Chapter 4), in the course of which Ó Neachtain refers to Lloyd as 'staruidhe' (historian), but I have failed to trace anything published by Lloyd in that field. It is evident, at any rate, that Lloyd was something of a linguist: in addition to English and Irish, he must have had a good knowledge of French, Spanish, Portuguese, Italian and Latin.

In a letter to Pope Clement XII in August 1733 Lloyd thanked the pope 'from his place of refuge' for his financial help and described himself as 'ill, having serious eye problems, distracted by cares, broken by labours'.[33] From the summer of 1735 onwards Lloyd's eye trouble appears

32   C. W. Russell and J. R. Prendergast (eds), *Carte manuscript report*, (London, 1871), pp. 11-12.
33   Ignatius Murphy, op. cit., p. 63.

to have worsened. He spent most of the next two years on the Continent seeking a cure in the waters of Spa and Aachen. But the possibility of a cure was only one reason for being on the Continent. He still liked to think of himself as an agent involved in secret service for the Pretender.

The state of his eyes gave rise to a measure of sympathy for him from the pope and the nuncio in Brussels. We learn that on 30 June 1735 Lloyd left Brussels for the waters of Spa to see if he could recover his sight which he had almost completely lost 'because of the sufferings he had undergone in his large, unhappy diocese'.[34] On 5 August 1735 we find the nuncio in Brussels informing Cardinal Firrao in Rome that he (nuncio) cannot refrain from recommending Bishop Lloyd to the cardinal in the hope that he will obtain some assistance for the prelate from the pope; that this most worthy bishop is in bad health because of the hardships he has endured in his diocese; that he is almost completely blind and has to come to Flanders to take the waters at Spa; that he is there at present but has no money whatsoever. The nuncio goes on to say that Lloyd's outstanding gifts and meritorious qualities, as well as his pitiable condition, has induced the nuncio to make this appeal on his behalf.[35]

On 28 October 1735 the nuncio pressed Cardinal Firrao to pay the 200 scudi sanctioned by the Pope for Lloyd who 'is in dire need'.[36] Again in a dispatch to Cardinal Firrao dated 2 September 1735 the nuncio states that, because of his infirmities, Lloyd is in Flanders and has taken the waters at Spa and that he is going to Aachen for the same purpose. Lloyd has called on the nuncio and told him of the sorry condition he is in because of the wretched state of his diocese, that he is broken in health as a result of his great zeal and his untiring labours and that his sight is almost completely gone. Consequently he requires more money to provide for his needs and to pay his debts. The nuncio has given him some assistance which was sent for the bishop of Limerick, but the amount is not sufficient. Moved by compassion and by his sense of justice, the nuncio encloses a petition from Lloyd in the hope that the pope will come to the aid of this worthy prelate, and at the same time expresses the desire that there were many more bishops of Lloyd's calibre in Ireland.[37] On 30 December 1735 the nuncio reported that Lloyd was then in Brussels 'on his way back to his diocese'.[38]

34 Cathaldus Giblin, op. cit., no. 9 (1966), p. 49.
35 Ibid., no. 9 (1966), p. 51.
36 Ibid., p. 54.
37 Ibid., p. 52.
38 Ibid., p. 56.

These dispatches from Brussels to Rome on the state of Lloyd's sight are paralleled by letters from Lloyd to Col. O'Brien in Paris, and intended for the ears of the Pretender. Lloyd's eye trouble is constantly alluded to but this apparently did not curb his ardour when a little spying in the Pretender's cause was called for. Thus on 28 October 1735 he writes to O'Brien from Brussels to say that

> the famous Bishop Strickland came to this town five or six days ago. The day before yesterday he dined with Count Harach, Grand Master, and after dinner came home very pensive to his lodging. He had then with him an Irish Franciscan father who was formerly a Protestant minister of whom he is very fond, and to whom he began to talk in a very different strain from what he had usually done before. He speaks of the German Empire as in decay and ruin, betrayed by its ministers and abandoned by its allies. He said the government of England was in the same condition by the treachery and folly of Sir Robert Walpole and his friends. This, says he, is the Chevalier's [Pretender's] turn. A little good management now would restore him. For my part, says he, let people think what they will, I wish it from the bottom of my heart and would contribute to it as much as any man. He then told this good father as a secret that he would in a few days go to Paris and lodge probably in the seminary of St Sulpice. All this I had from the friar this morning. What this inconsistent prelate means or with what design he spoke in this manner, you will judge much better than I can. I know he spoke a different language from this at the nuncio's table when he was last in town.[39]

Lloyd then adds this postscript:

> Since my writing the above I am assured from good hands that this Court has received advice that the peace is concluded without the intervention of the Maritime Powers [Britain and Holland]. If this be true, it may be a key to Strickland's change of language.

From the account of Bishop Strickland's career given in Chapter 6, it will be apparent that Lloyd had good reason to be highly suspicious of that prelate's activities, in particular his sudden championing of the Pretender's cause. Strickland at this point had returned from England, where he had

---

39 Stuart Papers, RA SP(M) vol. 183/130, MFR 802.

Bishop of Killaloe 141

been unsuccessful in his efforts, at the behest of the emperor, to bring Britain into the War of the Polish Succession on the side of Austria, and no doubt found himself at a bit of a loose end when, as noted by Lloyd, that war was concluded without the intervention of Britain. As will be gathered from a further letter dated Brussels 9 November 1735 from Lloyd to Col. O'Brien, Strickland had left Vienna 'with a flea in his ear' presumably because of the failure of his English mission:

> I was at Louvain when your letter came to the nunciature and that is the reason it did not come to my hands so soon as it should have done. I came immediately to this place and have made use of all my industry to find out and watch the gentleman in question's motions. He is now at Namur but is soon expected in this town. Whether he goes to Paris or no is not known, though the person I had my information from assures me of it. I spoke this day carelessly of him to the Nuncio. He thinks he has lost all credit at the [Emperor's] Court and, though he shows a fine cross which he says the Emperor gave him, yet the Nuncio thinks he left Vienna with a flea in his ear. I have such spies upon him that I think he cannot stir without my knowledge. This I know that he talks of our Master in a very different style from what he formerly did. If I hear anything new I will write again soon.
>
> I shall go from hence to Liege in a few days and shall not be back here till the week before Christmas, when I am to ordain some young Hollanders by the Nuncio's orders. If you have in the meantime any commands for me, please to direct to Puntal a Liège.[40]

In December 1735 Lloyd has Strickland still under surveillance. Spying on other people was a rather odd occupation for a man who was supposed to be nearly blind, and the question must be asked—did Lloyd exaggerate his eye trouble? In any event this is the news he conveyed to O'Brien in Paris:

> I gave you last week an account that the gentleman of Namur [Strickland] was to set out for Paris the 26th of the last month. This account he himself gave the Nuncio by letter of the 24th wherein he took his leave and desired to be excused for some time having a lawsuit to manage. He two or three days ago wrote again that the coming of the German troops into the neighbourhood of Namur

---

40 Ibid., RA SP(M) vol. 184/22, MFR 802.

hindered his going so soon as he expected but that he must go as soon as the present hurry is over. This the Nuncio's auditor communicated to me yesterday. I shall be on the watch and give the best account I can of him.[41]

It has already been noted that at the end of December 1735 Lloyd was in Brussels on his way home to Ireland. When he returned to Brussels in June 1736 on his way to Spa, he deposited with the administrator of the nunciature, Francis Goddard, a document[42] signed by nine members of the Irish hierarchy—three archbishops and six bishops—granting power of attorney to James O'Daly, canon of Tournai and non-resident bishop of Kilfenora, to oppose the project for the reorganisation of the Irish College in Paris, which was the principal source of secular priests for Ireland throughout the eighteenth century. Since he was entrusted with conveying the document to the nunciature, it can be assumed that Lloyd was one of the nine signatories. Originally all students entering the college were already ordained, but from 1707 the college had been taking some younger students who were not ordained. Under the proposed reorganisation persons who were already ordained would not for the future be accepted as students. These proposals emanated from the superiors of the college, in particular John Bourke, and gained the support of Cardinal Imperiali, protector of Ireland. Bourke in a letter dated 27 June 1736 to the Pretender castigated the students, who were already priests, as uncouth and illiterate 'who for the most part enter into orders without a call'. He claimed:

> They were priests of this kind that denounced to the government the Bishop of Cork and some estated gentlemen as collectors for your Majesty, upon which they were pursued so that the bishop could not appear in his diocese almost these three years past. The Primate of Ireland, Doctor Lloyd, the Bishop of Limerick and the Bishop of Raphoe were denounced by unruly priests and obliged to disappear.[43]

The only noteworthy supporter of the reorganisation of the college was Hugh MacMahon, archbishop of Armagh. The main reason for the opposition of the other bishops to the plans was the fear that their hold over the ordination of priests would be thereby undermined. As John Bourke put it:

41 Ibid., RA SP(M) vol. 184/108, MFR 803.
42 Cathaldus Giblin, op. cit., no. 9 (1966), p. 61.
43 Stuart Papers, RA SP(M) vol. 180/114, MFR 801.

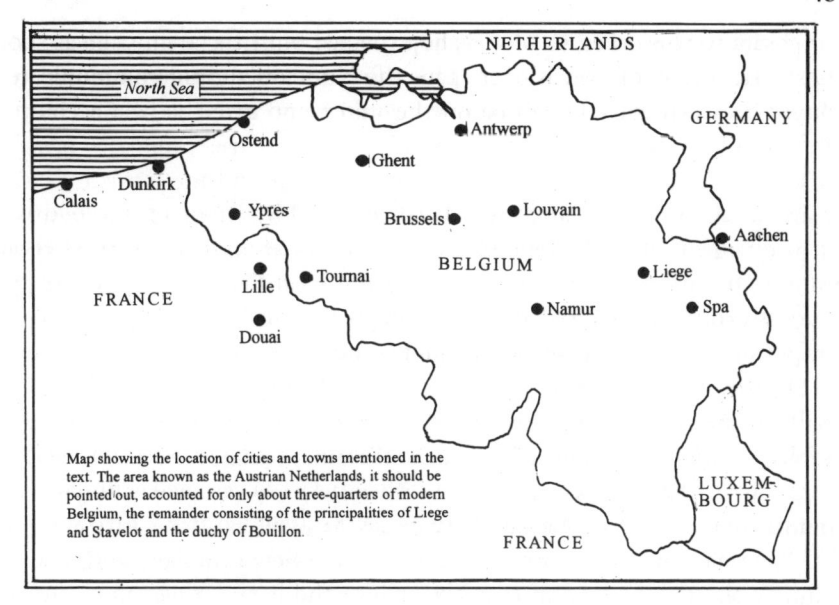

7 The Austrian Netherlands

Though we write to the bishops of Ireland that by the new regulation they are to have a sufficient number of subjects and that a smaller [number] of well-formed subjects would do more good and less noise than the great number they have of impudent, ignorant and indisciplined priests, they are still alarmed as if hindering 'em to make priests in Ireland were to condemn them to starve with hunger.[44]

It could also be argued in favour of the old system that, given that a knowledge of the Irish language was essential for nearly all priests at that time in rural areas, an ordained man coming to Paris at a mature age and remaining at the college a shorter space of time, was much less likely to lose his knowledge of Irish while abroad, than persons coming as youths to the college and remaining there for a much longer period.[45] Compromise

44 Ibid., RA SP(M) vol. 187/173, MFR 805.
45 There was also the danger that the students might lose their English. It is noteworthy that one of the proposals put forward by Fr. Myles MacDonnell in 1745 for reforming the various Irish colleges on the continent was that each community should be obliged to make a purchase of some English books, in particular those which treated of Religion, History, Controversy etc, in order to maintain the students' fluency in English. It is interesting that MacDonnell spoke of English as the maternal language (see Stuart Papers RA SP(M) vol. 266/150b, MFR 839).

proposals were worked out by Bishop O'Daly with the Irish College, the most significant of which was that, while ordained students would no longer be accepted, unordained ones would be accepted as subdeacons at the age of twenty-one.[46] But even these compromise proposals proved unacceptable to the hierarchy generally and in the end the status quo was maintained. However, later on, a limit imposed by Rome on the number of priests an Irish bishop could ordain acted as an indirect restriction on the number of priest students entering the Irish College.[47] Down to the later decades of the century the college continued to take in a high proportion of its students as ordained priests.

During the summer of 1736 Lloyd was also in touch with Dr Robert Witham, president of the English College at Douai. Witham had in 1730 published his translation of the New Testament under the title *Annotations on the New Testament of Jesus Christ*. It was in two volumes, the annotations accounting for nearly twice as many pages as the actual text of the New Testament. In Ireland the need for a new catholic translation to counter the flood of protestant bibles into the country had been recognised for some time. The Rhemish testament, the product of the English College at Douai, published at Rheims in 1582, had with the passage of time become dated in language and in some places near incomprehensible. A new translation had indeed been published by Dr Cornelius Nary, the Dublin divine, in 1718, but it had been quite undeservedly banned by the Holy See in 1722.[48] Dr Witham's translation would in these circumstances be seen by Lloyd and his brother bishops as an important element in the religious instruction of priests and laity alike, and it is not surprising then that Lloyd gave Witham a substantial order.

A note on the title page of the (English) Douai College diaries records that on 9 July 1736 a box containing 163 sets of Witham's New Testament were consigned to Dunkirk by Witham's orders. Witham added the following comment:

> These were to be sent to Bishop Lloid [sic] not as a present but who pretended to pay me for them by Retributions of Masses said by the priests of his diocese at the value of 6 livres, French money, for each set which makes 978 livres French.[49]

46 Stuart Papers RA SP(M) vol. 190/98, MFR 807.
47 See Hugh Fenning, *The undoing of the friars of Ireland*, Louvain, 1972 for further information on this matter of limiting ordinations.
48 See Patrick Fagan, *Dublin's turbulent priest; Cornelius Nary 1658-1738* (Dublin, 1991), pp. 79-91 for further information on Nary's New Testament.
49 'The Douai College Diaries' in *Publications of the Catholic Record Society*, vol. 28, (London, 1928), p. 1. Witham's New Testament was in two volumes, which are here described as a set.

From the tone of the above it seems unlikely that Witham, who was to die two years later, was ever paid the money owed to him.

August 1736 finds the good Bishop Lloyd again at Spa hobnobbing with the nobility and no doubt doing his eyes a power of good. He reports, this time to George Waters, a Paris banker friend of the Pretender, on the goings-on in that watering-place:

> I have been here fifteen days and every day hoped to have something the next day worth the telling but am still as far to seek as I was in the beginning. I delivered your letters to the Duchess, who seemed greatly pleased with my return, but from the moment she read them to this she has not had an opportunity of saying a syllable to me, she has been so taken up and hurried with the preparations for a great entertainment she has at length given to all manner of persons without distinction, that I must persuade myself she has not leisure to think of anything else. Now that it is over, I may perhaps hear from her. I must not omit telling you she is prodigiously devout. One Lydded, a Church of England minister, reads prayers at her house three times a week to all the Protestants who thirst for to hear him, and I was told two days ago by Mrs Pulteney that Mr Zachy Hamilton, who has been here these three weeks past, took it very ill that he was not the person employed to perform that service, and that the reason why he was not employed was because it was presumed he would not pray for George [George II] and his family as Mr Lydded does. Since I speak of Mr Hamilton, pray can you tell me what brought him thither. The Duchess told me she was not at all pleased with his coming. I have observed him narrowly. He seems to be angry with everybody and not pleased with himself. He travels like a fencer with a Scotch sword and target which he shows to everybody. He says he is Grand Master of a military order of knighthood, and shows to all sorts of people a ring as a badge of that honour, which he can confer. In a word he talks a little too freely of things past and present and does not in certain humours spare the most Sacred Persons. He has something in his looks and ways that make me fear his head is turned.
>
> Mr Pulteney is still here and speaks of going away for England next Saturday. I cannot express how civil he and his lady have been to me, and how freely he talks to me on every subject but one. When I delivered Mr Chavigny's message he answered very warmly that he would neither go to Paris nor write to him, for that whatever opposition he had made to the English Court on its maladministrators, he would

not, however, betray it with any foreign court, which was what he may well have understood Mr Chavigny intended to draw him into. He has often but very unaffectedly talked to me on the danger of corresponding or writing by post anything that ought to be a secret, for he plainly told me that the English Ministry had a thousand ways both at home and abroad of peeping into letters and that there were at this time in this very place people employed for that purpose. He repeated this so often that I concluded it was intended as a caution.

Lord Cornbury is here and seems to be extremely taken up with entertaining and diverting his sister, who is the giddyest of all womenkind. He visits the Duchess often but does not appear to be in any degree of intimacy with any other person or family here.

The Lords Scarborough and Lonsdale are here. The former and Mr Pulteney seem to be very intimate. They often ride out together. The Duke of Queensberry does not seem to have any thought or desire at all. Dumville is as busy and as prying as anybody can probably be. The Bishop of Namur came here two days ago to visit Mr Pulteney who has, I can assure you, at bottom no manner of esteem for him.

I have been obliged at the request of my Lord Fingall to write you a letter in favour of one Mrs Cullen, which pray forgive me. If you see Mr Chavigny, pray assure him that I am starving.

Postscript: Upon further enquiries I can't say that Mr Pulteney will not go to Paris by way of Lille.[50]

This letter introduces us to the unreal world of the watering-places of Spa and Aachen, where Whig, Tory and Jacobite socialised quite amicably together. The exalted company he kept and the esteem in which he was apparently held, is a measure of Lloyd's standing as a knowledgeable man of affairs, an interesting conversationalist and a lively raconteur.

The duchess mentioned by Lloyd was the duchess of Buckingham, natural daughter of James II and so a half-sister of the Pretender. Her first marriage to the third earl of Anglesey, whom she divorced on grounds of cruelty, has already been noted in Chapter 4. After Anglesey's death she married John Sheffield, duke of Buckingham (1648-1721), a vicar-of-Bray type who served (to his own advantage) under Charles II, James II, William III, Anne and George I. Her second choice of husband was scarcely any better than her first. Following his death she was involved in

50 Stuart Papers, RA SP(M) vol. 189/72, MFR 806.

several lawsuits in consequence of the reversionary interests which Buckingham left in his will to his natural children. She had five children by the duke, all of whom predeceased her. She died in 1743, aged sixty-two. Her haughtiness was proverbial. Horace Walpole described her as 'more mad with pride than any mercer's wife in Bedlam'. It is of interest that, following her death, there was a trial at bar to prove who was heir-at-law to the duke, when the Misses Walsh of Ireland were found to be his heirs.

In 1731 the duchess had been involved in a Jacobite plot to the extent that she was sent to England to sound out support for the Pretender amongst certain highly-placed people there. She met Robert Walpole, who gave her the impression that he was sympathetic to the Pretender, whereupon she revealed the Jacobite plans to him. She appears, however, to have remained on good terms with Walpole for she named him as a trustee in her will.

The Mr Pulteney mentioned by Lloyd was more likely Daniel Pulteney MP, rather than his more famous brother, Sir William Pulteney, Walpole's parliamentary opponent over many years. In 1725 Sir William had sent Daniel to Flanders to seek evidence in regard to a rumour that Walpole had received an enormous bribe from the Ostend Company, which, as already noted, had been set up by Austria to develop trade with the East Indies in opposition to British trading interests in that region. Daniel may have been on a similar information-gathering mission when he met Lloyd, whom he no doubt cultivated for his knowledge of current affairs.

With regard to the remaining people mentioned by Lloyd in his letter of August 1736, Zachy Hamilton was apparently, like Lydded, a church of England minister, but I have been unable to discover any further information concerning him. Theodore de Chavigny was a French career diplomat, who in the course of his career represented France in several major European countries. At the date of this letter he had just completed a five year stint as French minister to Britain. Henry Hyde, styled Viscount Cornbury, was Tory MP for Oxford university from 1732 to 1751. Lord Scarborough followed a military career, rising to the rank of Lieutenant-General. Lord Lonsdale was notable for having raised 10,000 men to oppose the Jacobite rising in 1715. He held various Government appointments, including that of Lord Privy Seal from 1733 to 1735. The duke of Queensberry's apathetic state was no doubt attributable to the change in his career prospects following his wife's disgrace at court, already mentioned in this chapter. He was not to come back into favour until after the death of George II in 1760.

By mid-September 1736 Lloyd is back in Liege. Bubbling over with the latest news, he writes on 22 September 1736 to Col. O'Brien in Paris:

> I came to this place with Mr Pulteney and his lady. They are gone off for England. They go to see the city of Lille but do not go to Paris. I cannot express the civilities he and his lady have shown me. I believe he is no enemy but I cannot venture to say more. The Duchess was affronted at Spa by the musicians she employed at a great entertainment she gave at Spa. I have managed so that the rascals will be punished, having been this morning to the Chancellor who has promised that the insolent fellows shall be mauled. I have had many discourses with the Duchess since my last letter but cannot learn anything more but that she is very zealous and, I think, very discreet too.
>
> Mr Pulteney showed me a very kind letter that he wrote without any solicitation of mine to Mr Chavigny. I beg you may second it. He sent it yesterday.
>
> There is some jealousy beginning between the sister of Lord Cornbury and the Duchess. I am afraid it will occasion at last a coolness between him and the Duchess. I hope I shall be able to give you some more distinct accounts soon. I am just returning to Spa. I have promised to correspond with Mr Pulteney and his lady. The Duchess intends to remove from Spa to Aix la Chapelle [Aachen].
>
> I congratulate with Madam O'Brien from the bottom of my heart on the safe delivery of a son. God preserve them both. The Grand Prior is at Spa.
>
> Mr Pulteney has been just now affronted at the gates agoing out. He and his family have been arrested and brought to their inn by a villain who is director of the Public Voitures. One presumes that he [Pulteney] should have hired carriages from him. I went again to the Chancellor, who called a Privy Council, when I appeared and had an order for punishing the fellow, but he came and put himself on his knees and was forgiven.[51]

We have here two instances of Lloyd's initiative in having abuses corrected—his action against the musicians who had affronted the duchess of Buckingham and against the Liege official who had given such short shrift to Mr Pulteney and his family. The letter written by Pulteney to Chavigny was, one suspects, in regard to a French clergy pension for Lloyd.

51   Ibid., RA SP(M) vol. 189/169, MFR 806.

Subsequent references indicate that Lloyd was to be disappointed in this.

An *avviso*, or news bulletin, from the nunciature in Brussels for 5 October 1736 tells us that at the end of the previous week the Duchess of Buckingham, accompanied by Bishop Lloyd of Killaloe, arrived at Brussels on her way back from Spa and Aachen; and that on the previous Tuesday the bishop continued his journey to England with the duchess and waited on her as far as Calais.[52]

But in fact the bishop never got any further than Calais on that occasion. He explains to Col. O'Brien in a letter dated 16 October:

> I stand at Calais . . . whence on Saturday last the Duchess embarked with a fair wind for Dover. I should have gone with her but she thought it better I should stay for some time longer on this side. She made a will where she went off, and deposited it in the hands of a friend at Calais with an order endorsed on the back that it should be delivered into my hands if anything happened to her.
>
> The Abbé and Colonel were with her but knew nothing of the will. She is a good and zealous woman, God Almighty prosper her in all her undertakings. I have promised to correspond with her. If you have any commands, I can send them safe. I am on my way to Brussels where I must stay till I know what Mon. Chavigny can do for me. I can with truth assure you that I have not at present as much as can keep me in clothes. For God's sake, Sir, let me know what hopes you have and direct as before to Brussels.[53]

During the winter of 1736 Lloyd visited a physician in Leyden in Holland; at that time Leyden university was famous all over Europe as a centre for the study of medicine. He availed of this visit to Holland to administer the sacrament of Confirmation to some Dutch catholics. The catholic Church in Holland was then subject to an even greater degree of repression than in Ireland. There were no resident bishops, and the nuncio in Brussels, who numbered Holland among his responsibilities, was no doubt glad to avail of Lloyd's visit there to have some people confirmed.[54] It will be recalled that the previous winter Lloyd was engaged to ordain some Dutch priests on the nuncio's orders.

52 Cathaldus Giblin, op. cit., no. 9 (1966), p. 67.
53 Stuart Papers, RA SP(M) vol. 190/105, MFR 807.
54 Cathaldus Giblin, op. cit., no. 14 (1971), p. 57. Cardinal Firrao, in a despatch to the Brussels nunciature, remarked that this recent worthy deed by the bishop (Lloyd) for the good of religion and the Holy See was in keeping with the high opinion the pope had of him; that the pope was moved by his (Lloyd's) extreme need and was considering means of providing him with some relief.

The departure of the governor general, Count Harrach, to Vienna and the arrival in Brussels of the new nuncio, Archbishop Tempi, are the main items of interest when Lloyd writes to O'Brien from Louvain on 16 March 1737:

> I, in my last, gave you an account of Count Harrach going to Vienna. He is gone and some say he is not to return. Others say he is to act here as the Marquis de Prie did when Prince Eugene was Vicar General. The Arch-duchess has been very ill and it is said that she is not at all pleased with her removal from hence. . . .
>
> Our new nuncio thinks he is to be removed from hence as soon as the Duke of Lorraine is declared governor. He thinks his mission will not allow the duke any person higher than an internuncio. If this should happen, I hope Mr Goddard will be continued here, if not as internuncio, at least as administrator. I would not have him stay otherwise.[55]

Due to straitened circumstances Lloyd is unable to go to Spa, and he must perforce soon make for home. It is in rather hurt tones that he writes to Col. O'Brien from Brussels on 26 March 1737. He dwells at some length on the new nuncio:

> I have had no answer to my two last letters. All I have to tell you now is that want of money hindered me from going to Spa, and that the same cause obliges me now to make the best of my way to London. I propose leaving this place on Monday next. I beg to receive your commands at Ostend directed for me at Mr John Gould, merchant.
>
> Our new Nuncio meets with some difficulties here. They will not allow him the same extent of power that his predecessor had and he will not stay on any other terms. This is, I believe, a very honest man, but he has not the parts of his predecessor. Mr Goddard is still here and it is said that he is to be continued here in the administration, if the Nuncio should remove as it is believed he soon will. He is a very worthy, goodnatured man but as I can conceal nothing from you, I fear he has gone a little too far with Davenant who, though he may be turned to account, is not at all to be trusted, for, besides other reasons, he cannot keep a secret. If I can give credit to some of his innuendos and to some other appearances, the letters I wrote to you,

---

55 Ibid., RA SP(M) vol. 194/161, MFR 808.

or at least some part of their paragraphs, have been communicated to Mr Goddard from the City [i.e. Rome]. You will not, I hope, imagine I write this without strong motives of suspicion. Our Master ordered me long ago to correspond with you and I never wrote you anything but what I thought my duty to tell you, and what I wrote of late was, I thought, for our Master's service without any prejudice to Mr Goddard, whom I esteem. I beg you will keep this letter to yourself and endeavour by some prudent method to find out whether any friend of Mr Goddard or any enemy of yours or mine could possibly have seen my letters at Rome. I shall be very impatient until I hear from you.

I have an account from the D. of B. that her great trial is to come on before the Lords on the 28th, Old Style. I hope to be at London on that day. She told me at parting that she would perhaps in the Spring send me on some business to a certain part of the world. Pray let me know as a friend to whom I always have been and forever shall be faithful, whether you think it would be agreeable to our Chief. If not, I will in the most prudent manner decline it. I here put my life into your hands. If you do not write to me, I shall take it for granted that I ought not to be concerned, and shall for the future content myself with praying for your success in everything.[56]

By April 1737 Lloyd had reached London on his way home. In what was to be his last letter to Col. O'Brien he reports on 8 April 1737 on the trial of the Duchess of Buckingham and upon some internal English affairs:

I was honoured with yours at Ostend under Mr Q——'s cover. I had a good passage hither where I arrived safe the day after our friend lost her great cause. It is true the law was against her but the hardship was so great that any other lady but herself would have had the law interpreted in her favour. I made her your compliments and they were, I assure you, very gratefully received. Mr Pulteney is not in town but is expected next week. I shall stay to see him and then go homewards. It is hard that I do not hear from Mr Chavigny. I believe I shall be forgot.

Mr Ulick Burke is here. He has been, it seems, lately in the South. I can't say all that I would say. As for news you must know, or already do know, that upon a motion made by the famous Alderman Barnard,

56 Ibid., RA SP(M) vol. 195/28, MFR 808.

the Commons have passed a bill for reducing the interest of money from four to three per cent. This has alarmed the Citizens so greatly that they have agreed to take all their money out of the Bank and the run upon it is so great that it is believed it will not be able to stand many days.

I have been told, and by no bad author, that there is a Scheme on foot for making some alterations in the Government with regard to the Dominions in Germany. He writes that after the death of the present king all and every of his successors shall resign to the next in blood, so that no king after the present shall be Duke of Hanover. I am assured that the Prince has already agreed to this Scheme, but whether his father will or not is the matter in doubt. It's believed that all the foreign powers will find their account in this Scheme.[57]

The case mentioned above, in which the duchess of Buckingham was involved, arose out of the will of her husband, John, duke of Buckingham, who died in 1721. The provisions of the will led to a very complicated situation when his only legitimate son, Edmund, duke of Buckingham died in 1735. The details of the case are highly complex and legalistic and need not concern us here. Suffice it to say that the decision of the high court in chancery in the case was very detrimental to the duchess's financial position. This decision was later upheld by the house of lords.

Ulick Bourke, mentioned above, was, according to himself, an uncle of the then earl of Clanrickard. Following his visit to England he submitted a report to the Pretender in August 1737 advocating a Jacobite uprising in Ireland and Scotland. Since the Irish were mostly disarmed, he proposed the sending of 6,000 stand of arms into 'the west of Connaught to some places I should direct in the Lord Clanrickard estate'. He considered that Galway, Limerick and Athlone could be easily taken in a surprise attack. He claimed that he himself could find a way of levying 12,000 men, 'and more if necessary', in the province of Connaught.[58] Burke's scheme must have appeared impracticable to the Pretender and his advisers. In any event, nothing came of it.

Sir John Barnard was MP for the City of London from 1722 to 1761, and was lord mayor of London in 1737. Like most of the city members in the eighteenth century, he was usually associated with the Opposition. He

57   Ibid., RA SP(M) vol. 195/68, MFR 809.
58   Ibid, Vol. 200/94, MFR 811.

had a reputation as an able financier but he refused the post of chancellor of the exchequer under Lord Bath (the former Sir William Pulteney) and Granville, when they tried to form a ministry in February 1746.

The suggestion in regard to Hanover reflects the British government's disillusion with that acquisition. While to George I and George II Hanover was a treasured possession, British politicians regarded it as a very mixed blessing inasmuch as it involved Britain too literally in the hornet's nest of German and north European politics. The earl of Chesterfield put the situation succinctly: 'Hanover robbed us of the benefit of being an island, and was actually a Pledge for our good behaviour on the Continent.'

There is little information on Lloyd's movements for the rest of 1737 and for the whole of 1738. There is an interesting paragraph about him in a letter dated 12 September 1737 from Goddard, administrator of the Brussels nunciature, to Edgar, the Pretender's secretary:

> As to Mr Lloyd I really have a double compassion for him, both in regard to his personal merit and his miserable circumstances, having lately received a letter in which not only he has declined being postulated for the vacant see of Armagh, but intends to renounce his own bishopric, not being able with his habitual affirmities [sic] to subsist any longer, except he be in some manner provided for, having hitherto lived a kind of dependent life, from those friends who have contributed to his subsistence; and as he was pleased to ask my advice upon this article, I persuaded him to take patience a little longer and not think of renouncing; for to do him justice his is almost the only diocese from which, since my living in this country, there has been no complaints, a great instance of his wise and prudent conduct; but what will make me watch for some benefice in the Pope's gift in these countries is the hearty, sincere zeal he has for H.M. and the Royal Family.[59]

How anyone could be seriously thinking of postulating for a man who was supposed to be half blind as archbishop of Armagh is difficult to credit, particularly as Armagh was a much more exacting proposition than Killaloe. Nevertheless, the Pretender appears to have given some consideration to nominating Lloyd to the Armagh vacancy, but decided against him, anticipating perhaps opposition from the Vatican to such a move.[60]

59 Ibid., RA SP(M) vol. 201/144, MFR 811.
60 Ibid., RA SP(M) vol. 200/187, MFR 811.

Goddard's reference to Lloyd's handling of his diocese only serves to show how little he (Goddard), from his perch in Brussels, knew about the Irish scene. Indeed, one correspondent severely criticised Lloyd for living in Dublin at this time and for having no residence in his diocese. He said that people who saw Lloyd reading, writing and walking in Dublin unaccompanied, could not accept that his sight problem was as bad as he claimed.[61]

However, while Lloyd may have neglected his diocese, his time in Dublin during 1737 and 1738 was not wasted, for in 1738 he again ventured into the catechetical field with the publication of a catechism in English and in Irish, called the Douai catechism. It is not clear as to why it should be so called. It may be that it was intended to give the impression of some association with Henry Turberville's much longer Douai catechism of the mid-seventeenth centry. The earliest copy I have been able to trace is in the National Library of Ireland and was printed by Ignatius Kelly of St Mary's Lane, Dublin in 1752.[62] That this is indeed Lloyd's catechism is clear from the legend at the end—'in usum clerii et populi Laonen: S.L.' (i.e. for the use of the clergy and people of Killaloe: S.L.). A catechism in English and Irish printed in 1742, which appears in the catalogue of the King's Inns Library, Dublin, may also be Lloyd's but it appears to have been mislaid. The 1752 edition is stated to be 'for the use of children and ignorant people'. Octavo in size, each page consists of two columns of questions and answers, the left column in English and the right column in Irish. Having dealt with the nature of Christianity—'What is a Christian?'—the catechism proceeds to expound The Creed, Hope, Charity, the Lord's Prayer, Hail Mary, The Commandments, Seven Sacraments, Cardinal Virtues, Gifts of the Holy Ghost, Works of Mercy, Eight Beatitudes, the various kinds of sin and the Four Last Things (Death, Judgment, Heaven and Hell). At the end there are two-and-a-half pages of instructions on how to learn Irish.

But Lloyd cannot claim any great credit for this catechism since the English version is to a predominant extent a repetition of O'Kenny's 'Galway Catechism', first published in Paris in 1725. The Irish version is a literal translation into Munster Irish, and we do not know whether this is all Lloyd's work either or whether some unknown Irish scholar helped him with it. Fr Nicholas O'Kenny was a native of Galway and a doctor of Paris university. His catechism was reprinted by M. Langlois of St

---

[61] Ignatius Murphy, op. cit., p. 67.
[62] *The Doway catechism in English and Irish for the use of schools* (Dublin, 1752).

Stephen's Street near St James, London (year not given) when it was stated to be for the use of the three kingdoms. A copy of this edition is in the National Libtrary of Ireland. The catechism proper is followed by some forty pages of morning and evening prayers, *modus absolvendi hereticos*, the true church proved by scripture, profession of faith, and prayers and ceremonies used at the reception of new converts. These additions are not included in Lloyd's catechism.

While Lloyd followed O'Kenny closely, he did make a number of alterations where he deemed it necessary. Firstly, he corrected the many printers' errors and errors of syntax which occur in O'Kenny. Unlike O'Kenny he set out the text of the Creed (short form), Lord's Prayer and Hail Mary before expounding these prayers. Other substantial alterations made by Lloyd are as follows. He omits an incomprehensible passage occurring at page 30 of O'Kenny. Where O'Kenny speaks of fasting 'by the custom of Ireland' (p. 62), Lloyd for some reason which is not clear has altered this to 'by the custom of England'. In answer to the question 'What is Contrition?' Lloyd adds to O'Kenny's answer: 'with a firm purpose of not sinning for the future' (p. 96). In answer to the question 'What is required to a good Confession?' Lloyd adds to O'Kenny's second requirement: 'taking care and time to make an Act of Contrition' (p. 97). In the definition of Heaven Lloyd is somewhat more restrained than O'Kenny; while to the latter Heaven was a place where 'the chosen and faithful servants of God, who die in the state of grace, shall live and reign with Him in happiness and glory for ever and ever', Lloyd simply says that they 'shall live with Him forever in His kingdom' (p. 124). Lloyd has omitted O'Kenny's claim that remembrance of the Four Last Things 'mightily contributes towards preserving us in the state of grace' (p. 107).

So much for the differences between the two texts. A few further general comments are relevant. Lloyd's text of the Creed contains such archaicisms as 'the Quick and the Dead' and 'the Resurrection of the Flesh'. It is interesting that his Lord's Prayer commences 'Our Father, *which* art in Heaven', a version which today is regarded as peculiarly protestant. Some answers to questions are highly simplistic—for example: Q. When was Christ born? A. On Christmas Day. Q. When did Christ die? A. On Good Friday. Q. Who are my neighbours? A. All mankind, especially Catholics. The expression 'the wicked President Pontius Pilate' sounds rather odd to modern ears. Finally, the sins that cry to Heaven for vengeance, according to both Lloyd and O'Kenny, are: Wilful murder, the sin of Sodom, oppression of the poor and to defraud labourers of their wages.

The provision of a catechism in English and in Irish by Lloyd could be seen as a conscious effort on his part to mitigate the effects of not residing in his diocese. A simple, uncomplicated catechism, which the literate among his flock would have little difficulty in reading, and which could be used by priests and schoolmasters in expounding to the flock generally catholic teaching, was clearly a means by which he could achieve from a distance a great amount of good. It seems probable that his vicars-general and other holders of ecclesiastical office visited him in Dublin (when he was to be found there in between his visits abroad), for the purpose of discussing the affairs of the diocese and arriving at decisions about the more important matters. Fr Peter Creagh's visit to him in 1738, noted below, is an example of this. It would seem likely too that he continued to pay occasional visits to the diocese for, while he might be fearful of taking up residence there in the wake of the Hennessy affair, it is difficult to see how there could be any great danger in flying visits by him, advance notice of which would be known only to a few. For a man so fond of travelling, such visits, far from being a chore, would surely have had a positive attraction.

It appears that some time during the summer of 1738 Lloyd travelled to the north of Ireland to assist at the consecration of Ross MacMahon as bishop of Clogher, for in a letter dated 15 May 1745, when he was in exile in the south of France, he recalled that Peter Creagh, who had just then (1745) been appointed his coadjutor in Waterford, had accompanied him from Dublin 'to help to consecrate one Mr MacMahon bishop of Clogher, who had been his [Creagh's] schoolfellow in Rome'.[63] Ross MacMahon was appointed bishop of Clogher by papal brief dated 17 May 1738.[64] He had previously been parish priest of Clontibret, an extensive parish to the south-east of Monaghan town. It seems probable, then, that the consecration took place somewhere in Clontibret parish. According to the Report on Popery 1731 there was no regular masshouse, only 'altars', in the parish of Clontibret, as indeed was the case in the majority of the Clogher parishes.

---

63 Stuart Papers, RA SP(M) vol. 264/172, MFR 838.
64 Ibid., RA SP(M) vol. 206/168, MFR 813.

THE QUESTION OF A COADJUTOR

From about 1736 onwards Lloyd was pressing either for a transfer to another diocese or for the appointment of a coadjutor with the right to succeed him in Killaloe. On 26 January 1737 in a long letter to Col. O'Brien, already noted, Lloyd remarked cryptically at the end: 'The bishop of Kildare is dead. Remember Mr Morgan of London.'[65] Morgan is described elsewhere as a man of merit who had spent twenty years on the English mission, and had been chaplain at the Savoy Legation in London.[66] The fact that Morgan's sister, during the summer of 1736, had been in France actively canvassing on his behalf for promotion to a diocese in Ireland, shows what back-stairs methods were at this time brought into play in the quest for a mitre.[67] While it did not prove possible for the Pretender to nominate Morgan for Kildare, he was quite prepared to nominate him as coadjutor in Killaloe, remarking that 'this solution for his [Lloyd's] relief is preferable to a transfer, which I might find difficult.'[68] Although Morgan was apparently 'a good friend of Lloyd', the latter for reasons which are not apparent did not want Morgan as his coadjutor. Following Lloyd's refusal of Morgan, the Pretender evidently found it difficult to keep his patience with Lloyd for on 1 April 1738 he remarked to his secretary: 'After this you should drop the idea, as I have made my last effort to find a coadjutor for the bishop.'[69]

However, a short time later the Pretender is again in an accommodating frame of mind when, following a letter from Lloyd, he remarks: 'But in regard to giving him [Lloyd] some other coadjutor than Morgan, he has only to make a proposal and I shall see what can be done for his satisfaction.'[70] But a week or so later we find the Pretender again adopting a hard line with 'As to this last I have no more to say on the affair of a coadjutor to him.'[71] By September 1738 Lloyd himself appears to have given up the idea of a coadjutor, for on 13th of that month secretary Edgar wrote to Goddard, the administrator of the nunciature in Brussels, in regard to a further letter from Lloyd:

---

65 Ibid., RA SP(M) vol. 193/142, MFR 808. Fr Robert Morgan was a Jesuit.
66 Cathaldus Giblin, op. cit., no. 10 (1967), p. 72. The Vatican encouraged catholic countries to open, at their embassies in London, chapels for the use of London's catholics. Chaplains at these embassy chapels were commonly Irish priests (see H. Fenning, op. cit., in note 16, Chapter 6, p. 617).
67 Stuart Papers, RA SP(M) vol. 189/75, MFR 806.
68 Ibid., RA SP(M) vol. 203/64, MFR 812.
69 Ibid., RA SP(M) vol. 205/159, MFR 813.
70 Ibid., RA SP(M) vol. 206/13, MFR 813.
71 Ibid., RA SP(M) vol. 206/75, MFR 813.

Since this last [Lloyd] does not now seem to incline to take a coadjutor, H.M. says there is nothing more to be done in this matter, and by his directions these papers are laid by amongst others relating to the Irish Mission.[72]

A FRENCH PENSION?

In the first half of the eighteenth century several Irish bishops were in receipt of pensions from the French clergy. The reason for such pensions was that some dioceses were so poor as not to be able to provide an income for their bishop as well as for their priests.[73] In the absence of a French pension, a bishop often depended on his own family and relations to provide him with an income, and a point often made in postulating for a particular person for promotion to bishop was that he had this extended family to provide for him, or that he was of independent means or was otherwise provided for. The problem did not arise to any great extent where a parish priest of the diocese was being promoted to bishop because he could usually depend on being allowed to retain his old parish as a mensal parish, although this did not follow as a matter of course, as Linegar was to find out when appointed archbishop of Dublin in 1734.[74] The problem arose in its acutest form when a bishop was effectively imposed on a diocese, as often happened when the new bishop was a Regular. The new bishop in such circumstances could find himself faced with a measure of non-cooperation, if not of hostility, which boded ill for any chance of an adequate income from the dues of the clergy.

The main drawback of a French or any other pension, where the good of the Church generally was concerned, was that it encouraged non-residence on the part of the recipient; since a bishop with a pension was not beholden to his diocese for an income, the incentive to perform his episcopal duties was lacking and there were instances of such bishops seldom setting foot in their dioceses. But persistent non-residence could result in the pension being withdrawn, as happened to Ambrose O'Callaghan, the Franciscan bishop of Ferns, in the early 1740s.[75]

During his early years in Killaloe Lloyd was dependent on dues from the clergy and laity, although it seems he found them slow to pay and

72   Stuart Papers, RA SP(M) vol. 209/71, MFR 814.
73   For further information on this subject see Francis Finegan 'Irish pensioners of the French Clergy 1686-1778' in *Irish Ecclesiastical Record*, no. 105 (1966), pp. 73-92.
74   Cathaldus Giblin, op. cit. no. 9 (1966), p. 39.
75   Stuart Papers, RA SP(M) vol. 241/95, MFR 828.

indeed put as much on record in a letter already mentioned.[76] However, following the virtual abandonment of his diocese from 1733 onwards, his entitlement to an income from that source must have become questionable. But it is interesting that as early as August 1730 the Pretender had in mind the possibility of a French pension for Lloyd when he wrote:

> I should be very glad if Matthew [code name for Lloyd] could obtain a pension from the French Clergy, but should be sorry if anything you have said should discourage their giving the like to the archbishop of Armagh, tho' I don't know particularly the want he may have of it.[77]

We have already noted how in August and September 1735 the Brussels nuncio was endeavouring to get some financial assistance from the pope for Lloyd.[78] It is noteworthy that Lloyd then blamed the 'wretched state of his diocese' for his lack of resources, although his true position was that he had been forced to abandon his diocese and could not therefore expect much in the way of income from it.

In October 1736 the hard-up Lloyd, then in Ghent, complains to O'Brien that he 'had not as much as can keep me in clothes'.[79] About this time representations appear to have been made on his behalf to the French diplomat, Chavigny, for a French clergy pension[80] by Pulteney, an English politician, but nothing came of this. Later in Brussels in March 1737 he is still down-and-out but more hopeful in this cri de coeur to Col. O'Brien in Paris:

> I hope God will provide for me. A very little matter will make me easy. I beg you will let me know whether they have as yet disposed of the benefices for it seems I am to have 400 Crowns upon some one of them.[81]

But efforts to secure a French pension for him seem to have failed. On 25 September 1737 the Pretender again raised the question of a pension when he remarked that 'the archbishop of Armagh had a little benefice in Flanders for which I recommended Bishop Lloyd to Cardinal Corsini, such esteem had I for the bishop.'[82] Unfortunately for Lloyd, in this

---

76 Ibid., RA SP(M) vol. 130/176, MFR 778.
77 Ibid., RA SP(M) vol. 138/176, MFR 782.
78 Cathaldus Giblin, op. cit., no. 9 (1966), p. 51.
79 Stuart Papers, RA SP(M) vol. 190/105, MFR 807.
80 Ibid., RA SP(M) vols. 189/169 (MFR 806), 190/105 (MFR 807) and 195/68 (MFR 809).
81 Ibid., RA SP(M) vol. 194/133, MFR 808.
82 Ibid., RA SP(M) vol. 200/187, MFR 811.

instance a certain Father Bohily was quicker on the draw and in the words of secretary Edgar 'made interest for himself for the same benefice and has carried it, so that Bishop Lloyd must have patience till another occasion'.[83] But in a further letter in November 1737 to Goddard in the Brussels nunciature, Edgar is still hopeful that something can be done for Lloyd:

> The King took note of what you say favourable of Bishop Lloyd, and of his present bad situation, and as H.M. is desirous to befriend and favour that good bishop, he directed to get that article of your letter translated into Italian, which he is to give to Cardinal Corsini. I should be very glad something could be done for his ease and advantage, and I am very hopeful that may be compassed, towards which your endeavours, I am sure, won't be wanting, and that you will be on the watch to give speedy advertisement here of what may fall out in your parts, or in French Flanders, in the Pope's gift for his advantage, which I look upon as the readiest and surest way of making him easy.[84]

Lloyd's translation to the bishopric of Waterford and Lismore in 1739 (see Chapter 8) meant that the question of a pension could no longer be an issue, since he was once more a working bishop who could expect an adequate income from a rather wealthy diocese. The assignment to him in 1743 of Trinity parish in Waterford city as a mensal parish further enhanced his financial position,[85] but it was to prove a short-lived boon, for after the persecution in the following year, he was forced to flee to France. There we find him in May 1745 plaintively asking the Pretender's secretary to recommend him to Cardinal Corsini, Protector of Ireland, for some additional remuneration, and complaining that he had not £30 a year by his diocese, 'and all that is spent before I can gather it from among my priests.'[86]

Following this appeal he appears to have been granted some kind of pension, for in the last letter from him in the Stuart Papers, dated 11 February 1746, we find him as ever hard-up and complaining that:

> I must pledge two rings and cross to pay my debts and shall be quite undone if Mr Pontin fails to send me what is due of my pension. I

---

83 Ibid., RA SP(M) vol. 201/61, MFR 811.
84 Ibid., RA SP(M) vol. 202/113, MFR 812.
85 Ibid., RA SP(M) vol. 253/188, MFR 833.
86 Ibid., RA SP(M) vol. 264/172, MFR 838.

received nothing since the month of March last, so that I hope, dear sir, that you will be so humane to speak feelingly to him.[87]

Since these words were addressed to Edgar in Rome, it can be concluded that this pension was provided from a Papal source and that Lloyd continued to enjoy it until his death in August 1747.

POPULATION OF DIOCESE OF KILLALOE IN LLOYD'S TIME

The hearth money returns are the only available basis on which to arrive at an approximation of population levels in Ireland in the first half of the eighteenth century. Under the Hearth Tax, introduced by an act of 1662, each householder was required to pay a tax of two shillings per annum in respect of each hearth in his/her house. Householders in receipt of alms were exempted from the tax. K. H. Connell in his book *The Population of Ireland 1750-1845* questioned the reliability of house numbers derived from the hearth tax. He came to the conclusion that for the country generally the hearth tax returns were 50% deficient and proceeded to arrive at estimates of population for different dates on this basis.[88] While a more recent investigation[89] has accorded the house numbers in the hearth money returns a much higher credibility rating than Connell, it does seem prudent to provide for some deficiency (say, 20%) to take account of poor households not subject to the tax and so not included in the returns, and for some wild, inhospitable terrain where hearth money collectors might fear to tread.

For 1732 the hearth tax collectors were required to make returns showing the number of catholic and protestant householders in their areas, and there is extant a pamphlet showing in respect of each county and the cities of Dublin and Cork the total number of catholic and protestant householders.[90] The diocese of Killaloe stretches over part of four counties, for which these are the relevant figures:

87   Ibid., RA SP(M) vol. 272/153, MFR 842.
88   K. H. Connell, *The population of Ireland 1750-1845*, (Oxford 1950) p. 13. I note that Ignatius Murphy, op. cit., p. 250 has estimated the population of the diocese of Killaloe in 1700 at 125,000 but this figure appears to be extrapolated in some way from Connell's assumptions. Feargal Grannell, on the other hand, arrived at an estimate of 14,000 catholic *families* during Sylvester Lloyd's term as bishop; this would correspond to a total catholic population of about 63,000. It will be seen that the figure I have arrived at is 80,000.
89   S. Daultry, D. Dickson and C. O Grada, 'Eighteenth century Irish population: New perspectives from old sources' in *Journal of Economic History*, vol. 41, no. 3 (September 1981) p. 613.
90   *An abstract of the number of Protestant and Popish families*, Dublin, 1736.

	Clare	Tipperary	Offaly	Limerick
Protestant households:	665	1,627	1,237	2,056
Catholic households:	9,348	16,465	6,677	14,820

It will be apparent from these figures that in County Clare one household in every fifteen was protestant, in Tipperary one in eleven, in Offaly one in six and in Limerick (including the city) one in eight. On the basis that the diocese of Killaloe comprises approximately four-fifths of Clare, one-third of Tipperary, one-sixth of Offaly and, say, one-twentieth of Limerick, we arrive at a rough estimate of 1,383 protestant and 14,819 catholic households in the diocese of Killaloe in 1732. If we allow 4.5 persons for each household a total population of 72,900 is arrived at, of which 6,224 (say, 6,200) were protestants and 66,686 (say, 66,700) were catholics. Allowing for the suggested deficiency of 20% in house numbers, an estimated catholic population of 80,000 emerges.

CONDITION OF THE PEOPLE

Bishop Patrick MacDonnogh, who succeeded Lloyd as bishop of Killaloe, was one of the Irish bishops who were opposed to the proposal to terminate the system under which the bulk of the students entering the Irish College in Paris were already ordained. His main argument against dropping the old system was that students who were already ordained on entry (and were therefore mature men) were much more likely to be able to withstand the rigour of the Irish Mission than unordained students who had, MacDonnogh goes on:

> lived in Paris since they were boys, and consequently [were] quite unfit to serve in such wild and miserable countries [i.e. counties], where none hardly remains but the common people, who can't speak a word but Irish, who feed for the most part upon oaten bread and potatoes, lying on straw in their poor thatched huts and cottages.[91]

In the process of driving his point home, it seems that MacDonnogh here presents us with a description of conditions in the diocese which is distorted and highly coloured. In County Clare, which accounted for about half the population of the diocese, catholic ownership of the land in

91   Spicilegium Ossoriense, vol. 3, p. 163.

1703 was about 25%[92] (as against a national average of about 14%). This favourable position arose from the transplantation of catholics into the county under the Cromwellian settlement, Clare being regarded as part of Connaught for the purposes of Cromwell's dictum 'To hell or Connaught'. It is also a fact that many of the catholic gentry of Clare were officers in the Jacobite army in Limerick in 1691, and so benefited from the clause in the treaty providing that they and their heirs should 'hold, possess and enjoy all and every their estates and freehold which they enjoyed . . . in the reign of Charles II'.

While Tipperary is not one of the counties specifically mentioned in the treaty, many of the catholic gentry there similarly benefited from the article mentioned. It has been claimed that as the century progressed conversions of the gentry to the established church substantially eroded this high degree of catholic ownership of land in Clare and Tipperary, as indeed elsewhere, but the convert rolls show that such conversions in the first fifty years of the century were much less than in the remainder. For example, in the case of County Clare the total number of converts for the period 1704-1789 according to the convert rolls was 278, but only sixty-five of these conformed prior to 1750.[93] MacDonnogh's claim that none hardly remained but the common people can only be described as exaggerated. Such a claim can hardly be reconciled with the fact that in 1728 a postulation in favour of Denis Crowe as bishop of Killaloe was signed by 117 gentry and, to judge by the surnames, it appears that these were mainly from the north Tipperary-south Offaly part of the diocese. As many more of the gentry class could be found in County Clare at that time.

In this context it is also necessary to bear in mind catholic *occupancy* of land as tenants as well as catholic *ownership* of land. All through the eighteenth century catholic tenants occupied a high proportion of land in Munster, and some of these would have been substantial farmers, who lived in thatched houses, showing little outward signs of wealth. Furthermore, the catholic bishops at this time came predominantly from the gentry class and were likely to look askance at peasants living in thatched houses, even though some of them might be prosperous.

That the majority of the catholic gentry in counties Cork and Limerick survived as large tenant farmers rather than as land owners is clear from a postulation by gentlemen from those counties in July 1747 in favour of John O'Brien as bishop of Cork and Cloyne:

---

92   Ignatius Murphy, op. cit., p. 34.
93   James Frost, *History and topography of the County Clare*, (Dublin 1893), p. 630 seq.

And as to the private condition of his [John O'Brien's] parents in the late circumstances of this distressed and reduced country, we likewise declare and attest that we have known them to have always preserved the sentiments and good principles of their ancestors, from whom they have never degenerated by following any vile or mechanical profession, but have always lived in a decent and credible manner in the farming way, as all other Roman Catholic gentlemen of this Kingdom are obliged to ever since the Cromwellian and Revolution forfeitures of Irish estates.[94]

The position can safely be assumed to have been much the same in counties Clare and Tipperary, although, as argued above, there would at this time have been a higher proportion of catholic land *owners* in county Clare. Although they might be only tenant farmers the innate snobbery of the gentry class rings through in the extract above in their contempt for anyone who followed 'any vile or mechanical profession'.

It can be concluded then that conditions in the diocese were not nearly as critical as Bishop MacDonnogh would have us believe. Granted, the majority of the people knew little else but poverty and privation, but this should not be allowed to obscure the fact that substantial numbers of the gentry continued to be catholics as well as the bulk of the strong tenant farmers, and in the towns there were many catholic merchants, shopkeepers, tradesmen and medical men.

USE OF IRISH

Again, Bishop MacDonnogh, in the quotation above, gives an exaggerated notion of the extent to which Irish was spoken in the diocese in the 1730s and 1740s. While Irish would have been almost the only language in the country areas, in the towns and larger villages English would have been widely spoken. Bishop John O'Brien of Cloyne gives a more balanced account of the extent to which Irish was spoken in Killaloe when, in opposing the candidacy of William Egan for bishop of that diocese, he remarked that Egan had no knowledge of Irish and therefore was not capable:

> of instructing the people *in the country districts*, who fortunately know no other language, and make up the majority of Irish catholics. The

---

94 Stuart Papers, RA SP(M) vol. 119/40, MFR 773.

instruction which the bishops give them during their visitations and particularly when they administer the Sacrament of Confirmation is essential for the preservation of the Faith and the good conduct of this poor people, whose aversion to the English language and everything English is one of the means used by Providence for the preservation of the catholic faith amongst them.[95]

---

95 Cathaldus Giblin, op. cit., no. 10 (1967), p. 136. The italics in the piece quoted are mine.

8

BISHOP OF WATERFORD AND LISMORE

The spring of 1739 saw Lloyd upon the move again, and this time his destination was to be Rome, a city which, despite all his travelling on the continent, he had not visited since 1713 when he spent a probationary period at the Franciscan college of St Isidore. Presumably he travelled via London, Brussels, Paris, and somewhere along the way he would have learned of the death of Richard Pierce, the bishop of Waterford & Lismore who had spent nearly all of a long episcopacy as an exile in France. Lloyd had been thinking for some time now of a transfer to a less exacting diocese than Killaloe, not that he had troubled himself much (for reasons which have been explained in the last chapter) with the ecclesiastical business of that diocese for some years. But, as mentioned briefly in the last chapter, complaints had been made in 1738 to Rome about the non-residence in their dioceses of certain Irish bishops, including Lloyd, and he may have judged that the best way to meet these complaints was by a transfer to a less demanding diocese, where residence would not be too much of a cross. Furthermore, the Pretender was quite receptive to the idea of a transfer. In the course of instructions to his secretary, Edgar, he had stated that 'if he [Lloyd] feels that in his case there is sufficient to authorise a transfer, I will see what can be done for his satisfaction in that regard'.[1]

Waterford & Lismore was now vacant. Though much smaller in area than Killaloe, it was reckoned to be much richer. Also, if a quick get-away proved necessary there was a busy port with ships continually plying with France. To make assurance doubly sure he would go in person to Rome and there prostrate himself before his king, who could hardly refuse him the necessary nomination after all his years of service.

The Palazzo Muti in Rome had been given to the Pretender as an official residence by Pope Clement XI in 1719. A building of no great

---

[1] Stuart Papers, RA SP(M) vol. 202/54, MFR 811.

architectural distinction, it was built around a square courtyard with a fountain in the centre. Here for the previous twenty years the lawful king of Great Britain and Ireland had kept a frugal court, protected by a papal guard and subvented by a papal pension. To escape the searing heat of the Roman high summer the pope had considerately further provided him with the Savelli Palace at Albano as a rural retreat.

From this Roman palace the Pretender spun a web of intrigue which at some time or other involved every European power of any account, with his restoration to the British throne as the desired end. Here the dispatches arrived continually from his agents in the major European capitals—from Count Owen O'Rourke in Vienna, from Col. Daniel O'Brien in Paris, from Sir Charles Wogan in Madrid,—all with the purpose of keeping the Pretender abreast with developments in those capitals. Here, with his advisers, the Pretender plotted and planned year after year, often thwarted, often brought to the brink of despair, but never giving up hope. While actual attempts at invasion or insurrection in England or Scotland had been attempted in the years 1708, 1715 and 1719, there had hardly been a year when the Pretender was not plotting, though sometimes with no tangible results, with some European power or other with invasion of Britain as the intended outcome. In this year of 1739 a ridiculous incident in the West Indies had sparked off a war between Britain and Spain—a war which is known to fame as the War of Jenkin's ear—and hopes were high in the Palazzo Muti of a Spanish invasion of Britain, with Jacobite assistance. As in the case of Ireland, England's difficulty was invariably the Jacobites' opportunity.

But despite a busy life of intrigue and not a little adventure, the Pretender always found time to take very seriously his right of nomination to vacant Irish catholic bishoprics, perhaps indeed for the very good reason that this was about the only real power left to him. Although appointment to vacant bishoprics was ultimately a matter for the pope, it is clear, from the importance attached to a nomination from the Pretender, that such a nomination was the critical factor, the papal appointment nearly always following as a matter of course. Thus when Sylvester Lloyd desired a transfer to the diocese of Waterford, it was not with the pope he sought an audience, but with the Pretender.

The Pretender had a high regard for 'good bishop Lloyd' as he called him and well he might have, for Lloyd had served him well over the years. That he was looking forward to meeting Lloyd is evident from a letter he wrote to John Hay, then living in Avignon: 'I received yesterday yours of the 30th, and by what you say I suppose Bishop Lloyd may soon be here, though we've had some very bad weather of late, but I hope it will settle again by next week.'²

In the beginning of April 1739 Lloyd was in the papal city of Avignon in the south of France, where he met with Patrick MacDonnogh, a Clareman who was Abbé of Fleaux, and between them they appear to have hatched out a little arrangement whereby, if Lloyd were transferred to Waterford, there was the distinct possibility that MacDonnogh might succeed him in Killaloe. The Abbé, writing in French to the Pretender, put it this way:

> Having come here two days ago with the design of going to Rome, to have the honour of rendering my very humble homage and my respectful duty to your Majesty and their Royal Highnesses, a slight but very inconvenient indisposition obliged me to postpone my journey until next month. Mr Lloyd, bishop of Killaloe, does me the honour while passing through here [Avignon] to call on me at Fleaux, and to ask me to accompany him to Rome, telling me he was going there to resign his bishopric and to represent in the same sense to your Majesty that he knows no other priest of the natives of that diocese who would be more agreeable to the clergy and gentry than me, and who would be better able to support himself since all the chief families are my relations or connections. I know better than anyone else my lack of capacity but whatever my limitations, I dare to flatter myself that my long experience of administration for nearly thirty years in a parish, which was composed for the most part of Huguenots when I was first put in charge of it, but which, when I left it to my nephew, were all good Catholics, has rendered me less inept than most of the others to fill the duties of Pastor [i.e. bishop]. I would be following in the footsteps of Mr Lloyd who, unfortunately finding himself through the loss of his sight in an unfit state to traverse as often as is necessary so vast a diocese, prefers the diocese of Waterford, which is much less extensive and has just been vacated by the death of Dr Pierse. If I have the misfortune, Sir, not to be successful on this occasion the good intentions which your Majesty has been good enough to testify on all occasions for twenty-three years past, must incline to do me good. I would never dare to have the hardihood to importune you for this sort of appointment without persuading myself that it is the will of God that I should fill it. I

2 Ibid., vol. 215/50, MFR 817.

submit myself with a full heart, accepting you, Sire, as the one to dispose of my fortunes and the way in which the Lord ordains me to follow. Whatever happens from this affair, I have resolved to go to throw myself at the feet of your Majesty to assure you of the profound respect and submission and the entire devotion with which I have the honour to be etc.[3]

Lloyd reached Rome about mid April and did not delay in paying his respects at the Palazzo Muti. The Pretender was clearly impressed:

Before I received yours of the 5th and 13th of April, I already had a good dale (sic) of conversation with Bishop Lloyd who came here some days ago. I am much pleased with him for he knows so many things, and so many persons that the time passed without having any left to speak of himself, which I put off until another time. I received a letter from Abbé MacDonnogh. The only objection I have for giving him my nomination on a proper occasion, is his being so intent on having one. But in this particular, as in all these matters, I shall endeavour to act to the best of my judgment and conscience.[4]

The Pretender lost no time in nominating Lloyd to the diocese of Waterford and he was duly appointed to that see by papal brief dated 29 May 1739.[5] MacDonnogh was nominated for Killaloe and was duly appointed by the pope.[6]

But in a sense Lloyd was walking himself into trouble by coming to Rome at this particular time, for the Vatican had taken very seriously the complaints about non-residence by Irish bishops and were determined to put an end to it. Early in May the secretary of Propaganda Fide, taking advantage of Lloyd's presence in Rome, wrote to Cardinal Petra, prefect of that congregation, suggesting that the complaint that Lloyd had not in five years spent a month in his diocese, should be brought to Lloyd's notice. On the other hand, on 26 May Cardinal Spinelli—the same Spinelli who had been nuncio in Brussels many years before—suggested to the secretary of Propaganda that he should meet Lloyd, since a meeting might be of some value in view of the particular congregation on Irish affairs which it was intended to convene.[7] Although, then, the Vatican

3 Ibid., vol. 215/43, MFR 817.
4 Ibid., vol. 215/102, MFR 817.
5 Ibid., vol. 216/18, MFR 817.
6 Ibid., vol. 216/139, MFR 817.
7 Hugh Fenning, 'John Kent's report on the state of the Irish Mission, 1742' in *Archivium Hibernicum*, vol. 28 (1966), pp. 60-1.

authorities were bent on chastising Lloyd for non-residence, they were nevertheless prepared to canvass his views on the state of the Irish church, and at the same time his appointment as bishop of Waterford was being proceeded with.

While in Rome Lloyd stayed in the Irish Franciscan College of St Isidore's.[8] His stay there gave rise to a further unfortunate interference by him in the affairs of another diocese, this time Meath. John Pettit, a member of the St Isidore's community and a native of the diocese of Meath, was informed by Lloyd that the parish of Mullingar was vacant and that Fr Gorman, a Franciscan, who had served in the army in Italy or Spain for the previous eighteen years, was the *presentator* of the parish (i.e. he had the right to nominate the parish priest). Apparently on the assumption that Gorman would not be interested in exercising this right, Pettit, as a fellow Franciscan applied to the pope for the parish of Mullingar and in July 1739 was granted a document by the datary placing him in charge of it. When Pettit arrived in Mullingar to take over the parish he was to find that the bishop of Meath, Stephen MacEgan, some eighteen months previously had appointed Barnabas Barnewall, a Dominican, as parish priest. Nevertheless Pettit attempted to take over the parish on the basis of the Vatican document in his possession, and it was only after an appeal to Rome by Bishop MacEgan that Barnewall's right to the parish was upheld. It emerged in the course of the dispute that the person holding the right of presentation to the parish was not Gorman at all but one Matthew Casey, who was regarded as having acquired that right because he had built the new chapel in Mullingar.[9] Thus it will be seen that the information given by Lloyd to Pettit, which sparked off an unseemly wrangle, was incorrect on two counts—Mullingar was not vacant and Gorman did not hold the right of presentation.

Lloyd, now bishop of Waterford, left Rome towards the end of July and reached Brussels in mid August 1739. He presumably was back in Ireland by early September. He then disappears from view until August

8   Stuart Papers, RA SP(M) Box 1, no. 153.
9   Cathaldus Giblin, 'Catalogue of material of Irish interest in the collection Nunziatura di Fiandra, Vatican Archives' in *Collectanea Hibernica*, no. 10 (1967), pp. 82–5. It later transpires that the right of nomination for the parish of Mullingar was previously held by the Pettit family, of which Fr John Pettit was a member. Because he was away soldiering, Fr Pettit's eldest brother failed over a number of years to exercise his right of nomination, and found the right had lapsed when belatedly he nominated Fr John Pettit for the parish. Fr John Pettit had, therefore, a certain amount of right on his side. How Fr Gorman came into the picture is something of a mystery (see C. Giblin, op. cit., *Collectanea Hibernica*, no. 14 (1971), pp. 61-2).

1740, when in a letter from Waterford to Mary Rosa Howard of Norfolk, he fills us in on what has been happening to him in the meantime:

My Dear Madam,
It gave me unspeakable joy to see a letter from you at a time that I began to imagine that every friend, nay everybody, had forgot me. The bad state of my health for these many years past reduced me to so low a degree that, as I was really unfit either to serve myself or any one else, so concluded that nobody thought me worth the corresponding with. I was, it is true, in the City [Rome] last year where my best friend, and the best of men, took notice of me, and did good things for me, which no man but himself would do, or perhaps could do. Our old friend, Mgr Spinelli, recommended honest Mgr. Adami to me for an employment in the City, which nobody could acquit himself of either so effectually or so honourably for our advantage as he. Our Master, as well as Protector, approved of the Scheme very much, but it was thought proper that I should on my return for Ireland propose it to our Chief Farmers for their approbation. I had on my arrival in Ireland the affliction to find our Parliament sitting and greatly fermented against all those of our persuasion and with great passion carrying on new Laws and Schemes for our utter extirpation. I had therefore only time to speak to the Gentleman of Dublin upon Mgr. Adami's subject and brought him to a very warm approbation of the project, but before I could go farther I was all on a sudden struck of an apoplectic and paralytic fit, which deprived me of speech and all kind of motion of one side, and I lay the whole winter (a severe one it was) in that miserable condition till about the beginning of May when I returned to some use of my limbs and the Parliament being then up after a terrible stroke at us which had driven many of our gentry into England, I began to think seriously of Mgr. Adami's affair. I came down into this country, though not well able to stand. The Gentleman of Cashel is rejoiced at the project and in the most humble manner is ready to go into anything that is done for Mgr. Adami; the Gentleman of Dublin is in the like disposition and the Gentleman of Armagh being lately in Dublin was applied to by him in the warmest manner; he approves of the Scheme but boggles at contributing to Mgr. Adami's maintenance. All this I have under the Vicar of Dublin's hand. Tuam is vacant, which does not signify much at the present, nobody dare oppose it, so that nothing is wanting but that he be immediately named by our Master and the protector; as for

an allowance for him a little time will complete that too. I am surprised he does not acknowledge the receipt of a long Latin letter which I wrote him a little before I fell sick. I directed it for him at Cardinal Ottoboni's and sent it by a very safe hand to Paris to be forwarded in the proper manner. I beg you will acquaint him with this whole transaction. I will write to him myself soon; in the meantime if you will be so good to send him this very letter to be shown to my honoured and dear friend, Mr Edgar, it will for the present answer the end. I shall keep safely the letters of Dublin and Cashel as a testimony of their approbation and I doubt not but we shall soon bring in the rest to bear. Nobody loves Mgr. Adami better than I do and I shall be greatly rejoiced to see ourselves in so good hands.

For God's sake, dear Madam, if there be anything I can do in this part of the world, command me freely; tell my good friend Dr Meagher that I made Father Hacket write to him as soon as I came to the use of my speech, to have his opinion of my going to Spa, but he did not think fit to make us any answer. I love him sincerely but I think he has quite forgot me. I was agoing to tell you a long story of something like an information which your good cousin, Julia Browne, gave of me to two of our Privy Counsellors when she was last at Spa, but I shall say no more, God forgive her.[10]

In the foregoing letter 'my best friend' and 'Our Master' are presumably the Pretender. 'The Protector' was Cardinal Corsini, Protector of Ireland at Rome. The proposal mentioned was that Mgr. Adami would be appointed agent for the Irish bishops at the Vatican, and it will be seen that Lloyd had obtained the agreement of the three Chief Farmers (code for archbishops), although the archbishop of Armagh was worried as to where the agent's salary was to come from. Despite Lloyd's hopes for the scheme, nothing appears to have come of it. About this time, according to some sources, Fr Denis Byrne, parish priest of St Michan's in Dublin, was in Rome as agent for some Irish bishops but that appears to have been a temporary assignment.[11] As regards the activities of the Irish parliament in 1739, that body met every two years and normally continued their

10   Stuart Papers, RA SP(M) vol. 225/155, MFR 821. Lloyd had good reason to complain of the harshness of the weather, for this was the winter of the Great Frost of 1739-40. The Julia Browne mentioned towards the end of the letter is presumably the same lady who has been already mentioned in Chapter 7 in connection with her efforts to found a refuge in Brussels for Irish Dominican nuns.
11   John Meagher, 'Glimpses of Eighteenth Century priests' in *Reportorium Novum*, vol. 2, no. 1(1958), p. 145.

deliberations into the following year. There was no new legislation against Catholics enacted in the 1739-40 session; what was involved was a reactivation of the existing legislation. The measures taken were apparently stringent enough to drive some Catholics to seek refuge on the continent. We read in an *avviso* from Brussels nunciature of 16 October 1739 that great numbers of Irish Catholics were arriving in Flanders, where they had fled to avoid the persecution which was threatening at home; all of them were going on to France.[12] This reactivation of the penal laws was triggered off by rumours of the Spanish-backed invasion of the country by the Jacobites, already mentioned.

Meanwhile Rome had been taking further action with regard to nonresidence by Irish bishops. In October 1740 the nuncio in Brussels obtained from a trustworthy source in Ireland further information on this subject, and at the same time warned bishops that they must live in their dioceses. Six defaulting bishops were named, viz. Patrick French of Elphin, Stephen MacEgan of Meath, Michael MacDonogh of Kilmore, Ambrose O'Callaghan of Ferns, James O'Daly of Kilfenora and Sylvester Lloyd.[13] Remarkably, all these came from the ranks of the regular clergy— French, Lloyd and O'Callaghan were Fransciscans, MacDonogh and MacEgan were Dominicans and O'Daly was an Augustinian. O'Daly could scarcely be faulted for clinging to his secure canonry at Tournai in Flanders rather than taking up residence in the poor, tiny, non-viable diocese of Kilfenora in the north-west corner of Clare. In the case of MacEgan the complaint was scarcely justified inasmuch as it was easier for him to administer the diocese of Meath (which, in addition to county Meath, includes five-sixths of Westmeath, about a quarter of Offaly and a small portion of Cavan) from a base in Dublin, with coaches plying to the main towns in the diocese, than from a town within the diocese. The non-residence of so many regular bishops derived, firstly, from the fact that, unlike secular bishops, they usually had no roots in the dioceses to which they were appointed and found it difficult to settle down in a new and often hostile environment. Secondly, a regular bishop was much more likely to incur the wrath of the authorities since the government's attitude from the beginning of the century had been to tolerate a certain number of secular clergy, while giving short shrift to the regulars. Thirdly, a secular priest, promoted bishop, could go on living in his old parish, and so his promotion, unlike a regular's, might often go unnoticed by the authorities.

12   C Giblin, op. cit., no. 10 (1967), p. 82.
13   Hugh Fenning, op. cit., p. 61.

Following a further examination of these complaints, as well as the problem of the newly established protestant charter schools, Pope Benedict XIV took the matter personally in hand and sent to Ireland as special visitor Father John Kent, President of the Irish College at Louvain, with orders to examine the situation on the spot under sixteen specified heads.[14] Kent spent some weeks in Ireland during the summer of 1742, but, instead of moving around the country and seeing the position at first hand, he divided his time between Dublin and Waterford, of which latter he was a native, contenting himself with listening to the views of a few people , in particular those of Dublin's archbishop, John Linegar.

While in Waterford Kent is believed to have approached Lloyd for his views, but he nevertheless did not show Lloyd any great partiality when he came to report on him, as will be seen from the following translation of the relevant portion of his report, which is in Latin:

> Sylvester Lloyd, bishop of Waterford, of the Order of Minors of the Strict Observance was translated from Killaloe to this diocese because of a defect of the eyes; where he has four Regulars as pastors, and he has united the parish of St John [Waterford city], which had begun to be administered by a Franciscan, to a convent of his own [Franciscan] confreres. He is possessed of a strange desire to journey to even foreign parts and to sojourn in Dublin amongst his friends, acquaintances and nuns of his own order [Poor Clares]. He governs his diocese quietly.[15]

In the section of his report on Irish nuns Kent reported that the setting up of a convent of Dominican nuns in Waterford was proceeded with by the Dominican order despite the lack of any tradition of a Dominican presence in Waterford and in spite of opposition from other orders. He went on to state that Sister Wyse, a native of Waterford, was transferred from the Dominican sisters convent in Dublin as superioress of the Waterford foundation and that she subsequently admitted two girls as novices, one of them her niece. According to Kent the local bishop, Lloyd, refused to examine both of these novices with a view to profession for the reason that the convent, for want of authority, was not seen as stable. Kent maintained that, in any event, the convent could never be financially viable, since Sr Wyse had left her dowry behind her in Dublin, her niece had no dowry, and, while the second novice had a dowry of £200, the interest on this sum would not be sufficient to support three sisters.[16]

14   Ibid., pp. 68-9.
15   Ibid., p. 95.
16   Ibid., p. 85.

The facts of this case are, however, somewhat different from the position as set out in Kent's report. In 1725 Father William O'Meara, in his capacity as a vicar general of Waterford diocese, gave written approval for the setting up of a convent of Dominican nuns in Waterford city in accordance with the order of the Dominican general chapter of 1725. O'Meara stated that such a convent 'will be an ornament here to the Catholic religion, [and] a means to instruct the young ladies of this city and country [i.e. county] in piety and Christian education.' The Dominican provincial later sent two nuns to found the Waterford convent— Anastatia Wyse from their Dublin convent and Margaret Browne from their Galway convent. They duly rented a house in Waterford where they set up a small boarding school. Sister Wyse later gave the habit to Catherine Wyse, her niece, with the approval of Bishop Lloyd shortly after the arrival of the latter in the city. The admission of a new postulant, Mary Pilkington, was then mooted. But doubts as to whether the convent had a proper legal title arose and Lloyd applied to Rome to have the position regularised in a letter dated 13 July 1740 in which he stated, *inter alia:*

> I shall most willingly not only approve of such measures as they [Dominican authorities] shall take, but shall most earnestly recommend to our superiors the advantage it will be to the public that the said Mrs Wise her house be built upon a solid foundation, beyond all contradiction for the future.[17]

The pope in May 1742 issued a brief regularising both the new foundation and the profession of novices.[18] However, Kent proved to be right about the financial viability of the project, for the convent was forced to admit of failure and to close down by the late 1750s.[19]

While Kent furnished a lengthy and very interesting report on the state of the catholic church in Ireland at that time, no action towards reform was taken by Rome until 1751. In the meantime the complaints about non-residence had had a salutary effect on some at least of the bishops concerned, more particularly as bishops who continued to live outside their dioceses, were threatened with the appointment of coadjutors. O'Callaghan of Ferns settled down more or less in Wexford, while Lloyd appears to have lived most of his time in Waterford.

17 Hugh Fenning *The Irish Dominican province 1698-1798* (Dublin, 1990) pp. 152-5.
18 Ibid., p. 155.
19 Ibid., p. 356.

When Lloyd took over his duties as bishop in May 1740, Waterford had not had a resident bishop since 1701 when Richard Pierce briefly appeared in the diocese, and was protected for a time by two Colonel Butlers. It is not clear whether he left of his own volition or was transported, but, at any rate, he feared that if he returned to the diocese, he could be charged with high treason, a capital offence. Efforts were made by Rome to persuade Pierce to return to his diocese in the early 1730s, but he repelled these, citing his position in Ireland *vis-à-vis* the law.[20] In 1736 when efforts were apparently being made to persuade him to accept a coadjutor, Pierce had this to say in a letter dated 21 September 1736 to the Pretender;

> I can assure your Majesty that I have no need of a Coadjutor to govern my diocese. In truth I have only forty parish priests to manage. Each of these has three or four parishes to care for, without which [pluralities] they would not be able to live, for there is not a tithe to be had in fixed revenue. To superintend them [the P.P.s] I have four vicars-general in the four corners of the diocese. Mgr. Butler, archbishop of Cashel, lives all the time with his family, fixed in my diocese, right in the middle of everything.[21]

With regard to conditions in Waterford city, Catholics there ever since the restoration had been accorded some degree of toleration. During the reign of Charles II there were four chapels functioning in the city,[22] although admittedly Catholics were required to have their services over and done with by the time protestants assembled for their services.[23] Catholics were briefly top dogs during the reign of James II, who granted the city a new charter, resulting in the appointment of a catholic mayor and sheriffs in 1688 and 1689. Following the inception of the penal code with the Banishment act of 1698, we find the Catholics of Waterford petitioning the city council in 1700 that they might be allowed to build a chapel in Bailey's Lane, off Barronstrand Street, which they described as 'an obscure passage not much frequented by the citizens'. They cited the

---

20 C. Giblin, pp. cit., no. 14 (1971), p. 53.
21 Stuart Papers, RA SP(M) vol. 189/161, MFR 806. Pierce's original letter is in French. Although Archbishop Butler's family home at Kilcash in south Tipperary was in the diocese of Waterford & Lismore, it is not correct to say that it was right in the middle of that diocese.
22 P. M. Egan, *Waterford* (Kilkenny, *c.*1895), p. 519.
23 Emmanuel Curtis, *Blessed Oliver Plunket* (Dublin, 1963), p. 209.

8 View of Waterford city in 1736

example of Dublin where 'under the eye of the government they have divers chapels in the city, and are graciously permitted'.[24] The petition was acceded to by the Council and the chapel erected.

Under the 1704 act for the registration of Popish priests, six priests were returned for the city as parish priests of the civil parishes of St John's, St Peter's, Holy Trinity, St Patrick's, SS. Michael's and Stephen's and St Olave's.[25] But these were not all separate catholic parishes. Rather it was a ploy to take advantage of the act, under which a parish priest could be registered for each civil parish, even though in practice two civil parishes or more might be joined to form one catholic parish. The Report on Popery 1731, which is such a mine of information for some other dioceses, is very sketchy in so far as it relates to the diocese of Waterford & Lismore. However, a return in respect of Clonmel, one of the Tipperary parishes in the diocese, stated that the mass-house there had

24 P. M. Egan, op. cit., p. 519.
25 Edmund Downey, *The Story of Waterford* (Waterford, 1914), pp. 248-9.

been 'since the first year of the reign of George I repaired and all slated, and very much improved, with three large galleries therein'.[26]

The Report on Popery also gives some particulars in respect of four of the civil parishes in Waterford city, viz. St Patrick's, St Peter's, St Stephen's and St John's. Of these St John's was the only one credited with a masshouse and it had been built before the first year of the reign of George I and was served by three friars. The popish parishioners of St Patrick's, St Peter's and St Stephen's, we are told, attended Mass at the mass-*houses* in Trinity parish adjoining, implying that there were two mass-houses in Trinity parish. One friary, with five friars, was returned for St Stephen's parish; the friars were said to officiate 'mostly abroad in private houses in the country'. This friary was presumably one and the same as that reported to be in Stephen Street in 1744. No private chapels or nunneries were returned for the four parishes in question. With regard to education, there were reported to be two popish Latin schools in St Patrick's parish and one Latin and one English school in St John's parish. In the Lismore part of the diocese there were two schools which were reputed to teach philosophy—one in the parish of Kilbarrymeaden and one in the parish of Newcastle and Gilcagh.[27]

When Charles Smith published his 'The history, topography and antiquities of the county and city of Waterford' in 1746, he tells us that there were then three mass-houses in Waterford city—one in the city proper and two in the suburbs. He has left the following description of the chapel in the city:

> . . . a fine modern building, the aisles supported by stone pillars, the panels of the wainscots carved and gilded and the galleries finely adorned with paintings. Besides the great altar there are two lesser, one on either hand, over each of which there are curious paintings. Facing the great altar is a large silver lamp and chain of curious workmanship; round the house [sic] are niches filled with statues of saints.[28]

Smith does not tell us where this large chapel, or the two smaller chapels, were situated, while he tells us the location of all the Protestant churches. It seems to have been a point of principle with protestant writers of guide books and topographical works of the eighteenth century to ignore as far

---

26 'The Report on the state of Popery, 1731' for the diocese of Waterford & Lismore as published in *Archivium Hibernicum*, vol. 2 (1913), p. 155.
27 Ibid., p. 156.
28 Charles Smith, *The ancient and present state of the city and county of Waterford* (Dublin, 1746), p. 181.

as possible the majority catholic persuasion. The large chapel appears to have been on the site of the chapel built c.1700 already mentioned. The present cathedral, dating from 1793, is on the same site off Barronstrand Street.

This large chapel was apparently what was later to be known as 'The Big Chapel', and probably had been already built when Lloyd arrived in the city in 1740. Waterford Catholics were no less to the fore in taking steps to ensure that a catholic school was available for the education of their children. The establishment of a free protestant school for the education of poor children under the Bishop Foy foundation, was seen as an agent for proselytising catholic children, and to counteract the effects of that school Walter Harris tells us that 'in order to frustrate and subvert the glorious design of the founder [of the Bishop Foy school] a Popish school, supported by subscriptions, was erected, which gave the same encouragement by teaching children gratis to read, write and cast accounts'.[29]

Charles Smith, in his book already mentioned, also gives a description of a catholic old womens' home, known as the Holy Ghost Hospital and situated near the ruins of St Saviour's Abbey. It consisted of two great rooms, and at the end of the longer room there was a chapel, enclosed with a rail and adorned with paintings and images. Here the poor, Smith tells us, had Mass celebrated once a week. Twenty-four widows of the popish religion were accommodated and besides their lodging each of them received two guineas a year. The women were accepted by the master on the certificate of the Roman clergy. The hospital, which was funded by the Walsh family of the Canary Islands, was built in 1718.[30]

In the matter of catholic merchants engaging in trade, Waterford corporation were inclined to blow hot and cold as the century advanced. In 1704 Kilkenny merchants were admitted to the freedom of Waterford city 'as catholic inhabitants, traders are', which meant that they were required to pay 6d. per lb. duty on goods. In 1706, however, the corporation ordered that 'all Popish merchants inhabiting this city be exempt from paying any other city duties on wool or other goods than protestant freemen pay from 25th March next'. But in September 1717 the corporation had second thoughts about such a liberal ordinance when

29 Quoted in Downey, op. cit., p. 261. A lamp bearing the inscription 'This lamp was given by Thomas Nunezeal to the Most Holy Sacrament 1738' used to hang before St Joseph's altar in the present cathedral. Since a donor would be much more likely to present such a lamp to a newly-built chapel rather than to an old chapel due for demolition, the probability is that the date the lamp was presented (1738) is also the date the new chapel opened. Presumably this was 'the large silver lamp' which Charles Smyth stated was 'facing the great altar' c.1746.
30 C. Smith, op. cit., p. 183.

they resolved that no catholic in future be admitted to freedom without paying a sum not less than £5 together with such fees as the corporation might think proper.[31] This imposition on catholic merchants, known as quarterage, also obtained in Dublin and other cities. The catholic merchants in Cork eventually challenged in the courts the legality of these quarterages and obtained a decision for their abolition in 1758.[32] However, it is of interest that Catholics in Waterford were being admitted as freemen on the same basis as protestants from the 1730s but in much smaller numbers.[33]

The diocese of Waterford & Lismore embraces practically the entire county of Waterford and about one-sixth of the area of county Tipperary. According to a census of catholic and protestant householders conducted in 1732 by the hearth money collectors, there were then in the county (including the city) of Waterford a total of 10,992 households, of which 10,165 were catholic and 827 were protestant, giving a ratio of twelve Catholic for every one protestant.[34] The total population might be estimated as follows:

City	2,000 houses approx. with 7 persons per house	14,000
County	9,000 houses with 4.5 persons per house	40,500
	Total:	54,500

Of this total, about 50,000 were Catholics and about 4,500 were Protestants. If we add on say 10,000 Catholics in respect of the Tipperary portion of the diocese, a figure of 60,000 emerges as the catholic population of the diocese in 1732, but allowing for a notional deficiency of 20% in the house numbers upon which this figure is calculated, the actual figure could be something of the order of 72,000. This compares with a catholic population of about 89,000 in 1766, as extrapolated from the Religious Census of that year.[35]

---

31   E. Downey, op. cit., pp. 249 & 276.
32   David Dickson, *New foundations: Ireland 1660-1800* (Dublin, 1987) p. 136.
33   National Library of Ireland MS Pos. 5559, *Minute Book of Waterford Corporation*.
34   *An abstract of the number of protestant and popish families*, (Dublin, 1736). For the number of houses in Waterford city around this time see Arthur Dobbs, *Essay on the trade and improvement in Ireland* (Dublin, 1731), part 2, p. 6. The protestant proportion of the population was much higher in Waterford city than in the county. Figures from the Religious Census of 1766 for the diocese of Waterford & Lismore - see William H. Rennison *Succession list of the diocese of Waterford and Lismore* (place of publication not stated, 1920) p. 233 - show that at that date 25% of the population of the city were protestant; the proportion would have been even higher in the 1730s.
35   W. H. Rennison, op. cit., pp. 233-5.

When Lloyd arrived in the city in 1740 it had a population of perhaps 15,000. A view of the city in 1736 shows a quay of four-storied houses stretching for about a quarter of a mile westwards from Reginald's Tower to Barronstrand Street, with four or five church towers visible in the background. The quay has ever been the pride of the city and not less so in the eighteenth century when Charles Smith claimed it was 'not inferior to but rather exceeds the most celebrated in Europe'.[36] Although the city had no less than seven civil parishes, Smith tells us that 'considerable tracts of each parish extend into the country'.

Lloyd was not long in his new diocese when a disastrous famine struck. There was a severe frost in 1739-40 which destroyed potato and other food stocks in rural areas. It has been estimated that one-eighth of the population of Ireland died in the ensuing two years from starvation and disease. The famine was particularly severe in all the counties of Munster despite its rich farmlands. In Waterford city an unusually large number of the inhabitants applied for doles from the corporation during 1740, resulting in the mayor taking up a loan of £2,000 for the purchase of corn for the relief of the starving poor.[37] Bishop George Berkeley of Cloyne in a letter of 19 May 1741 to Thomas Prior of Dublin commented:

> The distresses of the sick and poor are endless. The havoc of mankind in the counties of Cork, Limerick and some adjacent places hath been incredible. The nation probably will not recover this loss in a century. The other day I heard one from the county of Limerick say that whole villages were entirely dispeopled. About two months ago I heard Sir Richard Cox say that five hundred were dead in the parish, though in a county, I believe, not very populous. It were to be wished people of condition were at their seats in the country during these calamitous times, which might provide relief and employment for the poor. Certainly, if these perish the rich must be sufferers in the end.[38]

But in normal times Waterford & Lismore was a generally prosperous diocese with a relatively high proportion of well-to-do catholics. In the city of Waterford, as in Cork and Limerick, catholics had become prominent in trade. David Bindon was of the view that:

---

36 C. Smith, op. cit., p. 196.
37 E. Downey, op. cit., p. 320.
38 Quoted in John Mitchel, *The history of Ireland from the Treaty of Limerick to the present time* (Dublin, 1869), vol. 1, p. 65.

Ireland would flourish more if we permitted the Papists to take leases of lives and purchase lands, for now we drive them into trade and almost all the money of the Kingdom is in their hands. They are the greatest traders and especially the greatest runners of prohibited goods, to the ruin of the fair traders, who are generally protestants.[39]

In Waterford city also there were many wealthy catholic shopkeepers, as well as catholic physicians and surgeons, the medical profession never being subject to any penal restrictions. The county of Waterford and the portion of south Tipperary in the diocese, as well as having their share of the foregoing, had a large number of catholic tenant farmers, working sizeable acreages. But this is not to overlook the fact that the vast majority of catholics were poor labourers or small struggling farmers.

Information is scant on the day-to-day administration of the diocese in Lloyd's time. One presumes that he carried out some visitations of parishes, administering Confirmation, preaching to the people, admonishing clergy and laity alike. With regard to the clergy, Fr Patrick Power in his history of the diocese of Waterford & Lismore tells us that during his episcopacy in Killaloe Lloyd promoted priests to parishes, not by seniority, but by concursus (i.e. competitive examination of candidates) and that it could be assumed that he followed the same practice in Waterford & Lismore.[40] But it will have been noted from John Kent's report that the carrying out of his episcopal duties was punctuated by visits to Dublin, if not further afield.

Ill health continued to plague him to such an extent indeed that he felt compelled to seek a coadjutor. In a letter dated 1 May 1743 he complains thus to the pretender's secretary, Edgar:

> I must ask you now to represent me in the most humble manner at the feet of our King, and to inform him that I am now become so weak-sighted, and so incapacitated by a paralysis in my right side, as to be scarcely able to go about my district on horseback. This being the case, it will be absolutely impossible for me to fulfil the indispensable duties of my office. In one of his circular letters, the Pope recently promised us that he would provide coadjutors to those who because of their advanced age or sickness should prove incapable of carrying out their duties in person.

39 '*Diary of the First Earl of Egmont*' published by Historical Manuscripts Commission, London, vol. 3(1923), p. 329. Bindon's views appear in the diary under the date 21 January 1729.
40 Patrick Power, *Waterford & Lismore* (Dublin and Cork, 1937) p. 30.

For this reason I beg our King to nominate as my future help and comfort Mr Thomas Stritch, a gentleman of about 38 years, a native of this country [county], elected by the clergy to be their vicar general during the last vacancy, and continued by me in the same office to the great satisfaction both of the clergy and people. He was educated in Rome under the direction of Father [Alexander] Roche who upon any enquiry will bear testimony to his life and manners for the period during which he lived with him. And I take it upon my conscience to assert that his life has been equally irreprehensible since he returned to this kingdom.

He comes from a very ancient and honourable family, both on his father's side and on his mother's. That family, long ago, enjoyed great credit and esteem in this country. In one word, I do not know a man more zealous for the honour of God and more faithful in the service of our King than Mr Thomas Stritch. Hence it is that I humbly implore, with the greatest insistence, that he and no other be granted to me as coadjutor with the right of succession and with all the other prerogatives which are customary in similar cases. I hope that His Majesty will graciously deign to interest himself in this matter, because to put me into the hands of any other Coadjutor would be to send me down in my old age with affliction into the grave.

I pray you to present my most humble offices to their Royal Highnesses. May God in His infinite mercy make them prosper in everything they undertake.[41]

The Fr Roche mentioned in the foregoing was Father Alexander Roche, president of the Irish College in Rome, which had places for a total of nine secular students from the Irish Mission. Stritch died within a year of his being appointed as coadjutor. Fr Patrick Power states that he does not appear to have been ever consecrated bishop; symptoms of insanity are said to have manifested themselves which prevented consecation.[42] On the other hand, it seems odd, if he were never consecrated, that Lloyd should refer to him in a letter which will be noticed shortly as a brother bishop. Furthermore, Stritch is called 'the late incumbent' of the diocese in a letter dated 22 February 1745 from Fr James MacKenna to Edgar.[43]

---

41 Stuart Papers, RA SP(M) vol. 249/98, MFR 832. What appears in the Stuart Papers is a translation into Italian of Lloyd's letter which we can assume was in English. For the translation back into English I am indebted to Father Hugh Fenning OP.
42 P. Power, op. cit., p. 30.
43 Stuart Papers, RA SP(M) vol. 262/187, MFR 838.

On 21 November 1743 Lloyd wrote to Edgar on the question of having assigned to him as a mensal parish the Cathedral parish in Waterford city:

> It was with the utmost joy that I received an account from Mr Goddard of the health and welfare of your whole family; the Great God preserve and bless them in all their undertakings. The favour granted to Mr Stritch was very agreeable to this whole county and to me in particular. I hope we shall never give the Master reason to complain of either of us.
>
> We have had an account that Mr William O'Meara has been lately promoted to a farm in the county of Kerry. He has been for some time past in possession of a small farm within this city, which was likewise within the precincts of the Cathedral, and is by his present removal vacant in your City [Rome], and custom makes it in some measure as my right. Such is at present the practice in Dublin, Kildare, Ossory, Cork and so forth. I hope the like favour will not be refused to me, for I am in great want of some help, having now a younger brother, as you know, to maintain, and being very well able with the help of an under-servant to acquit myself of my duty. All that I expect from my friends is that they will solicit for me before another runs away with this little farm which is according to custom my right. I have no reason to doubt your zeal in anything that regards me.
>
> *Postscript*: Mr Goddard, to whom I wrote last post, can give you an account of my pretensions to this farm.[44]

The 'farm in the county of Kerry' is of course the diocese of Kerry to which William O'Meara was appointed bishop by papal brief dated 20 November 1743. Likewise 'the small farm within this city' is the cathedral parish which Lloyd sought as a mensal parish. This would make him financially more independent since it would provide him with a dependable income and free him from the necessity of trying to extract contributions from reluctant parish priests. When Lloyd speaks of having a younger brother to maintain, he does not mean a real brother but a brother bishop in the person of Thomas Stritch. It will be noted that, while on 1 May 1743, when he was seeking a coadjutor, he had become so weak-sighted and so incapacitated as to be scarcely able to go about his district on horseback, he is now well able with the help of an under-

---

44 Ibid., vol. 253/188, MFR 833.

servant to acquit himself of his duty. It might be concluded from this that Lloyd was able to vary the state of his health to suit the particular case he wished to make, and that he often exaggerated his ill health when it suited the particular circumstances.

In the parliamentary session of 1743-44 there was further discussion in the Irish parliament of a reactivation of the laws against Catholics, resulting in a proclamation by the lord lieutenant and privy council dated 24 February 1744. This was again fomented by a Jacobite invasion scare, which indeed proved to be more than a scare the following year when the Pretender's son, Charles Edward, landed in Scotland and rallied the clans with such effect that the British administration had a nasty shock.

The proclamation of February 1744 commanded all justices of the peace and other magistrates strictly to put in execution the several laws against popish archbishops, bishops, vicars-general, deans, jesuits, monks, friars or other regular popish clergy and of all popish clergy exercising ecclesiastical authority. A reward of £150 was offered upon conviction of any of these before 1 October 1745. Monasteries, friaries, nunneries and other popish fraternities and societies were required to be suppressed and papists to be disarmed. A reward was also offered for the discovery of harbourers of popish archbishops and bishops. Searches were only to be made between the rising and setting of the sun, except in cities and towns.[45]

There was an immediate response to the proclamation from magistrates and other upholders of the law. In Dublin a number of the regular clergy were arrested. In March it was reported that in Youghal and many other corporate towns the mayors and magistrates had furnished themselves with arms and ammunition so as to be ready to oppose any invasion or insurrection that should be attempted, and that they had been searching the houses of catholics for arms but had so far found none.[46] On 10 March at the assizes at Drogheda the grand jury made presentment of five Dominicans, four Augustinians and four Franciscans from the town. On 20 March the grand jury at Maryborough (Portlaoise) made presentment of a reputed popish bishop, two vicars-general and six friars.[47] In Kilkenny the grand jury presented Colman O'Shaughnessy,[48] Dominican

---

45 John Brady, *Catholics and Catholicism in the Eighteenth Century Press* (Maynooth, 1965), p 65.
46 Ibid., p. 66.
47 Ibid., p. 66. The 'reputed Popish bishop' is named as Bryan Moore but there was no catholic bishop of that name in Ireland then.
48 *Old Kilkenny Review*, vol. 13 (1961), p. 43. The hounding of some other bishops was quite severe. O'Callaghan of Ferns died in Dublin in August 1744, worn out, it is said, by his efforts to avoid arrest. MacDonogh of Kilmore had to change house twelve times in two months because high treason was sworn against him (H. Fenning, op. cit., note 17, p. 188).

bishop of Ossory, on a charge of being a domestic chaplain to the Pretender. In the same city it was reported that 'all the masshouses here are shut up and the friers and priests dispersed and absconded.'[49]

But presentment was one thing: discovering the whereabouts of those presented, arresting them and bringing them before the courts was another. Besides, there was a reluctance on the part of many magistrates, conscious of their personal vulnerability in a country for the most part overwhelmingly peopled by catholics, to become involved. It is not surprising then that the Drogheda friars were still at large in August when they were again presented by the grand jury and warrants were left by the judges of assize to apprehend them.[50]

One measure which could be accomplished fairly easily was the closing down of chapels and masshouses, and this was done with some dispatch in Dublin and other centres. This led to temporary, makeshift chapels springing up, and the collapse in February 1744 of an old house in Pill Lane, Dublin, in which Mass was being celebrated, resulted in the deaths of the celebrant priest and nine others.[51]

In Waterford Sylvester Lloyd appears to have judged it expedient to leave his normal place of abode, for when the officers of the law came looking for him he was not to be found. The mayor, Cornelius Bolton, rather lamely reported on 14 April 1744:

> In obedience to the Order of the Lord Lieutenant and Council transmitted to us by you, we have made diligent enquiry within our jurisdiction for the names and places of abode of all persons being or reputed to be Popish archbishops, bishops, vicars-general, deans, jesuits, monks, friars or other regular popish clergy and of all papists exercising ecclesiastical jurisdiction.
>
> And we find that Sylvester Lloyd, reputed to be popish titular bishop of Waterford, resided in the city of Waterford for some time past but upon search being made for him pursuant to the proclamation, we find he has lately absconded and cannot be found. We find that William O'Meara, reputed to be Popish dean of Waterford, resided in the city of Waterford for some time past but upon search for him, he has absconded as aforesaid. We find that John St Leger, Felix Cleary, William Sexton, Peter Macnamara, Peter Costello, Luke Kelly, William Shee, John Bray and William Brown to be reputed

---

49 Alderman William Colles to his wife in Primm papers, no. 87/1 National Archives, Dublin.
50 J. Brady, op. cit., p. 67.
51 Ibid., p. 65.

monks, friars and jesuits and that they or some number of them dwelt together for some time past in a house in Stephen Street called the Friary, but upon search made in aforesaid house and other places, we find they have absconded as aforesaid.

All the persons listed above were regulars, except for William O'Meara, who was included presumably because he had occupied a position of authority, that of dean. This bears out the general experience that secular clergy were not disturbed unless they were known to occupy positions of authority, although admittedly the closing down of chapels and masshouses rendered even the ordinary secular priests ineffective.[52]

While a report in *Faulkner's Dublin Journal* of 13 March 1744 that 'the titular bishop of Waterford hath surrendered himself to the mayor of that city' is evidently incorrect, there is no doubt but that Lloyd was actively pursued by the forces of the law, and the Brussels nuncio was later to claim that he made good his escape 'by a miracle'. Although blind and so paralysed as to be hardly able to mount his horse, he avoided his pursuers for three weeks and took ship by night. He reached the island of Jersey in five days and went on thence to La Rochelle, where he appears to have arrived towards the end of April.[53]

Archbishop Linegar of Dublin in August 1744 reported to Corsini, the cardinal protector of Ireland at Rome, that Ireland was grievously afflicted by misfortunes and persecutions, the most recent of which began the previous February and threatened to wipe out every trace of catholicism in the country, and that, because of this, the archbishop was compelled to have recourse to the cardinal who was such a vigilant and sympathetic protector.[54] In Madrid Dr John Lacy translated the proclamation of February 1744 into the different languages and circulated it to the catholic courts in Europe in the hope that pressure might be brought to bear on the British government to have the persecution brought to an end.[55] The best hope of such an intervention lay with the Austrian empress, Maria Theresa, Britain's catholic ally in the War of the Austrian Succession then raging. It so happened that the Austrian representative in London at that time was Count Taaffe, who made it his business to see for himself conditions in Ireland at first hand and had the personal experience of not

---

52 William P. Burke, *Irish priests in penal times* (Waterford, 1914), p. 369.
53 H. Fenning, op. cit., in note 17, p. 188. The nuncio's letter is dated Brussels, 2 May 1744 and is in the archives of the Congregation de Propaganda Fide (S C Irlanda 10, ff 147-8).
54 C. Giblin, op. cit., no. 10 (1967), p. 99.
55 Stuart Papers, RA SP(M) vol. 258/168, MFR 836.

being allowed to attend Mass in Dublin because the chapels were closed down.[56] The representations which Taaffe subsequently made to George II, whom he knew personally from campaigning together on the continent, were instrumental in easing the repressive measures.

As to how this persecution compared with previous ones, Thomas Burke, later bishop of Ossory, who himself narrowly escaped arrest at the Dominican convent in Bridge Street, Dublin, was later to claim that the 1744 persecution was the only *general* one since the death of Queen Anne in 1714.[57]

Later, from his refuge on the Continent, Lloyd is said to have written 'a letter of defiance' to the mayor of Waterford. This letter does not appear to have survived; the evidence for it is contained in a letter from one Fr James McKenna to the Pretender's secretary, seeking a nomination for himself to the bishopric of Waterford. McKenna claimed that the bishopric was then vacant, that Lloyd had 'ceded it during the late persecution' and could not return to it because of the letter of defiance he had written to the mayor.[58]

It may well be that the enforcement of the proclamation of February 1744 was pursued with greater vigour in Waterford than elsewhere. Its bishop was one of the few, perhaps the only one, compelled to flee the country at that time. Admittedly Lloyd would have been a marked man in the eyes of the authorities. They would have looked upon him as a renegade to his own class and no doubt they had some inkling of his Jacobite activities over the years.

The proclamation continued to be enforced in greater or lesser degree throughout 1744. The summer of 1745 brought the Jacobite rising in Scotland and, left to its own devices, the Dublin parliament at its new session commencing in the autumn of that year would in all probability have introduced even harsher measures against the catholics, for any Jacobite invasions or rumours of invasions had in the past been invariably marked by repression of catholics. On this occasion, however, any inclinations of the Dublin parliament in that direction were effectively stymied by the British government, who apparently had decided that the best way to neutralise Irish catholic support or sympathy for the Jacobites was by conciliation. Accordingly, in September 1745 a new Viceroy, the amiable and liberal, but firm earl of Chesterfield, was sent over to Dublin

56 Patrick Moran, *The Roman Catholics of Ireland under the penal laws of the eighteenth century* (London, 1900), p. 54.
57 H. Fenning, op. cit., in note 17, p. 188.
58 Stuart Papers, RA SP(M) vol. 262/187, MFR 838.

to implement a policy of allowing catholics the free exercise of their religion.[59] Although Chesterfield's term as viceroy was one of the shortest—a mere seven months in fact—it was later viewed as a watershed in the treatment of catholics. The fact that Ireland played no part on the side of the Jacobites in the '45 was not forgotten, and never again was there any attempt to reactivate the religious provisions of the Penal Laws.

Chesterfield's liberal views are perhaps best exemplified in a letter many years later to the protestant bishop of Waterford, Richard Chenevix, where he stated:

> I would only require the priests to take the Oath of allegiance simply, and not the subsequent oaths which in my opinion no real papist can take, the consequence of which would be that the least conscientious would be registered and the most conscientious ones excluded.[60]

Lloyd's poor health and his absence from his diocese meant the appointment of a coadjutor to replace Stritch would have to be proceeded with sooner or later. Evidently he opposed the appointment of a further coadjutor, presumably for financial reasons, but on this occasion he was quite firmly over-ruled by the Pretender, whose secretary, Edgar, wrote to Lloyd on 13 April 1745:

> I received some time ago yours of 5th October from Mr Creagh [Abbé Creagh], unto whom, upon your recommendation, I did all the service I could, and charged him to tell you so with the assurance of my humble respects. Now I come to tell you that, having received lately yours of 20th February, I did myself the honour to lay it before the King, and by his directions this serves to let you know that, though

---

59 Just how firm Chesterfield was prepared to be with catholics, if the need arose, can be gleaned from the following excerpt from a letter he wrote to the duke of Newcastle on 24 October 1745 from Dublin Castle: 'The Papists here are not only quiet but even their priests preach quiet to them. The most considerable of them have been with me to assure me of their firm resolution not to disturb the Government, and to thank me for not having disturbed them, as usual at this time. I told them very fairly that the lenity of the government should continue so long as their good behaviour deserved it, but that if they gave the least disturbance, they should be treated with a rigour they had never yet experienced' (see John Bradshaw ed., *The letters of Philip Dormer Stanhope, earl of Chesterfield* (London, 1892), vol. 2, p. 686.

60 John Bradshaw (ed.) op. cit., (London, 1892), vol. 3, p. 1116. Chesterfield's remark to Chenevix was in fact made in a letter dated 29 January 1755 in connection with the form of oath to be included in a bill for registering catholic priests, which in the event was withdrawn. Chenevix had been Chesterfield's chaplain for sixteen years and he maintained a regular correspondence with Chesterfield after he was appointed a bishop in 1745. Most of Chesterfield's views about Irish affairs were expressed, not during his period as Lord Lieutenant, but in correspondence with Chenevix and others over a period of more than twenty years after he left Ireland.

H.M. has a particular esteem and regard for you and would willingly contribute on proper occasions to your ease and satisfaction, yet your state of health having been represented to him in such a manner as to make another Coadjutor to you in your diocese absolutely necessary, H.M, after weighing the matter seriously and having at the same time all due consideration for you, has thought it proper to name Mr Peter Creagh of Limerick your new Coadjutor, and the Pope has actually accepted of the nomination, the Bulls are expending, and upon this subject Cardinal Corsini will probably write to you in a post or two. H.M thought that the real good of the Mission required his taking this step without loss of time, and is persuaded, when you reflect seriously on it, you will approve of it, and the more that Mr Creagh bears one of the best Characters, and that, had you been to choose yourself, you could not have pitched upon a more proper person. This H.M. commands me to say to you and to assure you of many kind complements in his name.[61]

Peter Creagh was duly appointed coadjutor in Waterford by papal brief dated 5 May 1745.[62] Lloyd accepted the appointment with a good grace. On 15 May he wrote to Edgar from Bagnères, a watering-place near the present shrine of Lourdes;

Dear Honoured Sir, I received the honour of your kind letter of April the 13th, forwarded to me from Avignon to the Irish Community at Toulouse and from thence by the Superior of the Community to this place, where I have been these five weeks and have gone through the whole course of the waters and hot baths. I am a good deal better in my sight, and generally so of my Palsey and Rheumatism. The physicians of Montpellier, as well as of Toulouse and Bagnères are all of opinion that my blindness as well as the heaviness in my right side is owing to a thickness in my blood and that the very pungent pains I felt were rather Rheumatick than Paralytic pains, and that if I exercise continually by riding and walking, it will probably restore me quite. They likewise desire I should take the cold baths winter and summer, and this, dear Sir, is my present situation. God Almighty shower down his choicest blessings upon our dear King and upon the Royal Issue. God prosper them and crown all their undertakings with

61 Stuart Papers, RA SP(M) vol. 264/50, MFR 838.
62 Ibid., vol. 264/147, MFR 838.

success, and that I may see and hear it is so before I die, is my continual prayer. If I had not been so weak as I was, I would have followed his Royal Highness wherever he went, though it were only to hear from him every day, for I scarce hear a word of him in this place, which breaks my heart.

His Majesty thinks better than I do. His zeal and piety makes him study our good more than we do ourselves. I own Mr Peter Creagh is as fit a man as could be given to help me. The hope of my recovering my health made me think of not troubling his Majesty to name me another Coadjutor, for it is very hard to meet with two men of Mr Stritch's and Mr Creagh's meek and peaceable disposition. I was very happy in Mr Stritch and make no doubt but I shall be so in Mr Creagh. I know him and the sweetness of his temper very well. He lived in my diocese of Killaloe until he was made Dean of Limerick. I had many opportunities of knowing him and his learning, for I have employed him to compose some wrangles among the clergy in my diocese. He accompanied me from Dublin into the North of Ireland, where I went to help to consecrate one Mr MacMahon bishop of Clogher, who had been his schoolfellow in Rome. Mr Creagh is welcome to the bottom of my heart and I shall give him an account of the honour the King has done him. His relations are in very good circumstances and well able to support him in any disappointments he may meet with, but while I have half a loaf, he shall have half of it. I begged already you would do me the honour to recommend me to Cardinal Corsini for I really want some additional bread. I have not thirty pounds a year by my diocese and all that is spent before I can gather it among my priests. Lay me at his Majesty's feet with the greatest submission, assure him I shall forever be pleased with what he does. Give my duty to the Duke of York. I have a flying report that he was to serve a campaign somewhere in Italy. God Almighty bless him wherever he goes. Pray give me leave to give my humble service to my Lord Dunbar and beg he would speak to Cardinal Corsini to do something for me, for I must go for Bordeaux immediately to strive to get me passage for Ireland. Necessity drives me. I cannot stay in this country any longer.[63]

When he says 'while I have half a loaf, he shall have half of it', he means that he is determined that the bishop's dues will be split evenly between

63   Ibid., vol. 264/172, MFR 838.

himself and the coadjutor. But the eternally hard-up and optimistic Lloyd is still hopeful that some kind of a pension will be found for him. As for his intention of returning to Ireland, there is no evidence that he ever did so. The following November Creagh applied to Propaganda Fide for full episcopal faculties, citing Lloyd's great age, blindness and residence in France,[64] but this request was not apparently granted at that time.

On 11 February 1747 Lloyd wrote to Edgar what was to be the last of his letters to be preserved among the Stuart Papers. He is at Nantes on the west coast of France:

> Honoured Dear Sir, I wrote to Father O'Brien, the guardian of St Isidore's, and I again wrote to Abbé Creagh and in both letters desired my humble service might be given to you and begged they would acquaint you with my misfortune on the coast of Brittany in August last, when being taken by a Guernsey privateer, I had the misfortune to fall between the ship and the boat and was sorely bruised which had like to have cost me my life. I was put ashore at Port Louis where I lay sick for above a month and then was sent in a horse litter to Nantes, where I have lain ever since in a very weak condition, but am now, I thank God, much better than I have been at any time ever since I came into France and do resolve with the first opportunity to make another push to go into Ireland, for I am not able to live longer in France. I have been forced to borrow some money from an old acquaintance I met here and on that I have subsisted all the while I have been here. I must pledge two rings and a cross to pay my debts and I shall be quite undone if Mr Pontin fails to send me what is due of my pension. I received nothing since the month of March last, so that I hope, dear Sir, you will be so humane to speak feelingly to him and persuade him to send me an account of what was then paid and how much he sends me yearly. I am in the greatest want and cannot do without this money. I can make a shift to eat and drink in Ireland but as things stand can expect nothing else.
>
> You know much better than I how affairs stand with our Prince. We have here the greatest hopes of his good success, and for my part I always hoped in God that he would do better without the French assistance than with it, and, forgive me if I speak wrong, I fear their late flutter in his favour at Boulogne and Dunkerque did him more

---

64 Hugh Fenning (ed.), 'Letters from a Jesuit in Dublin 1747-48' in *Archivium Hibernicum*, vol. 29 (1970), p. 145.

hurt than good. If you did know how much the English despise and hate the French, you would expect no good from their meddling especially in so public a manner as they have done of late, nor do I believe that they have it in their hearts to do us any good, nor ever had since Queen Elizabeth's time, but especially since James the First came into England. For God's sake, dear Sir, give my most humble duty to his Majesty. The Heavens protect him and his royal issue. Since I can do no more, I must never cease to pray for them.[65]

The fact that Lloyd was taken prisoner by a privateer would seem to imply that he was at this time on board ship, but, if so, whither he was bound is not explained. In the course of the letter he speaks of making *another* 'push' to go into Ireland, and this might imply that, when taken prisoner, he was bound for Ireland, a hazardous undertaking with Britain and France still at war. Port Louis, where he was landed by the privateer, is a small port in Brittany some eighty miles north of Nantes. Lloyd's bitter words about the French have to be viewed in the context where the Jacobite invasion of England (under Prince Charles Edward) in late 1745 had failed because the expected French aid did not materialise, although France should have been cock-a-hoop at the time after her recent great victory at Fontenoy. Such a glorious opportunity of bringing Britain to her knees would not occur again.

From a letter dated 4 November 1746 from Fr Michael Fitzgerald SJ, rector of the Irish College in Rome, to Edgar, we learn that Lloyd's coadjutor in Waterford, Peter Creagh, had decided to make his home in Carrick-on-Suir 'as being more convenient for the administration of his diocese'. 'Besides', the letter goes on, 'his residence in that town will be attended with much less other inconveniences than in Waterford,'[66] It may well be that Creagh was profiting from Lloyd's unhappy experience of the authorities in Waterford by removing himself from their surveillance.

Fr Fitzgerald goes on to point out that, if Creagh's move to Carrick-on-Suir is approved, then Creagh would be pleased 'to pitch upon' Fitzgerald's brother, Fr Patrick Fitzgerald, as the man to succeed him in Trinity Parish, Waterford, which apparently Creagh held as a mensal parish. He mentions that Cardinal Corsini, protector of Ireland, would have the honour to dine with 'his Majesty' the following day when the proposals could be put before his Eminence who would 'have no difficulty to grant the bishop a request

65 Stuart Papers, RA SP(M) vol. 272/153, MFR 842.
66 Ibid., vol. 278/91, MFR 844.

which tends only to enable him to serve his diocese more effectually'. Fr Fitzgerald concludes that 'in that case, the parish of Trinity becoming vacant, can be given to my brother without offending Mr Loyd [sic] in the least, it being absolutely in the court of Rome's disposal'.[67]

It appears that Fr Fitzgerald was a bit over-optimistic in assuming that the proposals, which were approved, could be implemented without offending Lloyd, who in fact was very upset when he heard what was afoot, as the following letter dated Dublin, 3 February 1747 indicates:

> Mon trés cher ami, Mr Hennessy desires me to inform you that Dr Lloyd is now at Louvain in his way home as 'tis reported, and that there will be troubles between him and Mr Creagh. He fears likewise that he will make his collation of Carrick parish to Mr Fraher as good as he can and so oppose both Mr Creagh and Mr Patrick Fitzgerald.[68]

It appears then that Lloyd was bent on returning to Ireland to assert his authority as bishop by preventing Creagh from taking over Carrick-on-Suir as his mensal parish and consequently preventing Patrick Fitzgerald from becoming parish priest of Trinity parish, Waterford. In the event Lloyd never seems to have returned to Ireland. In fact he had only a few more months to live, for the next news we have of him is in a letter dated Paris, 13 August 1747 from Fr Matt MacKenna to a person unknown which states that Lloyd 'was buried in this town [Paris] last Thursday'.[69] He thus died early in August 1747 (à la Gregorian calendar in use on the Continent), or late in July 1747 (à la Julian calendar still in use in Ireland and Britain at that time). His last resting-place is unknown.

There only remains to mention the details of Sylvester Lloyd's will, made in Waterford on 9 August 1743. It reads as follows:[70]

> In the name of God. Amen.
>
> I, Sylvester Lloyd, being weak in body but of sound mind and understanding, and considering the uncertainty of this mortal life, have thought proper to make and publish this my last will and testament, revoking all former wills by me made, and declaring this alone and no other to be my last will and testament, of which I

---

67 Ibid., vol. 278/91, MFR 844.
68 H. Fenning, op. cit. in note 64, p. 145.
69 Stuart Papers, RA SP(M) vol. 286/96, MFR 848.
70 William Carrigan, 'Dr Sylvester Lloyd' in *Journal of the Waterford Archaeological Society*, vol. 3 (1897), pp. 38-39.

appoint the Reverend Mr Francis Phelan, and Messrs Andrew Fitzgerald and Maurice Hearn, merchants, of the city of Waterford, executors.

Imprimis, I bequeath my soul to God and my body to the earth, to be buried as private as possible.

What worldly substance I am possessed of or entitled to, I give, devise and bequeath the same in manner following:

I give and bequeath one shilling to each of my nephews and nieces by my half-sisters, Jane and Rebecca Lockington.

Item I give and bequeath one shilling to each of my cousin germans, and to each of my relations who may pretend a right to any part of my substance.

Item I give and bequeath my gold watch to Mr Richard Quane, bankier at Paris.

And finally I give, devise and bequeath to my said executors, after they have paid my just debts, the remainder of my worldly substance.

In witness whereof I have hereunto put my hand and seal this 9th day of August 1743.
　　　　　　　　　　Signed
　　　　　　　　　　S. Lloyd (Seal)

Signed, sealed and published
in presence of us,
T. Barron
John Cassin
Tho. White.

The within named Francis Phelan and Andrew Fitzgerald, the surviving executors of the within will named, were duly sworn as well to the truth of their belief as to the due execution thereof this 24th day of August 1748.
　　　　　　　　　　Before me
　　　　　　　　　　Edw. Thomas, Vic-General
Francis Phelan.
Andrew Fitzgerald
Probate was taken out August 24th, 1748.

The will is endorsed 'S. Lloyd, his will'. The Fr Francis Phelan mentioned as an executor was a curate in Trinity Parish at the time the will was made. He was later a parish priest in Waterford city and died at an advanced age in 1791. It will be seen that the will was not proved until over a year after Lloyd's death and that one of the executors, Maurice Hearn, did not live long enough to perform his executorial functions. The fact that Lloyd cut off several of his relations with a shilling is an indication of bad blood between them and Lloyd, deriving perhaps from Lloyd's having turned catholic in his youth. The ploy of bequeathing a paltry shilling to such relatives was intended to forestall, or at least render difficult, the bringing of an action for a share in the estate. It was quite common in wills of that time to make specific mention of personal articles of value such as a gold watch, but whether in the present case the Paris banker, M. Quane, ever succeeded in possessing himself of Lloyd's gold watch is doubtful. It looks like an item which Lloyd may have had to dispose of to provide a little hard cash during his impoverished last years in France.

EPILOGUE

General: Catholics in Ireland in Lloyd's time were undoubtedly second-class citizens, who existed as a sort of sub-culture, but within the limitations imposed by the penal laws they did not fare badly at all. In the cities and towns some catholics grew rich and prosperous as merchants, shop-keepers, tradesmen, manufacturers and in the medical profession. In the country the majority of the tenant farmers, outside of Ulster, were catholics, some of them with substantial holdings. But this is not to ignore that the vast majority were poor cottagers, dependent on their potato patches and the little they could earn as labourers. Despite the penal laws, the catholic church in the first half of the century expanded and developed, and carried on with its functions notwithstanding occasional reactivations of the laws by the authorities. Bishops went on their visitations, arbitrated in disputes and maintained a correspondence with their parish priests and brother bishops.

Lloyd, the bishop: Although he was a bishop for nearly nineteen years, his achievements were modest enough, due to his eye trouble, his involvement in the Hennessy affair (which rendered five or six of his ten years in Killaloe unprofitable) and his insatiable itch for foreign travel, which, one feels, would have come between him and the proper care of his diocese even if he had been allowed to carry out his duties unmolested. His first four or so years in Killaloe was a time of solid achievement when, according to Archbishop Butler, he journeyed from end to end of his large diocese confirming and preaching, and visiting places which had not seen a bishop for a hundred years—which does not say much for the activities of his predecessors in the diocese. There were many bishops in Ireland at this time who achieved a great deal more than Lloyd, but whose achievements went unnoticed and unrecorded for the simple reason that that was how a catholic bishop functioned best, given that he was tolerated only by connivance. Lloyd was fortunate in that he left behind him a volume of correspondence mainly in the Stuart papers of sufficient size to form the basis for a biography.

Lloyd, the traveller: From 1723 onwards he was constantly on the move. He must have crossed the Irish Sea two dozen times, undergone the fatiguing four-day journey by coach from Chester to London, thence to Dover and on to Calais. He then had several ports of call on the Continent—Douai, Ypres, Liège, Spa, Brussels and occasionally Paris. But anyone who looks in Lloyd's correspondence for information on the vicissitudes and hardships of eighteenth century travel will look in vain. There is hardly ever a word about the hazardous sea-crossing, the painful ride in the coach from Chester to London, the innumerable inns in which he must have stayed in England and on the Continent. He seems to have taken it all for granted and assumed, no doubt rightly, that any comments he might make on his sea or coach journeys or how he fared at the inns on the way would be of no interest to his correspondent.

Lloyd, the man: To be a catholic bishop in Ireland in the first half of the eighteenth century might not appear to most people as the desired goal of many clerics in view of the conditions under which bishops necessarily had to carry out their duties. It is difficult to reconcile, then, the unattractiveness of the job with the scrambles, and sometimes the unseemly wrangles, which marked the filling of most episcopal vacancies. Many clerics appear to have pursued their ambition of achieving episcopal rank with a single-mindedness more in keeping with the secular rat-race. The methods used by Sylvester Lloyd to achieve his ambition of being a bishop mark him out as a self-seeking, over-ambitious, worldly man. The policy he pursued of being useful to the Pretender was calculated to endear himself to that worthy with a view to obtaining from him a nomination to an Irish bishopric. The view of some pious men in Dublin on the question of his suitability for the archbishopric of Dublin was that he made many friends by his charm of speech and pleasant manner, but that he did not show signs of holiness and gravity meriting promotion to archbishop. He comes across as a gregarious man of considerable learning, a linguist who was well-informed about international affairs, a lively raconteur who could hold his own in any company from the table of the Nuncio in Brussels to the salon of a duchess. His visits to the Continent gave him an opportunity of cultivating the kind of company he loved—lords and ladies, statesmen, churchmen. These visits gave him access to a milieu which was largely denied him at home where being a catholic bishop meant exclusion to a predominant degree from what was called polite society.

Lloyd—the international dimension: There was an international dimension to Lloyd which is rare amongst Irish bishops. He apparently got an itch for travel early in life when he enlisted as a soldier in King William's army. His later defection from the army was to take him as far as Lisbon and back to Ireland by way of Rome. The first evidence of this international dimension was his translation into English of Pouget's monumental Montpellier Catechism, but far from earning him any kudos, his translation was to end up on the Index of Prohibited Books along with the original catechism.

Journeys to Paris in 1723 and 1725 were for the purpose of soliciting French support for the quashing of the 1723 Popery Bill but the extent of Lloyd's success in these missions is debatable.

The congress of Soissons in France, which commenced in June 1728, was again to prove a disappointment for Lloyd in that the question of religious toleration failed to make the agenda of the congress and Lloyd's hopes of cutting a figure as the representative of Irish and English catholics failed to materialise.

For the next ten years Lloyd was back and forth regularly to Flanders, and one suspects that these journeys were undertaken as much for the enjoyment of the company at Spa, as for any good the waters there might do his chronically-impaired eyes. Intelligence work for the Pretender was another aspect of his sojourns in Flanders which appealed greatly to him.

The successful organisation of opposition to a special catholic oath and to the catholic address to King George II in 1727, Lloyd would probably have regarded as his greatest achievement, but in historical retrospect this could only be described as a negative achievement, inasmuch as it entailed the commitment of Irish catholics to the doomed cause of the Pretender. Loyalty to the Pretender in the years ahead was to cost the catholics dearly. Indeed, it is not too much to say that had they shown the same loyalty to the house of Hanover in the 1720s as they were to demonstrate in the 1770s, the path to emancipation might have been greatly shortened.

INDEX

Aachen, Germany 139, 146, 148, 149
Abercorn, Lord 82
Adam & Eve's Franciscan chapel 36, 38, 39, 41, 42
Adam & Eve's inn 35, 36, 40, 41, 42, 43
Adami, Mgr. 171, 172
Address to king by catholics (1727) 86-102
   Lord Delvin's part in 88-90, 96-98
   Queries on 101-2
   text of 100
Albano, Italy 167
Allegiance, oath of for catholics 74-80, 97-98
Anne, Queen 138, 146, 188
Annesley, Arthur, 3rd earl of Anglesey 71, 146
Annesley, James, 5th earl of Anglesey 71
Annotations on the New Testament of Jesus Christ 144
Anthony of Padua 63
Ar bhfilleadh don Athar Silvester Lóid ón Fhraingc go hÉirinn 51
Arbuckle, James 138
Armagh 72, 153
Army in Ireland, Lloyd's report on 84
Articles of Limerick 88, 96
Arundel, earl of, see Howard
Athenry, Lord, see Bermingham
Athlone, Co. Westmeath 71, 152
Audoen's Arch, Dublin 44
Auersperg, Count 106
Aughrim, battle of 52, 65
Avignon, France 108, 109, 115, 167, 168, 190
Ayr, Scotland 106

Bagnères, France 190

Bailey's Lane, Waterford 176
Ballinakill, Co. Mayo 42
Banishment Act 1697 34-5
Barnard, Alderman 151, 152
Barnewall, Fr 35
Barnewall, Fr Barnabas 170
Bar-sur-Aube, France 76
Barronstrand Street, Waterford 176, 179, 181
Barron, T 195
Barry, James, earl of Barrymore 72
Bath, earl of, see Pulteney
Belem monastery, Lisbon l8
Benedict XIV, pope 174
Berkeley, George, C. of I. bp. of Cloyne 181
Bermingham, Fr 52, 54
Bermingham, Fr Francis 53
Bermingham, Francis, 14th Lord Athenry 72
Bermingham, Mr (Fr ?) 124
Betham Dr 117
Bindon, David 181
Bohily, Fr 160
Boin, France 57
Bolton, Cornelius, mayor of Waterford 186
Bolton, Theophilus, bp. and archbp. 75
Boulay, Lorraine 76
Boulter, Hugh, C. of I. archbp. of Armagh, 66, 90, 119
Bourke, Fr John 142
Bourke, John, earl of Clanrickard 65
Bourke, John Smith, earl of Clanrickard 152
Bourke, Theobald, Viscount Mayo 72
Bourke, Ulick, 151-2

Bowning, Mr 137
Bray, Fr John 186
Bridge Street, Dublin 42, 188
Brodrick, Alan, Viscount Midleton 67, 93
Brown, Mrs 38
Brown, Patt, solicitor 134
Brown, Fr William 186
Browne, Sir John 137
Browne, Sr. Julia 137,172
Browne, Sr. Margaret 175
Browne, Peter, C. of I. bp. of Cork 72
Brownlo, Mr 72
Bruree, Co. Limerick 12
Buckingham, duchess of 145, 146, 147, 148, 149, 150, 152
Buckingham, duke of, see Sheffield
Burke, Canon W.P. 45
Burke, Thomas, bp. of Ossory 188
Burrow's Court, Dublin 44
Burton, Edwin 46
Butler, Christopher, archbp. of Cashel 57, 128, 129, 176, 196
 and appointment of Vatican agent 171-2
 and Hennessy affair 134-6
 favours Crowe for Killaloe 121
 on Lloyd 126-7
Butler, Col 176
Butler, Edmund, 8th lord Dunboyne 15, 62
Butler, James 60
Butler, Thomas, 8th Baron Cahir 14, 15, 52, 60, 105, 109, 138
Byrne, Fr Denis 172
Byrne, Edmond, archbp. of Dublin 23, 25, 30, 40, 50, 52
Byrne, Fr Edmond OSA 26
Byrne, Fr John 26
Byrne, Fr 129

Cahir, Lord see Butler
Cahir, Co. Tipperary 15
Calais 113, 149, 197
Cambrai, France 106
Canary Islands 179
Carlingford, earl of, see Taaffe
Carlingford, Co. Louth 71
Carrick-on-Suir 193, 194
Carrigogunnell, Co. Limerick 59
Carroll, Fr Anthony 130
Carroll, Fr Daniel 130
Carte, Thomas, historian 15, 137, 138

Casani, Fr Joseph 29
Case of the Roman Catholics of Ireland, The 20, 49, 50
Casey, Matthew 170
Cashel, Co. Tipperary 12, 14
Castlerobertgore, Co. Limerick 13
Castletown, Co. Kildare 128
Caulfield, James, Viscount Charlemont 72
Celbridge, Co. Kildare 128
Channel Row, Dublin 72, 131, 137
Chapel Lane, Dublin 41
Chapel Yard, Dublin 39
Charlemont, Co. Armagh 72
Charles II 146
Charles V, emperor 18
Charles Edward, Prince 78, 185, 193
Chartres, France 57
Chavigny, Theodore, French diplomat 145, 146, 148, 149, 150, 159
Chenevix, Richard, C. of I. bp. of Waterford 189
Chester 125, 197
Chesterfield, Lord, see Stanhope
Clanrickard, earl of, see Bourke
Cleary, Fr Gregory 38
Cleary, Felix 186
Clement XI, pope, 166
Clementina, wife of Pretender 78, 109
Clinch, Fr John 26
Clogheen, Co. Tipperary 15
Cloncoragh, Co. Limerick 13
Clonmel, Co. Tipperary 177
Clontibret, Co. Monaghan 156
Cock Hill, Dublin 44
Coghill, Marmaduke, MP 128
Coke, Sir Edward, lawyer 102
Colbert, Charles-Joachim, bp. of Montpellier 20
Coleslogh, Adam 114
Congregation of hermits of St Jerome 18
Connell, Dr (Fr) 96
Connell, K. H., demographer 161
Conolly, William, speaker 93, 127, 128
Cook Street, Dublin 35, 36, 38, 39, 40, 41, 42, 43, 44, 45
Cook Street area, Dublin 43-5
Corc, king of Munster 12, 62
Cormack, Fr James 26
Cornbury, Lord, see Hyde
Corsini, Nereo, cardinal 159, 160, 172, 187, 190, 191, 193

Index

Costello, Fr Peter 186
Cox, Sir Richard, MP 72, 181
Creagh, Abbé 189, 192
Creagh, Peter, bp. of Waterford 156, 190, 191, 192, 193
Cromwell, Oliver 135
Crowe, Fr Denis 121, 123, 124, 163
Cullen, Mrs 146

Daly, Denis, chief justice 22
Daly, Poor 52
Davenant, Mr 150
Delaney, Mrs 38
Delvin, Lord 87
Derry 69
Dillon, General Arthur 53, 54, 55, 59, 64, 65, 66
Dominican nuns refuge in Brussels 137
Doneraile, Lord 134
Doneraile, Co. Cork 134
Donlevy, Fr Andrew 96
Donnelly, Nicholas, bp. and historian 39
Douai, France 15, 16, 60, 104, 113, 115, 144, 154, 197
Dover 15
Dowdall, Stephen, bp. of Kildare 136
Doyle, Mr 82
Drogheda 185, 186
Dublin archbishopric, filling of 52-5
Dumville, Mr 146
Dunbar, Lord 191
Dunboyne, Lord, see Butler
Duncannon, Co. Waterford 70
Dunkin, William, poet, 138
Dunne, Bernard, bp. of Kildare 55, 57, 105, 130, 131
Dunne, Abbé James 57, 58, 59, 87

Earl Street South, Dublin 52
Edgar, James, Pretender's secretary 94, 135, 153, 160, 161, 166, 172, 182, 183, 184, 189, 190, 192
Egan, William, bp. of Waterford 164
Elizabeth I, Queen 193
English College, Douai 60, 109
Ennis, Co. Clare 126, 132
Eugene, Prince 150
Exchange Street Lower, Dublin 39

Fagan, Luke, bp. and archbp. 18, 19, 23, 28, 130, 131

Farrell, James 38
Farrell's Court, Dublin 44
Fell, Charles (alias Dr Umfreville) 105, 108, 113, 114
Fenelon, Francois, archbp. of Cambrai 106
Fingal, earl of 87, 146
Firrao, Giuseppe, cardinal 136, 139, 149
Fitzgerald, Fr Andrew 195
Fitzgerald, Matt 137
Fitzgerald, Fr Michael 193, 194
Fitzgerald, Fr Patrick 193, 194
Fitzgerald, Fr 41
Flannery, Darby 131
Fleau, France 168
Fleury, André, cardinal 58, 59, 87, 96, 103, 109, 111, 112, 118, 119
Flynn, John 131
Fontenoy, battle of 193
Foras feasa ar Éirinn 46
Forbes, Arthur, 2nd earl of Granard 71
Forde, Mr 36
Foy, Nathaniel, C. of I. bp. of Waterford 179
Fraher, Fr 194
Franciscan Ho. of Studies, Killiney 32
Franciscan order 33-36
Francis of Assisi 33
Francis Street, Dublin 35
French, Patrick, bp. of Elphin 173

Gallagher, James, bp. of Raphoe and Kildare 142
Galway, Lord 35
Galway 152, 154
Garzia, John, priest hunter 40, 41, 42, 43, 96
Gay, John, playwright 126
George I 103, 104, 109, 115, 146, 153, 178
George II 86, 88, 90, 99, 101, 106, 111, 112, 188, 198
Gerane, Fr Matthew 131
Gernon, Fr Laurence 26
Ghent 159
Gibraltar 81, 103, 126
Gibraltar, seige of 80, 85
Giffard, Bonaventura, vicar apostolic, London 111, 115, 116
Gilcagh, Co. Waterford 178
Gillow, Joseph, biographer 11

Glinn, Co. Limerick 13
Goddard, Mgr. Francis 142, 150, 151, 153, 154, 157, 160, 184
Gore, Sir Ralph 127, 128
Gorman, Fr 170
Gould, John 150
Grafton, Charles, duke of 47
Granard, earl of, see Forbes
Grand Alliance, War of the 17
Grannell, Fr Feargal 16, 18
Granville, Lord 153
Gregory XI, pope 18

Hackett, Fr 172
Hamilton, Zachy 145
Hanging in Stephen's Green, Dublin 82
Hanover, Duke of 152
Hanover 153
Harach, Count 140, 150
Harold, Fr John 26
Harris, Walter 179
Hay, John, earl of Inverness 60, 78, 109, 167
Hearn, Maurice, merchant 195
Hennessy, Fr John 134, 135, 156
Hennessy, Mr (Fr) 194
Henry, Prince 78, 191
Hieronymite order 18
High Street, Dublin 45
Hoadley, Benjamin, C. of E. bishop 127
Hoadley, John, C. of I. archbp. of Dublin 127
Howard, Bernard 120
Howard, Henry, earl of Arundel 120
Howard, Sister Mary Rosa 119, 120, 171
Howard, Philip, cardinal 120
Huguenots 168
Hyde, Henry, Viscount Cornbury 146, 147, 148

Imperiali, Giuseppe, cardinal 31, 32, 120, 121, 124, 142
Ingleton, Fr 124
Ingworth, Fr Richard 33
Irish bishops, non-residence of 173-4
Irish Capuchin convents at Bar-sur-Aube and Vassy 76
Irish College, Douai 60, 109
Irish College, Paris 142-4
Irish College, Rome 183
Irish College, Seville 23

Irish House of Commons
    Catholic freeholders deprived of vote 93
    Lloyd's report on meeting of 127
    Whig majority in 93

James I 193
James II 11, 17, 47, 146
Jaret, Captain 41
Jenkin's ear, War of 167
Jersey 187
Jones, Fr 40

Keating, Fr Geoffrey, historian 46
Kelly, Carbery, bp. of Elphin 53
Kelly, Fr 124
Kelly, Edward, bp. of Clonfert 53
Kelly, Ignatius, printer 154
Kendal, duchess of 92
Kennedy, Fr Terence 26
Kent, Fr John 42, 180
    report on Irish church 174-5
Kilbarrymeaden, Co. Waterford 178
Kilbroderan, Co. Limerick 13
Kilcash, Co. Tipperary 129, 176
Kilcolman, Co. Limerick 13
Kilconnel, Co. Galway 36, 42
Kilfenora, Co. Clare 123
Kilfergus, Co. Limerick 13
Kilkenny College 17
Killaloe parish 132
Killaloe diocese
    catechism for 154-6
    condition of people 162-4
    extent of 123
    filling of vacancy in 123-4
    population in 1730s 161-2
    'state of popery' in 132
    use of Irish 164-5
Killeedy, Co. Limerick 13
Killybegs, Co. Donegal 82
Kilmoylan, Co. Limerick 13
Kilrush, Co. Clare 132
Kilscanell, Co. Limerick 13
King Street North, Dublin 40, 137
King, William, C. of I. archbp. of Dublin 48, 90
Kinnitty, Co. Offaly 123
Kinsale, Co. Cork 81
Kirk, John, 46

Index 203

Lacy, Fr John 187
Langlois, Mons. 154
La Rochelle 187
Lawless, Sir Patrick 50, 52
League of Augsburg, War of 17
Lehey, Fr Francis 32
Lercari, Nicola, cardinal 91
Leslie, Canon James 12
Leyden 149
Liège 141, 197
Lille 146, 148
Linegar, John, archbp. of Dublin 26, 158, 171, 172, 174, 187
Lisbon 16
Lloyd, Revd. Edward 12, 13, 14
Lloyd, John 14
Lloyd, Sylvester
  address to king 86-96
  'apostacy' alleged 45-6
  appointment to Killaloe 120-5
  in army of King William 17
  army in Ireland, report on 84
  assessment of 196-198
  bilingual catechism 154-6
  Carte's life of Ormond 137-8
  coadjutor appointed 182-3
  coadjutor, request for 157-8
  congress of Soissons 103-117
  conversion to Catholicism 17
  Cork bishopric, bid for 60-61
  death and will 194-5
  Dublin archbishopric bid for 52-55
  education 16-17
  episcopacy, early years 128-9
  eye trouble 138-9
  Franciscan in Cook Street 33-45
  Hennessy affair & aftermath 133-7
  Hieronymite order member 18
  Irish College Paris controversy 142-4
  Kent's report on 174
  Last years in France 189-198
  non-residence in diocese 173-4
  and oath for catholics 77-80
  parents and place of birth 11-15
  pension, presses for 158-61
  and persecution of 1744 186-7
  poem in Irish on 62-3
  and Popery Bill 1723 49-52, 56-9
  questing rights of friars 129-31
  refuge for nuns, Brussels 137
  state of Ireland, reports on 64-73
  smitten by apoplectic stroke 171
  Spa, visits to 145-9
  surveillance work for Pretender 140-1, 145-9
  translation of Montpellier catechism 20-32
  and Vatican agent 171-2
  visit to Irish House of Commons 127
  translation to Waterford 166-9
  Waterford, conditions in 176-82
Lloyd, Thomas (I) 12
Lloyd, Thomas (II) 13
Lloyd, Revd. William 12
Lockington, Edward 16
Lockington, Jane 14, 195
Lockington, John 16
Lockington, Rebecca 14, 195
Lockington, Richard 16
Locran, Fr 130
Lonsdale, Lord 146
Loop Head, Co. Clare 123
Lorraine, Duke of 150
Lorrha, Co. Tipperary 130, 132
Louis XIV 17, 80
Louis XV 53
Lourdes 190
Love, John, revenue collector 134
Lurgan, Co. Armagh 72
Lydded, Revd. 145

MacCarthy, Donagh, bp. of Cork 60
McCarthy, Thaddeus, bp. of Cork 62, 134, 136, 142
McCartney, General 81
MacDonnell, Fr Myles 43, 143
MacDonnogh, Patrick, bp. of Killaloe 126, 162, 163, 168, 169
MacDonogh, Michael, bp. of Kilmore 94, 173, 185
MacEgan, Stephen bp. of Meath 26, 84, 90, 120, 130, 131, 170, 173
MacGlaughlin, Fr Mark 60
MacKenna, Fr James 183, 188
MacKenna, Fr Matt 194
MacLaughlin, Fr 60
MacMahon, Hugh, archbp. of Armagh 57, 142, 159, 171
MacMahon Fr Michael 131
MacMahon, Ross, bp. and archbp. 156, 191

MacMahon, Terlagh, bp. of Killaloe 123
MacNamara, Daniel 132
MacNamara, Francis 132, 137
MacNamara, Fr Lucius 133
MacNamara, Fr Peter 186
Madden, Fr 130
Majorca 52
Mallow, Co. Cork 134
Manuel, king of Portugal 18
Maria Elizabeth, archduchess 137
Maria Theresa, empress 118, 187
Marlborough, duchess of 126
Maryborough (Portlaoise) 185
Mayo, Viscount, see Bourke
Meagher, Denis 52
Meagher, Dr 172
Meelick, Co. Galway 129, 130
Merchants Quay, Dublin 39
Michael's Lane, Dublin 44, 45
Midleton, Viscount, see Brodrick
Minorca 81
Moloney, Mr, solicitor 134
Montpellier 20, 190
Montpellier catechism 20-32
Moor, Fr Francis 40
Moore, Bryan 185
Morgan, Fr 157
Morley, Fr Martin 130, 131
Mosley, Mr 115
Mulhern, P. 21
Mullingar, Co. Westmeath 133
Murphy, Edward, archbp. of Dublin 55, 57
Murphy, Mrs 38
Murphy, Fr Paul 41
Murphy, Fr Simon 41

Nagle, Joseph, solicitor 134
Nagle, Francis 134
Namur 103, 141
Nantes 192, 193
Nantes, edict of 50
Nary, Fr Cornelius 25, 26, 49, 75, 76, 87, 97, 99, 138, 144
Neale, the, Co. Mayo 137
Nenagh, Co. Tipperary 132
Newcastle, Duke of 85
Newcastle, Co. Tipperary 178
Nicolson William, C. of I. bp. of Derry 75
Noailles, Louis, cardinal 20
Norfolk, Duke of 105, 110, 114

Nowland, Moses 83, 84
Nugent, Lady Mary 72
Nugent, Thomas, earl of Westmeath 72, 86, 87, 88, 89, 95, 97, 102, 104, 116
Nunezeal, Thomas 179

Oates, Titus, 109
Oath of allegiance for catholics 74-80, 97-8
O'Brien, Col. Daniel 59, 60, 65, 76, 77, 84, 90, 95, 104, 106, 109, 113, 114, 116, 118, 124, 125, 140, 141, 148, 149, 150, 157, 159, 167
O'Brien, Fr 192
O'Brien, John, bp. of Cloyne, 163, 164
O'Brien, Madam 148
O'Brien, General Morrough 59
O'Brien, Fr William 124, 125
O'Callaghan, Ambrose, bp. of Ferns 41, 56, 57, 103, 119, 135, 158, 173, 175, 185
Ó Casaide, S. 45, 46
O'Connor, Dermot, Gaelic scholar 46, 138
O'Daly, Fr Daniel 22
O'Daly, James, bp. of Kilfenora 142, 144, 173
O'Daly, Thomas Power, lawyer 18, 21, 22
O'Gara, Bernard, archbp. of Tuam 72
O'Hero, Fr 41
O'Keeffe, Cornelius, bp. of Limerick 131, 134, 136, 142
O'Kenny, Fr Nicholas 154, 155
O'Madden, Fr 60, 61
O'Meara, William, bp. of Kerry 175, 184, 186, 187
Ó Neachtain, Tadhg, Gaelic scholar 11, 12, 15, 52, 80, 138
Ormond, James, 2nd duke of 60, 71
O'Rourke, Count Owen 167
O'Shaughnessy, Colman, bp. of Ossory 185
Ostend 150, 151
O'Sullivane, Thomas, Gaelic scholar 46
Ottoboni, Pietro, cardinal 172

Palazzo Muti, Rome 166, 167, 169
Paolucci, Fabrizio, cardinal 57
Paulus Benignus 133
Pecha, Pedro Fernandez 18
Perpignan, France 59
Petra, Vincenzo, cardinal 169
Pettit, Fr John 170

Index

Petty, Sir William 14
Phelan, Fr Francis 195
Philip II 18
Philip V of Spain 80
Pierce, Richard, bp. of Waterford 166, 168, 176
Pilkington, Sr Mary 175
Pill Lane, Dublin 130, 131, 186
Plowden, Francis, historian 88
Plunkett, Oliver, archbp. of Armagh 135
Polish Succession, War of 115, 141
Pollen, J. H. 46
Pontin, Mr 160, 192
Pontius Pilate 155
Popery Bill 1723 47-52, 56-59
Port Louis, France 192, 193
Portmahon, Minorca 81
Pouget, Mgr. Francois 20, 32
Power, Thomas 22
Power, Fr Patrick 182, 183
Pozzobueno, Marquis de 50
Pretender, see Stuart
Prie, Marquis de 150
Prior, Thomas 180
Pulteney, Daniel 147
Pulteney, Mr 145, 146, 148, 150, 159
Pulteney, Mrs 145, 148
Pulteney, Sir William, earl of Bath 147, 153

Quane, Richard 195, 196
Queen Street, Dublin 126
Queensberry, duchess of 126
Queensberry, duke of 146
Quesnel, Pasquier 109
Quin, Co. Clare 132

Radcliffe, Revd. Stephen 87
Ramsay, Alan 105
Ramsey, Mr 105, 108
Raymond, Anthony 138
Redmond, Fr James 26
Reginald's Tower, Waterford 181
Rehill, Co. Tipperary 15, 138
Richard II 68
Richmond, duke of 95
Roche, Fr Alexander 183
Rocque, John, map-maker 36, 39, 43
Roscrea, Co. Tipperary 129
Rosemary Lane, Dublin 39, 41, 44
Ross (New Ross) 70

Russell, Fr 30
Ryan Denis 40
Ryan, Fr Laurence 130

St Albans 125
St Audoen's chapel, Dublin 41
St Bonaventure's College, Douai 16
St Catherine's parish, Dublin 52
St Germain, Paris 115
St Isidore's College, Rome 166, 170
St Jerome 18
St John's parish, Waterford 177, 178
St Leger, Fr John 186
St Mary's Lane, Dublin 154
St Mary's parish, Dublin 26
SS Michael & John's chapel, Dublin 39
SS Michael & Stephen's parish, Waterford 177, 178
St Michan's parish, Dublin 26
St Olave's parish, Waterford 177
St Patrick's parish, Waterford 177, 178
St Peter's parish, Waterford 177, 178
St Saviour's Abbey, Waterford 179
St Stephen's Green, Dublin 82, 83, 84
St Stephen Street, London 155
Savelli Palace, Albano 167
Scarborough, Lord 117, 146
Schoolhouse Lane, Dublin 44
Segovia, Spain 18
Segrave, Fr John 36
Seville, 23
Seville, treaty of 118
Sexton, Fr William 186
Shanagolden, Co. Limerick 13
Shannell, Co. Limerick 14
Shannon, Lord 67
Shanrahan, Co. Tipperary 138
Shee, Fr William 186
Sheffield, John, 1st duke of Buckingham 146, 147, 152
Sheffield, Edmund 2nd duke of Buckingham 152
Shrewsbury, earl of 115
Simpson, Elizabeth 14
Skipper's Lane, Dublin 44
Sloyan, G. S. 21
Smith, Charles 178, 181
Soissons, congress of 103-19
Southcote, Fr Thomas 108, 109, 110, 114, 117, 118
Southwell, Edward 48, 90

Spa, 139, 142, 145, 146, 148, 149, 150, 172, 197
Spanish Inquisition 29
Spanish Succession, War of 80
Spinelli, Giuseppe, nuncio and cardinal 17, 29, 30, 31, 49, 54, 57, 59, 90, 91, 111, 112, 119, 169, 171
Spinola, Giorgio, cardinal 31, 59, 111, 112
Stafford, Lord 108, 109
Stafford, Major 39
Stephen Street, Waterford 178, 187
Stones, Fr Edmond 134
Stonor, John, vicar apostolic 104, 109, 114, 115
Strickland, Thomas, bishop of Namur 104, 114, 115, 116, 140, 141, 146
Stritch, Thomas, coadjutor bishop of Waterford 183, 184, 189, 191
Stuart, Fr Francis 89, 125
Stuart, James Francis Edward, the Pretender 11, 17, 42, 56, 58, 59, 66, 70, 71, 74, 76, 78, 81, 83, 84, 89, 91, 94, 98, 99, 104, 105, 106, 109, 113, 115, 119, 120, 124, 134, 139, 140, 142, 146, 147, 150, 152, 157, 159, 166, 169, 172, 176, 183, 189, 191, 193, 198
 and archbishopric of Dublin 55
 and book proposed by Lloyd 94-5
 and coadjutor in Killaloe 157
 and coadjutor in Waterford 183, 190
 and Killaloe vacancy (1728) 120-5
 matrimonial troubles 77-8
 meeting with Lloyd 169
 and oath for catholics 78-80
 O'Brien his agent in Paris 59
 and pension for Lloyd 159-60
 portrait of 107
 rumours of Jacobite invasion in 1726 82-4
 and Soissons congress 104, 113-15, 119
Swan Alley, Dublin 44
Swift, Jonathan 126
Synge, Edward, C. of I. archbp. of Tuam 41, 48, 74, 78, 94, 98, 138
Synge, Edward, C. of I. bishop, 74, 87, 97

Taaffe, Theobald, earl of Carlingford 87
Taaffe, Count Nicholas 187, 188
Tagaste, Portugal 18
Tailor, Elizabeth 14
Talbot's Inch, Co. Kilkenny 50

Tempi, Luca, archbp. and nuncio 150
Thomas, Edward 195
Thorn, Poland 56
Tipperary town 133
Toomevara, Co. Tipperary 123
Toulouse 190
Tournai, Flanders 142
Trimleston Lord 87
Trinity parish, Waterford 160, 177, 178, 184, 193, 194, 195
Tubrid, Co. Tipperary 138
Turberville, Fr Henry 154
Tyrconnell, duchess of 40

Umfreville, Dr (i.e. Charles Fell) 105, 108, 113, 114
Utrecht, Peace of 80, 103

Valenti-Gonzaga, Silvio, cardinal 136
Vassy, France 76
Vesey, Revd. John 13
Vesey, Sir Thomas, C. of I. bishop of Ossory 71
Vienna, Treaty of 118

Wake, William, archbp. of Canterbury 48, 74, 75, 94
Walker, Fr 41
Walpole, Horace 147
Walpole, Horatio, ambassador 58, 59
Walpole, Robert, prime minister 59, 103, 114, 117, 126, 140
Walsh family 179
Walsh, Fr Francis 36
Walsh, Misses 147
Waterford & Lismore diocese
 catholics, treatment of 176-7
 big chapel in Waterford city 178-9
 famine in 1740-41 181-2
 catholic merchants 177-80
 population 180-1
 and persecution of 1744 186-7
 state of popery in 1731 177-8
 1739 vacancy, filling of 166-9
Waters, George 145
Werburgh Street, Dublin 86, 101
West, Richard 67
Westmeath, earl of, see Nugent
White, Fr James 131
White, Thomas 195
Whyte, Laurence, poet, 44

Index

William III 11, 17, 34, 72, 146, 198
Williams, John 36
Witham, Fr Robert 106, 109, 144, 145
Wogan, Sir Charles 167
Wood, William 66, 92
Wyse, Sr Anastatia 174, 175

Wyse, Sr Catherine 175
Youghal, Co. Cork 185
Ypres, Flanders 105, 106, 197
Yuste, Spain 18

Zinzendorf, Chevalier 118